CUTTING OUT

CUTTING OUT

The Making and Unmaking of a Surgeon

JAMES K. WEBER, M.D., F.A.C.S.

ARCHWAY
PUBLISHING

Archway Publishing books may be ordered through booksellers or by contacting:

Archway Publishing
1663 Liberty Drive
Bloomington, IN 47403
www.archwaypublishing.com
844-669-3957

ISBN: 978-1-6657-2857-7 (sc)
ISBN: 978-1-6657-2855-3 (hc)
ISBN: 978-1-6657-2856-0 (e)

Library of Congress Control Number: 2022921229

Print information available on the last page.

Archway Publishing rev. date: 1/16/2023

ADVANCE PRAISE

Jim Weber launched his surgical career from a position of privilege. But nothing would insulate him from life's great equalizers. In his case, these would include an emotionally distant alcoholic mother, the rugged physical demands and personal humiliations of surgical training, cutthroat hospital politics, and heartbreaking patient stories.

Weber shares the victories also: pioneering work in weight loss surgeries and teaching University of Washington family doctors.

While he tried to find life balance through his music and teaching, Dr. Weber's health paid a steep price. After several heart attacks rearranged his priorities, Dr. Weber developed a new career teaching yoga. Reuniting with the love of his life, he essentially started over.

Gritty and candid, this is the story of an accomplished physician healing himself.

Linda Gromko, R.N.,M.D.

Dr. Jim Weber describes how he fulfilled his dream to become a surgeon, only to find that despite his expertise, commitment, and passion, he was not truly satisfied. Enter a difficult transition period that led to his second calling: Yoga Doc.

Jim writes artfully and compassionately about his experiences in ways that make us all reflect on what is important to us, what is worth working for, and what brings us joy.

Jennifer Wisdom, PhD, Wisdom Consulting

When one's best friend in college writes a tell-all memoir that brings back long-buried memories, one gets worried. But Jim Weber's surprisingly entertaining description of his journey from privileged Gramercy Park upbringing, with education at Buckley School, Hotchkiss, Yale, and Columbia, to preeminent surgeon, to yoga doc is fascinating.

Surprisingly honest about his four marriages, his description of the road from high-flying surgeon and Seattle Symphony Board member, to being served with two lawsuits on the same day, to discovering that he loves teaching yoga makes this read hard to put down. His self-insight and hilarious anecdotes make for a great saga, even if I did not know some of the story already.

Who knew in addition to being a singer and surgeon and yoga instructor, he was also a gifted writer? A new career beckons!

Richard Peiser, M.B., PhD.,
Michael D. Spear Professor of Real Estate Development,
Harvard Graduate School of Design

ALSO BY THE AUTHOR

Overcoming Obesity Through Weight Loss Surgery

The Complete Idiots Guide to
Modern Manners Fast-Track

Joie de Vivre, As I See It:
Reflections on Youth and Maturity

Scribbling In My Spare Time (in progress)

This book is dedicated to Mary Monica Mitchell,
My wife, soulmate, and inspiration

CONTENTS

FOREGROUND

Reflecting Kahlo's *Roots*

What a wee little part of a person's life are his acts and his words! His real life is led in his head and is known to none but himself. All day long, the mill of his brain is grinding, and his thoughts, not those of other things, are his history. These are his life, and they are not written. Every day would make a whole book of 80,000 words—365 books a year. Biographies are but the clothes and buttons of the man—the biography of the man himself cannot be written.

Mark Twain, *The Autobiography of Mark Twain*

MEANINGS

We do not receive wisdom. We must discover it for ourselves, after a journey through the wilderness which no one else can make for us, which no one can spare us...

Marcel Proust,
Remembrance of Things Past

I

Writing this book has been on my mind for quite a few years. I kept pages of notes, mostly one-liners, to jog my memory of unusual or otherwise noteworthy experiences, the majority relating to my medical career. I kept adding more notes, for more than thirty years.

As I ultimately assembled them into a coherent narrative, a unifying story emerged, a story of one man's journey to move beyond a successful surgical career into the privilege of assisting more people in a different way. Reuniting with his true love provided the necessary affirmation that this was the right choice.

James K. Weber, M.D., F.A.C.S.
August, 2022

II

Like Dr. James Weber, I made significant changes in my professional trajectory. I gave up a career as a bench scientist for an administrative position in medical school, facilitating others with their research. Admittedly, the changes I made were not as radical as Jim's. Even so, I certainly can relate to the journey he details in *Cutting Out: The Making and Unmaking of a Surgeon*.

I had the opportunity of meeting Dr. Weber because of professional contact with his wife, Mary Mitchell. I found them to be two of the kindest and most interesting people one could ever hope to cross paths with. I have spent a great deal of time working with Mary, an expert on etiquette—also a deep introvert like myself.

Jim, on the other hand, is as extraverted as they come, and I admit that early on I was drained by his non-stop expressiveness and direct line of inquiries into my life. It's my recollection, probably flawed, that I met Jim in a hotel lobby as we waited to check out at the end of a National Postdoctoral Association conference. He started a conversation that was quite one-sided until Mary showed up and expressed joy that we had met. So began a friendship that has lasted many years despite our differences in upbringing, location, and careers.

I don't think I have any friends more different from me than Jim Weber. He is a generation older, grew up in what I'd consider a rich family, had an Ivy League education, and built a career as a surgeon. But what really matters is that he is a man who really cares about what he does and how it impacts others. He is serious about making the most of his life and helping others do the same.

I knew that Jim had retired from a successful career as a bariatric surgeon. I knew he'd gone to the finest schools in the land along the way, and that he had a wonderful wife with whom he lived in a fairy-tale house that floated on the water in Seattle.

In short, I knew Jim was a good guy who had a good life and for whom everything kind of went the way it was supposed to go. Then I read this book, and realized that so many of the things I'd assumed about him were wrong. Also, that many things I'd assumed were right, but I learned much more about why that was so.

This book takes you on a journey through time, as a young boy who seems destined to be a doctor like his parents does exactly that, but never feels he quite fits in. Even though most of us can't relate to the experience of being a surgeon in a family of physicians, we all can understand how it feels when we aren't quite where we should be.

Many of us spend a lifetime quieting the inner voice that urges us to try something else, even when the outcome is neither safe nor certain.

Some of us hear the voice for the first time later in life and dismiss it, either as midlife crisis or a childish cry to give up our soft but successful life.

Very few indeed, hear the voice late in life for what it is: the truth. It's our heart's true desire. It's the path to happiness despite pain. It's what we always wanted to do, rather than what we always thought we were supposed to do.

A *vanishingly small number* of that very few who hear the voice and recognize it actually heed the call.

Jim did it. He closed a successful practice, became a yoga instructor because he loved both teaching and yoga, and made personal fulfillment his greatest achievement. What more could any of us wish for, and how can we hope to do the same?

There are no great secrets in this book, but the stories are filled with humor, kindness, and wisdom. And, as so many of us have been forced by this pandemic to question what is really important in life, *Cutting Out* is even more timely. I applaud you for selecting this book, and urge you to take its lessons seriously.

In the end, choosing happiness over "success" is what life is all about, and Jim's tale can help you understand why this is so.

Keith Micoli, PhD,
Associate Dean, NYU School of Medicine

III

James Weber, a former weight-loss surgeon, has written an exquisite autobiography that takes the reader across many neighborhoods, states on the East and West Coasts and in the South, through leading institutions of learning and medical science. The author, a rare blend of physician and man of culture, reflects on his successes and reversals, high achievements, and all too human disappointments and foibles, with disarming candor, flashes of wit and humor, and infectious human warmth. There is inspiring growth and progress through his life and loves, capped with a tender, Odysseus-like reunion, after almost thirty years, with Mary, a college friend and now his soulmate.

An Ivy-League polymath and "well-rounded" personality, he has written a life story that encapsulates key chapters in the social, educational, and medical history of contemporary America, starting with the medical careers of his parents and relatives and leading to his own training and practice, and his latest incarnation as a yoga teacher and therapist. Here, then, Is a "summing up" of a life of meaning, reflection, and ever-growing gratitude—for which all readers will be grateful.

Vicki C. Petropoulos, DMD, MS, FACP
Diplomate, American Board of
Prosthodontics, Emeritus Faculty,
University of Pennsylvania SDM

IV

Healing

There is healing in the laying on of hands; in the letting go of fear, in asking for help, in silence, celebration, prayer. There is healing in speaking the truth and in keeping still, in seeking sunlight and not shunning struggle. Laughter and the affirmation of wholeness hold their own healing. When the soul dances, when the day begins in delight, when love grows and cannot be contained, when life flows from moment to moment, healing happens in the space between thoughts, and the breath before the first sung note. Healing is a birthright and a grace. When we dare to be open to the unknown, when we extend ourselves in caring, when we welcome in the vast expanse of life, healing comes from the heart, and blossoms from the inside out.

Danna Faulds, from her book,
Go In and In: Poems from the Heart of Yoga

PLAYGROUND

Appreciating Turner's *Norham Castle, Sunrise*

There was a roaring in the wind all night;
The rain came heavily and fell in floods;
But now the sun is rising calm and bright;
The birds are singing in the distant woods...

All things that love the sun are out of doors;
The sky rejoices in the morning's birth;
The grass is bright with rain-drops...

"This morning gives us promise of a glorious day."

William Wordsworth,
"Resolution and Independence."

MUSINGS

IN MEDIAS RES

It is 6 pm, June 30, 2008. I am turning off the lights and closing the door to my office for the last time, marking the end of my surgical career— a career that had spanned thirty-five years...

You cannot simply stop being a surgeon. Not unless you become physically unable or legally prohibited from continuing to practice. Neither situation pertained to me.

No, you must wind down. There are post-operative patients who must be doctored to full recovery. There are long-time patients who have come to depend upon you, and a reliable replacement must be found for them. There are letters to be written to colleagues. Charts to be put into accessible storage. Instruments, supplies, and other equipment to be parceled out. Books to be given away. Licensing bodies, hospitals, and insurance companies to be notified. But all this was the easy part.

The hard part was turning out the lights.

It was that slight flick of a finger, something I had done thoughtlessly so many times before. That's when it hit me. It was over. A renunciation was subsumed in that final act: abandonment, a cop-out, something irreversible. Had I just made the biggest mistake of my life? Surgeons cannot afford to make mistakes, do not forget.

I did not rush into this decision. I thought about it for years. Many years. Even as a pre-med in college, I began to question my planned career trajectory. Especially at exam time. I didn't enjoy science courses; my love was English literature. Science to me was cold, hard facts and formulae—black and white. Poems and stories were adventurous and emotionally evocative—technicolor. Lab assignments were drudgery. Required reading, given sufficient time, was a pleasure.

I had my doubts in medical school. I was motivated to help people, but, instead, I was inundated with facts seemingly unassociated with patient care. I thought long and hard about giving it up, as I struggled through a brutal, five-year surgical residency.

I thought about it when I first started practicing and realized I naively had joined up with a surgical bad actor.

I thought about it after my first, second, third, and fourth heart attacks. It was then that a plan started to take form.

Please understand that I'm not a quitter. With the

tenacity of a bulldog, I have finished every task and surmounted each obstacle that was set before me.

Yet, in the last years, something was gradually changing deep inside. Slowly, I was beginning to experience a sense of freedom, of possibilities I never considered. I began to feel happy, whole, loving, and lovable. I saw spiritual potential within and around me. I came to think of my heart attacks as the key to improved health.

After half a lifetime apart, I reunited with my soulmate, Mary. She led me to yoga. She taught me about gratitude. She helped me put my life into proper perspective. She provided the spark that ignited the torch, illuminating what has become a spiritual journey. She showed me the trailhead, beyond which lay a brighter path.

If I had turned off the office lights without her, I would have been left groping about in the dark.

MIND YOU

I am in an unfamiliar operating room. I have been asked to perform a relatively simple operation, an appendectomy. The patient has all the signs and symptoms. There is no need to order any further tests. All that remains is to remove the offending organ, and I am ready to do my job. The patient is anesthetized.

There are several extenuating circumstances that are making me feel distinctly uncomfortable. Although I am not on the attending staff of this hospital, no one seems concerned about that. In addition, I am no longer a practicing surgeon. Yet here I am, and I have accepted responsibility for this patient. No one is questioning my qualifications.

The operating theater is adequately staffed with supporting personnel, all unfamiliar to me. There is more than enough equipment on hand, not that I need much to remove an appendix.

The real problem is that I cannot convince the nurses to follow simple antiseptic guidelines. They keep contaminating the skin prep, and I can see that the surgical instruments have not been properly sterilized. I manage to keep my anger and frustration under control. After all, this isn't my home turf, so I am on my best behavior. Instead of raising my voice, I ask that the skin prep be redone, and the instruments be re-autoclaved.

This is not going well. Precious time is being wasted.

What should have been a straightforward procedure is becoming a nightmare. I can't perform the surgery under these conditions...

Suddenly, I am awake, startled. It was only a dream.

I've been plagued by a variation of this dream for over forty years. Sometimes, I am still a surgical resident having a hard time finishing the program. At other times, I am a pre-med student having trouble finding the registrar's office. I can't remember my schedule, and I know I have missed many classes. Frequently, I am teaching younger surgeons, showing them a better way of doing things, usually under less-than-optimal conditions.

Things have changed.

I have not performed surgery for fourteen years. I now teach yoga and offer yoga therapy. What I do makes me feel happy and fulfilled. I never felt this happy and fulfilled as a surgeon. Perhaps that is why I have never had a yoga-related dream. To be truthful, I never dreamed that I would be practicing, let alone teaching yoga. Yoga is the dream I never had that came true!

Yoga has made me more compassionate, more accepting, more contented, kinder, more truthful, and more loving. Teaching yoga allows me to encourage similar self-growth in others. Together, my students and I learn to look each day to find a better self inside, bring the improvements forward, and become an improved influence for the good to all around us. We learn that we can change the world, one (often unanticipated) interaction at a time. We celebrate the joy in the breath, the peacefulness and beauty in the moment, and the love all around us. This is reinforced each time we do yoga.

We realize that there is yoga in service to others, however it may be performed. That there is yoga in observing a flower, in writing a thank-you note, in smiling at others in the elevator. There is yoga in brushing your teeth before turning in. Sitting outside on a clear night and watching the sky is yoga. So is making salad.

The word *yoga* means to balance: the right and left sides, the masculine and the feminine, the active and the passive, the joy and the heartache, the hot and the cold, the intuitive and the obvious, the work and the play.

We energize through stillness. We heal our hearts by opening the heart space; therein is the route to compassion. We learn to move into an *asana*, a pose, by feeling, not by thinking.

I didn't learn any of this in medical school or in my surgical training or practice. I learned how to take care of sick people. In the process, I made myself sick. I've always been a teacher, but I taught facts; now I teach timeless truths. Through Mary, I came to yoga, and now I do what I can to inspire others.

Yoga works for everybody; all they must do is give it a try. It works for the devoutly religious; it works for the agnostic. It is as effective for the unemployed as for the captains of industry and those who labor under them. It can help the patient undergoing a kidney transplant, and it would add greatly to the level of care and compassion delivered by the transplant surgeon. It has worked for two thousand years, though hitherto for an insufficient number of practitioners. The whole world needs it now, more than ever.

MORTALITY

I came across a book recently that a medical colleague gave me years ago, *The Book of Questions*, by Gregory Stock, Ph.D. One question in particular resonated with me:

> *"If you knew that in one year you would die suddenly, would you change anything about the way you are now living?"*

My answer is: "Had this book not been written, I would have said that I would like to have had the chance to reach out to all my friends and loved ones, including ex-wives, and tell them how much they meant to me. I wish I could have expressed how I felt about them throughout my life, not near the end.

However, having written this book, I now hope that everyone who reads it can appreciate how I have poured my heart out in its pages. They will discover a lot about me they never knew and, I hope, will gain some insight into their own lives in the process.

I certainly hope I have more than a year left. The older I get, I realize that I still have much to learn, to teach, and to be grateful for. I intend to make as much of the time left to me as I can. I will continue to attempt to pass on this newfound appreciation to my family, friends, and students.

MISSPENT YOUTH

EARLY MEMORIES

As a child, I wanted to be a physician, in particular, a neurosurgeon. Both parents and my uncle were doctors, so they encouraged my childhood fantasies. My mother even introduced me to a prominent neurosurgeon while I was in high school. He gave me a biography of Harvey Cushing, the founder of American neurosurgery, with an exhortatory personalized inscription.

I never read the book; didn't even peruse the Table

of Contents. I was too busy with my studies and extra-curricular activities. By then, I was no longer thinking about neurosurgery anyway. I wanted to do well in school, be admitted to a top college, probably to be pre-med—but also to pursue a liberal arts education. I was self-motivated and driven to succeed. Having fun and cultivating friendships weren't that important to me. I certainly had never heard about yoga in those days.

I grew up in Manhattan, the borough that out-of-towners gravitate to when they visit New York City. Since my parents were doctors and worked full time, I had a governess. Nora Tyrell—Noreen to me—joined our house-hold when I was nine months old.

She came to us through the inattention of my fa-ther. He was sitting in the shade of a tree, working on a crossword puzzle, leaving me to munch on leaves. Nora's sister Lill saw this example of well-intentioned child neglect. She politely chastised Dad and went on to mention that she had a sister, recently "off the boat" from Ireland and in search of employment.

And so, Noreen was hired. She remained with our family for nearly twenty years, off and on, in various capacities. She was quite diligent in her duties and attempted to control everything in my environment. In particular, she did her best to isolate me from the potentially pernicious influence of my brother, Jonny, eight years my senior—which he resents bitterly, even to this day.

Mom and Noreen got along like oil and water much of the time. But Noreen would brook no challenge, even if it emanated from her employer. She was there to take care of me, and take care of me she did. She did such a good job that she became a kind of surrogate mother. This could make things difficult, as my real mother was on site as well.

I remember feeling particularly upset whenever the two of them went at each other. Mom would get nasty and imperious. Noreen, being Irish, would get defensive and stubborn and storm off to her room. I would be left not knowing what to do or say. Generally, I avoided taking sides and did the best I could with whatever limited options I had. And things always seemed better the next day, if I waited.

By the time I was four, I was enrolled in the Brick Church Nursery School. It was Eton suits every day—short pants, white shirt with rounded collars over a lapel-less jacket, with dress shoes and knee-high socks. You don't see many boys dressed like this anymore.

The school was coeducational. I wasn't to share a classroom with girls again, unless you count confirmation class, until my senior year in college!

Back in the '50s, Mom was busily transforming herself into a Presbyterian. Her parents, *émigrés* from Ukraine, were non-observant Ashkenazi Jews. Dad also grew up in the Jewish faith, but gravitated toward the secular humanism of Ethical Culture. By the time I was old enough to discuss theological matters with him, he simply labeled himself atheist and took little or no part in my religious training.

It was Mom's idea to raise Little Jimmy as a card-carrying Presbyterian, presumably with the acquiescence of the grandparents and a neo-atheist Dad. Not that anybody gave me a choice. What did I know anyway? I was four years old. Although I certainly wouldn't have minded a little exposure to Judaism along the way, I am grateful for the religious foundation that was provided me. It continues to inspire me to serve others with compassion and love, to pray, and to thank God for favors, large and small.

Mondays through Fridays was Brick Church School, and I went to Sunday school as well. I was really into the Bible. When I was ten, I was selected to be the Brick's representative on a Bible radio quiz show. Always the diligent student, I was pumped and knew my stuff. I also sang in the church youth choir.

After school, I liked to visit the medical offices that Mom and Dad shared with my uncle. The three of them were on the attending staff of Lenox Hill Hospital. Dad often took me there on rounds. He would leave me in the lobby with a book while he visited his patients. New York was a lot safer in those days.

Harvey Cushing's neglected biography notwithstanding, I've liked to read for as long as I can remember.

I also filled my head with baseball statistics, most of which I learned from a big anthology of baseball lore and history. I also enjoyed browsing through the family's *Compton's Encyclopedia*, which was kept on a shelf in the dining room as the ultimate arbitrator of not uncommon family dinnertime disagreements.

We lived in an upscale apartment building on East 86th St. for five years, but there were serious problems. We had an unsolved burglary, and there were gunshots in the elevator one day. It was time to move when someone committed suicide by jumping off the roof, just minutes before my brother came home from high school.

Our parents bought a five-floor town house in lower Manhattan, on East 19th Street, between Third Avenue and Irving Place, a lovely street known to this day as "Block Beautiful." The cost was $75,000, a lot of money in 1955. They lived there for thirty years.

This part of town is not only posh, but of considerable historical interest. Nearby Gramercy Park is one of the few private city parks in the Northeast.

There are some significant landmarks around or near the Park. The National Arts Club, of which Mom was a member, and The Players (another famous club) are both on the south side. The National Arts Club was the former home of Samuel Tilden, Governor of the State of New York. He came as close to winning the Presidential election of 1876 as did Al Gore in 2000.

The Players was created by a gift from Edwin Booth, the preeminent Shakespearean actor of his day and brother of the infamous John Wilkes. His gift of the mansion enabled the foundation of the club. Founding members included Mark Twain, General William Tecumseh Sherman, of Civil War fame, and Brander Matthews, famous educator and President of Columbia University. Actor's Equity was created by the founding members of The Players.

The former Friends' Meeting House, just north of our house, served as a major stop on the Underground Railroad. Isadora Duncan had her dance school in a townhouse on the north side, and Theodore Roosevelt was born two blocks west. Other famous residents included Thomas Edison, the Steinway family, John Steinbeck, Hart Crane, and, more recently, Julia Roberts, Uma Thurman, Jimmy Fallon, Rufus Wainright, Winona Rider, Ann Curry, Kate Hudson, and Chelsea Clinton.

We had some famous people on our block, too. Igor Cassini, brother of fashion designer Oleg and a syndicated gossip columnist, lived on one side of us. Skitch Henderson, jazz pianist and conductor/composer, lived on the other. Ann Morrow Lindbergh had a love nest across the street from our house, where she would secretly meet her lover, Dana Atchley, an internist at Columbia-Presbyterian.

Irving Place around the corner was home to Pete's Tavern, where O. Henry wrote The Gift of the Magi and other stories, mostly under the influence. At the bottom of Irving, on 14th St., was Lüchow's, a venerable German restaurant, founded in 1882, its walls festooned with entrancing oil paintings of scenes from Wagner operas. We would make sure to go there every holiday season, when lavish decorations were on display on a revolving circular table that surrounded a giant Christmas tree. Sadly, in 1982, as 14th St. became more and more run down—unlike today, when the whole of Union Square has been gentrified—Lüchow's burned down in a suspicious fire.

MISCHIEF

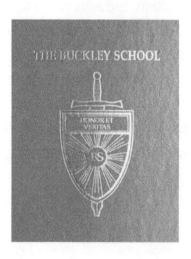

The Blue means the Truth;
The Shield means the Brave;
The White means Purity...
From the school song

My parents opted to enroll me in the rather exclusive Buckley School, on the fashionable Upper East Side. The determining factor likely was that Buckley offered French at every grade level. This had to have delighted Mom, since she was a died-in-the-wool Francophile. Some of the French idioms and proverbs I learned still rattle around in the back of my head. Sometimes they just pop out in conversation. Problem is that the usage is not always appropriate, occasionally embarrassing, and often requiring some effort at explanation.

The school, as my class knew it, was confined to a

single townhouse on East 74th St. It originally was first through eighth grades; today it is kindergarten through ninth. Four more buildings have been added since I graduated in 1962, and the student body is nearly half again as large, although still not coeducational. The tuition has increased sixfold. I learned all this a few years back, when I gave my first of what has become an annual, much-needed talk on table manners to the ninth grade. (Why me, you might ask? Read on. All will be revealed.)

Lunches were miserable fare. Today, the students get catered, tasty meals. Furthermore, the lunchroom can be converted to an auditorium, complete with tiered seating, by the touch of a button—in a mere five minutes. They showed me; I could hardly believe my eyes. How times change.

Coat and tie were required, as they were at the Brick Church School. We weren't allowed to wear long pants or jackets with lapels until third grade. Good riddance, Eton suits.

We had some memorable teachers at Buckley. Mr. Rotella, the music teacher, introduced us to Gilbert and Sullivan operettas, which became a lifetime of special enjoyment for me. I remember reciting Vachel Lindsay's poem, "The Congo" to Mr. Rotella's dramatic, bongo-drum accompaniment. I can still recite the first of the three longish sections, more or less correctly.

Dramatically. Yet only to myself; it's not at all PC. Look it up; you soon will see what I mean.

Mr. McLeod, in addition to being a good math teacher, was deadly accurate throwing erasers at misbehaving boys. The only tutoring I ever received at any level was from him. My parents felt that I needed some extra help in pre-algebra, so they shipped me off to his place on The Island (Long Island, that is) for a week after seventh grade. No matter that he tossed me out of class more than a few times for pranks and talking behind his back.

In eighth grade, I was made editor-in-chief of the school newspaper, *The Buckley Record*. And I worked hard at it. Most of the articles were written by me, and subsequently rewritten by our faculty advisor. A few of us would walk around the neighborhood, trying to sell ads. The barbershop, where most of us had our hair cut, was the easiest mark.

I worked hard at almost everything I did at Buckley. I graduated first in my class, with a solid educational foundation and study habits that stood me in good stead—we English majors, after all, generally gravitate toward alliteration—for the rest of my education.

MIND BLOWING

I was twelve years old the day Dad called me into his bedroom (Dad had moved into Jonny's room after he left for college) for a conversation I will never forget. "Your mother is an alcoholic," he said solemnly, hoping that I would be able to help him persuade Mom to mend her ways. No doubt, I had seen her quite out of it more than a few times—stumbling, slurring her words. She always had told me it was because she had taken an antihistamine for sinus congestion. Now it all began to make sense.

Dad and I tried everything we could think of to get Mom to stop drinking. We tried smothering her with loving appeals. We tried threats. I searched every closet, cabinet, and shoebox for bottles—and sometimes confronted Mom with my discoveries. She invariably would say, "I don't know how they got there." This made me feel angry, frustrated, and sad.

I pleaded with the owner of the corner liquor store to stop sending vodka bottles to the house. This took a lot of nerve for a boy still in grade school. I loved Mom and was in awe of her many accomplishments. I never took her drinking as a personal repudiation; I simply wanted her to be well.

Yet, no matter how hard I tried, nothing I did seemed to influence her behavior. Thankfully, she never embarrassed me in front of my friends. I don't think her patients had any idea that she had a growing addiction to alcohol, at least not in the early years of her medical practice. Years later, we started finding empty bottles stashed in her office.

With the situation worsening, Dad and I started going to Al-Anon meetings, for families who have loved ones addicted to alcohol. There, we were encouraged to talk about our feelings, something we rarely did at home. We were taught to hate the habit (since recognized as a disease), love the alcoholic, and acknowledge that we were powerless to change her behavior.

The willingness to get help had to emanate from Mom, and that wasn't about to happen anytime soon. She acted as though we were crazy to think she had a problem. Even when we told her that we were going to Al-Anon. Even when we showed her lipstick stains on the bottles! This was so very sad. It seemed as if nothing ever could make her well again.

What brought Mom to this sorry state? As a boy, I simply could not understand. She seemed to have everything going for her: a good career, a caring husband who also had a good career, two loving sons, both doing well, and a beautiful home.

Jonny and I believe we have the origins of her alcoholism pretty much figured out now. Just out of high school, while on a European tour, Mom had a love affair with a dashing Frenchman named Andre. She became pregnant around that time and, likely, he was responsible. She was sent away to the University of Wisconsin for her first year of college. She always maintained that this was because she was too young to enroll in Barnard, from which she graduated. But in reality, it was to have a baby. Immediately put up for adoption.

She remained in contact with Andre, meeting him years later in Paris, on at least three occasions that Jonny and I know of. I met him twice. By then, he was married, with two sons. She had several other opportunities to see Andre when she went back and forth to buy property and build her villa in the South of France. I have a letter she wrote in French to Andre but never sent (possibly a first draft?). There is reference to money she loaned him and much in it to suggest that she still carried a torch for him, after all those years. No wonder she turned to the bottle to ease her broken heart.

She never disclosed any of this to us. It is heartbreaking to think about her, stubbornly suffering alone, despite living with two sons and a husband. We would have done anything in our power to help, had she been willing to accept it.

Years later, our half-sister turned up at the house. She had searched the available adoption records and tracked Mom down. She first spoke with Dad, who knew nothing of her existence. Imagine his shock. She gave him a book she had written about searching for one's natural parents.

Dad allowed her to go to see Mom, who was convalescing at the time. She had suffered a stroke, a broken hip, eight months of alcohol rehabilitation, and two years of physical therapy. Mom's defense mechanisms were still operational, however, and she spent no more than a few minutes with her daughter. What they said to each other, no one will ever know.

Dad didn't tell me about this surprise visit until a year or two later. He said he couldn't remember the woman's last name or the title of her book, which he had discarded. I am sure he was trying to wish the whole experience away. I was the one who told Jonny. All we know is that her name is Ruth, and she was living in California at the time. She must be nearly ninety by now, if she still is living.

I never felt comfortable pressing Mom on the subject, and Dad really didn't want to talk about it, either. A prime example of the emotional closeting that my family honed to a fine art. I tried a Google search with what little information I had and came to a dead end.

I really would have liked to meet my half-sister. I am sure she dearly would have loved to hear about her mother. How disappointing that trip to New York must have been for her! Imagine having done all of that sleuthing to find her mother, only to be met with total rejection. It must have felt terrible to have the door slammed shut against any further contact.

I wonder if knowledge of what happened here explains why I find myself so often willing to give others a second or even (and herein you will see that it hits particularly close to home) a third chance. It helped me develop a deep sense of compassion, which I am learning through yoga and self-discovery to communicate better.

I have a fantasy:

My half-sister is still living. Somehow this book comes to her attention. She reads it, only to find out that she has two half-brothers who would love to meet her, to give her a hug, to share stories. That her mother had real regrets and wished she could have done better by her. Somehow...

MATURATION

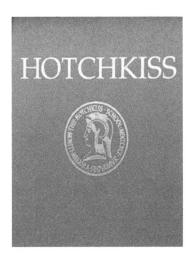

We'll cherish all the mem'ries dear,
That cluster 'round our sojourn here.
From the school song

After Buckley, I attended the Hotchkiss School, which
is in Lakeville, Connecticut. Five of my classmates from
Buckley joined me. Our entire graduating class went off
to boarding school, which was the thing to do among
my set.

I already was used to living away from home. At
age nine and again at ten, I attended an eight-week

summer camp in Maine. Most of my grade-school classmates had done the same. It helped us cope with homesickness and was deemed good preparation for boarding school.

Hotchkiss is located on 827 lovely acres, amidst rolling hills, in the northwest corner of Connecticut, a mile and a half outside of the nearest town, two miles from the New York state line, and six from the Massachusetts border. Back in the mid-sixties, the total enrolment was 320 students. Ninety percent of the class boarded, and all were male. Today, there are 600, and the school went co-ed in 1974. Tuition in my day was around $6,000 per year; today it is ten times that. Were it not for a large endowment fund of around $450 million—the seventh highest among American boarding schools—no doubt tuition would be even higher.

Speaking of education costs, my entire private school education from nursery school through medical school—the best that money could buy— cost my parents $142,000. In 2021, that same education, at the same schools, would have cost nearly a million dollars more!

My favorite teacher was Peter Beaumont, arguably the best teacher I ever had at any level. He taught second-year French, for which I was automatically eligible as a freshman, since I had plenty of French at Buckley. He was the kind of teacher who inspired his students always to strive to do their best. Dad came up for Parents' Day, sat in on his class, and declared him the finest teacher he had ever seen. High praise, indeed, considering what little French Dad understood.

We called Mr. Beaumont "*Petit* Pete, the *petit* tank," because he resembled a mini Sherman tank, small, but solidly built. His son, Charlie, was legendary at Hotchkiss. Some nine years before we had matriculated, he had set the national high-school javelin record. The high-school record, mind you, not just the boarding-school standard. Surprisingly, the javelin thrower ended up a classmate of mine in medical school.

Organized sports were emphasized, and I went out for soccer, swimming, and track. I was a goalie, a one-stroke swimmer, and a miler. Yet the real fun was playing stickball, which, weather permitting, we did frequently. I could throw a few surprisingly tricky pitches, thanks to the many whiffle-ball games Jonny and I played at home. We had some good hitters. I was not one of them, but Steve Greenberg could hit a tennis ball almost as far as the eye could see. And no wonder. His father, Hank, was a famous ballplayer, a Hall of Famer. Steve and I had gotten to know each other in eighth grade, even though he went to a different grade school.

Greenberg and I decided to room together in our third year and were assigned a primo room. It had been a quad, but we somehow secured it as a double. I am not exaggerating when I say that this was the best room I ever had in any school. Without the furniture, it was almost big enough to accommodate a regulation shuffleboard course.

I think we got the room because we were favorites of the Nort. George Norton Stone was the head of the math department and in charge of our dorm. We liked him so much that we named the stray dog we adopted Little Nort in his honor. I think he was secretly tickled, since he looked the other way. Keeping pets was strictly forbidden.

Heck, everyone knew Little Nort was up there living with us. We fed him doughnuts and table scraps, and he was in a permanent state of bliss. Then one sad day his owners showed up and laid claim to him, which we were in no position to dispute.

Hotchkiss had surprise holidays every once in a while. On those days, we were encouraged to hike, sail on the nearby lake, or otherwise commune with nature. Not I, you understand, but a number of classmates would head off into the woods with cigarettes and bottles of booze. At least five got caught and were expelled. Incidentally, drugs of any kind were unheard of at our school in those days.

Weekend debauches in New York City were another thing. The main activity was trying to get served hard liquor. Nobody was ever kicked out for this, as bartenders couldn't care less how old we were, so long as we could pay the freight. The legal age in New York at that time was eighteen, but so what?

We often had parties at my house. I remember one

weekend when I had invited so many classmates that Mom had to go around the neighborhood to borrow mattresses. Can you imagine? My mother, borrowing mattresses?

Holidays would find many of us at the hamburger joint that was halfway between the school and Lakeville. The food was mediocre, but the jukebox was cheap: six plays for a quarter. One time, my friend, Bob Small, and I put in three quarters and pressed the song "Norman" eighteen times. "Norman" was without question the worst song in the jukebox. It ranks among the worst songs ever.

We stayed around for the first two and a half plays before leaving. Later, we found out that after the fourth or fifth play, people were beginning to get irritated. Another time around, and "What the fuck?" was heard, here and there. By the seventh time, people began to throw things at the jukebox, whereupon the owner went over and turned it off. Such innocent fun.

I got in big trouble over another caper. It was Greenie's idea to remove our ditsy corridor master's clean laundry and replace it with an armful of our dirty athletic clothes. I thought this was a great plan.

Unfortunately, one of my jockstraps had my name sewn on the waistband, since Noreen had labeled all of my clothes before I went off to camp the summer before. So, I got nailed. Greenie never fessed up to sharing in the prank, and I took the fall like a man. As punishment, I was no longer entitled to be a proctor senior year. This was a real humiliation. Not only that, but I would have to move into less opulent digs. A real bummer.

Nevertheless, as senior year began, I really was proud to have been chosen as editor-in-chief of the *Mischianza*, our school yearbook. Its name came from *meschianza*, Italian for medley. I had talented co-editors, including an excellent satirical cartoonist. We put a huge amount of time, thought, and imagination into our work. The final product was one that continues to impress me today.

I played backup goaltender on the varsity soccer team. Greenie was first-string, and, not only that, he also was All-American. I spent most of my time on the bench. The coach occasionally would remember to put me in, so long as we either were ahead or behind by at least four goals.

Winter term, I had just gotten over strep throat, and my parents thought it unwise for me to swim. So, I went out for the varsity hockey team, even though I was a miserable ice skater. I solved that problem by taking on the role of team manager. Didn't have to skate at all. And we won the league championship. I'd like to think I made a difference. If nothing else, I was an enthusiastic cheerleader. Certainly had fun; winning is always such a tonic.

The *Misch* took up so much of my time that I dropped out of track. There were so many last-minute details.

Besides, the coach kept shortening my races from one year to the next, trying to find the right distance for me. I knew from running the 440 that I never would make it as a sprinter. What I ended up doing was teaching junior lifesaving to interested schoolmates, since I had recently obtained my Water Safety Instructor certification at camp.

The music scene was hugely important for me at Hotchkiss, as it was throughout my schooling. Important enough to warrant an entire chapter in this book. For now, I will just say that I sang in a variety of groups and greatly enjoyed studying Music History.

Hotchkiss introduced me to some other interesting characters. I was in Advanced Placement French with David Demaray, who was a strange little man. Typical of so many of the French, he always reeked of garlic, mainly because he always wore a clove of it, which he thought kept him in good health. This man was so facile in French, Spanish and English, and so quick of mind, that he could simultaneously translate back and forth in any combination of the three tongues. This is no mean feat. The United Nations frequently called upon him to pinch hit for translators.

Students and faculty alike venerated our senior English teacher, Dick Gurney. And rightly so; he was practically an institution in and of himself. You hardly ever could have a discussion at any of the reunions without his name coming up. However, it seemed to me that his main interest was in following the school football team. Since I was merely the backup varsity soccer goalie, his interest in me was desultory at best. But he did give us a strong background in and love for nineteenth-century American literature (Thoreau, Hawthorne, Emerson, Melville, and Whitman) and Shakespeare. I'm sure this was a major reason that Bob, Greenie, and I all ended up majoring in English at Yale. That, and the fact that the English Department at Yale was the finest in the country.

The social scene for me was formal dinners and dances and, as I said, consuming alcohol underage in the City. But never on campus; I followed the rules. Many of my classmates didn't and, again, a number of them paid a heavy price for this when they were caught. The expulsion of one of my classmates opened up the opportunity for me to be reinstated as a senior proctor. My roommate was Sandy Lord, a rather dissipated Rolling Stone devotee, who was editor-in-chief of the school newspaper.

Our room was certainly adequate, although nowhere near as vast as the room I shared with Greenie the year before. What was cool, though, was that a kid who occupied the room next door left school, and we convinced the faculty that we should have this room as well. We used it more or less as an office, since we were in charge of the yearbook and newspaper.

I excelled at answering multiple-choice questions and took the SATs and Achievement tests without any special preparation. I scored a 743 in Math and a 721 in Verbal. My English Achievement test score was 747 and French was 720 for the written, 727 for the oral ('Listening" was what it was called.).

The Stanford interviews were held at Hotchkiss. I was given an A rating, which meant that I would be accepted. With that assuredness, I limited my other applications to Yale and Harvard. Harvard put me on the wait list, but that wasn't a problem, because I preferred to go to Yale. And I wasn't alone. Twelve of the eighty-seven in my graduating class did the same, perpetuating a time-honored Hotchkiss tradition as a Yale feeder.

I graduated eighth in my class and was admitted to the National Honor Society. I really was a good student and actually enjoyed taking tests, writing papers, and memorizing facts. Like most students, I tended to cram for midterms and finals, which is not conducive to long-term recollection. Yet, cramming worked well for me. And it left my memory free for the really important things, like lyrics to Rock 'n' Roll songs and baseball stats.

Mom and Jonny came up from New York for graduation ceremonies. In fact, Mom always came to my graduations. Dad only came to the ones in New York City; his busy practice made it hard for him to get out of town. I truly believe that Mom supported me to her fullest capacity, considering how she had bottled up her emotions (a sad pun).

Hotchkiss continues to be important to me. I went back for both the Fifth and Tenth Reunions. These events were mostly about trying to impress each other with how well we were doing.

The Fiftieth was something else again; we were all just glad to see each other, in many cases for the first time in half a century. We toured the amazing sustainable farm and heating plants, sat in on some classes and lectures. We witnessed a spontaneous school meeting devoted to Black Lives Matter. Three of our former teachers were still healthy enough to join us for dinner.

We had an opportunity to look back through our personal files for the first time. That meant access to all the comments by the head of admissions, the dormitory and corridor masters, and miscellaneous letters to and from our parents. Some of the comments were pretty snarky. I could see why the school makes you wait until the Fiftieth Reunion before allowing you a peek. After all, by this time most of the faculty who wrote the comments are retired, or passed on.

Not surprisingly, I had been excoriated over our jock-strap prank, and described by the admissions director to be "obviously smart," but "not particularly attractive." What?

Even so, that was better than what he had said about Scotty McLennan: that he "looks like Mortimer Snerd." For any of you who may not have known, Mortimer Snerd was a grumpy, sneering, snarling ventriloquist's doll; Google him. Scotty got the last laugh, though.

The former Dean of Religious Life at Stanford, he was named Hotchkiss Man of the Year for 2018. Revenge of the Snerd!

Bob and I were charged with putting together the Fiftieth Reunion *Mischianza*, which truly was a labor of love. I offered a few yoga classes to the students, faculty, and the more intrepid of my classmates.

MAY DAY

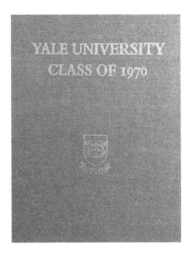

*Oh let us strive that ever we
May let these words out watch-cry be,
Where'er upon life's sea we sail:
"For God, for Country and for Yale!"*
From the school song

Small approached me about sharing accommodations at Yale. Thing was, Greenberg had made the same request of me. Naturally, being friends with both, I suggested that we apply for a suite, which we were able to finagle, on Yale's Old Campus, a gigantic quadrangle of classroom buildings and freshman dorms. Of course, Steve, being somewhat of a prima donna—former high school All-American goaltender and captain of the Hotchkiss baseball team, son of a Hall-of-Famer—had to have the single room. For the next two years, Bob and I shared the double. We lived on the first floor, which was handy whenever we stumbled back from parties in an inebriated state.

Yale had twelve residential undergraduate colleges at the time. Two more have been added since then. Our affiliation was with Jonathan Edwards, but we ate most of our meals with our fellow freshmen in the enormous main dining room. There were around 1200 of us—all men, of course, but that would change in three years. We had opted for J-E affiliation because Steve's big brother, Glenn—and I mean big: Yale football, drafted by the New York Jets, and all—was in J-E.

Because of my high grade-point average and SAT scores, I was invited to participate in an experimental honors program called Directed Studies (DS), then in its second year. This was an ambitious attempt to present the entirety of Western thought in a year, or year and a half. I felt that I was up to the challenge. The amount of material to which we were exposed was mind-boggling. I don't think I have ever completely recovered from the shock.

Looking back, this was a formative time. I began the life-long habit of over-extending myself, relentless in my quest not only to succeed, but to excel. This, I believe, eventually contributed to my series of heart attacks.

In our literature course, we were given a week to read the *Iliad,* another for the *Odyssey,* and one more for the *Aeneid.* You think this is doable, when you are also trying to master Locke, Hobbes, Rousseau, Hegel, Kant, William James, and Marx in the Western Political History course? While also studying the entire History of Western Art, Pre-Calculus, and Physics 101?

Oh, was I a mess, trying to keep up with all the reading, not to mention writing weekly papers on such works as Stendhal's *Le Rouge et le Noire*—thank God, read, or supposed to have been read, in English—*Measure for Measure* and *Antony and Cleopatra. La Commedia Divina* was a bit of an exception, having been a two-week assignment.

This was more than a human being, even one described as smart, should ever have had to do. It was a mental boot camp. Just imagine yourself trying to keep up. I swear, even my idol, Theodore Roosevelt, a voracious reader, would have found it nearly impossible to keep up with these assignments had he gone to Yale in 1970, instead of to Harvard in 1876. (More about him later.)

Frankly, the only way to get through this was to hone a helpful technique called bullshitting. And this we all learned rather quickly. It was a simple matter of self-preservation. One would read a bit and bullshit a lot. For instance, take Thucydides. I never got through more than ten pages of his *History of the Peloponnesian War* until forty-two years later, when I finally pulled it off my shelf and finished the assignment. Better late than never.

There was never any question in my mind that I would major in English. The strength of the English Department was the reason I chose Yale over Stanford or Harvard. There also was never any question of my not being pre-med. Clearly, I was influenced by my parents and uncle. The ethos of serving others always has been strong in me. Although no longer sure about what kind of doctor I wanted to be, I knew that I wanted to go on to medical school.

At the same time, credit my parents with inculcating in me an abiding love of the arts. Music, art, opera, and literature were all part of the backdrop of my upbringing. It never occurred to me that life could be lived without appreciation of, and participation in, these art forms.

Even though I gravitated toward liberal arts by nature, I was aiming for medical school, and grades in the lab sciences were of paramount importance. I had little aptitude and less appetite for lab sciences, least of all Physics. I had somewhat less than a clue about what was going on in the world of quarks; Avogadro's number stayed in my head only as long as I needed to regurgitate it for tests. Frankly, the demands of Directed Studies bedeviled any efforts I tried to make in any other course.

As you can imagine, I did not fare well on the Physics mid-term. That is putting it mildly. I received a 68, which was the lowest grade I ever received on any exam at any level of schooling. Frankly, I thought my chances of getting into medical school were torpedoed, then and there, part way into my freshman year. I was too ashamed to tell my friends or family how poorly I had fared. When asked, I just mumbled something like, "not too well," which was also about how I was feeling.

I do not know how I managed it, but I pulled a 96 on the final. That gave me an 89 for the semester, without really understanding much of anything about Physics. I only wanted to retain enough information to get me through the MCATs. That was all I needed from Physics.

I joined the Yale Freshman Glee Club and a small singing group, the Alley Cats. Practices and concert-izing were time consuming, yet great fun and a wel-comed break from the grind of studying.

In what spare time I had spring semester, I would take the train home, borrow a car and drive to Tenafly, New Jersey. The previous New Year's Eve, I had met Amee Wood, interestingly, at my own house, while hosting a party. That was the start of an eight-year relationship. Friendships with other young women, a couple of them serious enough, were no longer an option. College, and Amee, made everything different.

Amee's father, John Archibald Wood, M.D., was

an internist at Columbia-Presbyterian. His lineage was old New England and included a forebear actually named Amiruhami. Her mother, Louise Gaillard Wood, was from a venerable Southern family. One of her relatives was Francis Marion, the Swamp Fox of the War of 1812. Another was a famous Air Force Major General, Clayton Bissell, who had a controversial, although distinguished career through both World Wars.

Amee was a high school senior when we first met. She moved on from there to Skidmore College. After several years of dating, we decided that we would marry in 1971, when she finished college.

Getting back to academics, four lab sciences were required for pre-meds, and medical school applications had to be submitted in the fall of senior year. It was difficult to get all four courses in by then, since I really couldn't fathom taking two lab sciences in any one year. Who, in their right mind, would want to do that? So, I took Inorganic Chemistry at Columbia over the summer of 1967. The course was intensive. And so was the heat in the un-air-conditioned classroom and lab, especially with everybody's Bunsen burner turned on. The teaching was mediocre, but I got straight A's, and that was all that really mattered.

As sophomores, the three of us moved on to a quad-turned-triple in Jonathan Edwards College. We all declared as English majors, and I opted out of a second year in Directed Studies. I couldn't imagine what was left to learn anyway, since we had seemed to have covered just about everything freshman year.

To satisfy my Major, I took a course in American Literature, co-taught by Robert Penn Warren and Cleanth Brooks. Both were famous, the former as a novelist for *All the King's Men,* and the latter as a poet and co-author of the seminal standard, *Understanding Poetry.*

My lab science that year was Organic Chemistry. Challenging, smelly, and time-consuming—especially so at the end of the semester, when I still had six of the seven "unknowns" to figure out, with one week to go. Defining an "unknown" is not quite like trying to know the unknowable, only something along those lines.

That last week, I would arrive at the lab each morning, when the janitor opened the place, and he would kick me out at closing time. Talk about cramming. I am proud to say that I got all my unknowns correct. However, I only earned a B; the teacher said that it looked to him as though I had "skipped a couple of steps here and there." More like educated guesses.

I did elect a few broader course offerings. For instance, I studied Greek Tragedy under Eric Segal, he of *Love Story* and TV Olympic Marathon commentary fame. I loved that course. Segal was a little dynamo. Too bad he left Yale for Harvard.

I took a Music History seminar with a chain-smoking, odd fellow named Bailey. Music and music history remain a huge part of my life. I can still recall cramming to finish my twenty-page term paper on Brahms' Fourth Symphony. Rick Peiser, my best friend in college and a unique character himself, typed as I dictated, as Amee plied us with coffee. This marked the only time I ever wrote a paper that long and still loved what I had written about afterwards.

In the summer of 1968, I took a job at Columbia-Presbyterian Medical Center, as a lab technician for a pediatrician/researcher, Robert Winters. It was fairly dull work that didn't pay well, but I needed something medicine-related to make my application to medical school look more stellar. This was especially important, because I was an English major and hadn't opted for the usual science path preferred for pre-med students.

One day toward the end of sophomore year, Bob and Steve informed me that they had decided to stay in our suite in J-E, but that they would retain it as a double. This meant I was the odd man out. I was shocked and deeply hurt by this, considering I was the magnet that brought the three of us together in the first place.

For fifty-four years I had attributed their decision to personality differences between me and Amee, and Greenie's girlfriend. Just the other day, however, Bob made a clean breast of it and told me it was more because my schedule was so completely different from his—that I was crawling into the upper bunk at all hours of the night and waking him up. If he had taken Organic Chemistry, he might have been more sympathetic. Let's face it, telling me to move on was the only way he would ever get a bedroom to himself!

Be that as it may, I was so hurt about the split-up that I decided I no longer wanted to stay in the same residential college. I left J-E for nearby Branford College, feeling something akin to abject homelessness. I asked Charly Gates, a friend from the Alley Cats, whether I might room with him. He was kind enough to say yes, whereupon Charly, myself, and John Beattie (Charly's roommate from sophomore year), applied for a triple for junior year. Once again, I shared a bedroom, this time with Charly, like yours truly, a straightforward kind of guy.

John, on the other hand, is quite a character. His main passion in life—aside from endlessly writing Rachel Maddow in his quixotic attempts, first, in getting Mr. Trump removed from office and, now, prevented from ever attempting to run again—is solar eclipses. He travels to every total solar eclipse, renting airplanes so he can chase the path and gain a few more seconds of totality. John can remember the exact date and the minutes and seconds of totality of every solar eclipse he has witnessed!

I fulfilled my pre-med requirements with two semesters of Biology, which made more sense to me than Physics or Chemistry. Almost all the other courses I took were in the English Department. I had taken five courses each semester of my first two years in order to lighten my course load as a Junior and Senior.

I took a great Elizabethan and Jacobean drama course, which, in theory, was taught by Harold Bloom. In actuality, it was taught by his teaching assistants. I also took an excellent course on Chaucer and a marginally worthwhile one on Spenser. For my money, *The Faerie Queene,* with all of its endless allegory, is the most abstruse piece of writing in the English language after *Finnegan's Wake.* I may have the dubious distinction of being one of only a handful of Americans to have read the former in its entirety; as for the latter, I gave up after two pages.

The cool thing about my Spenser course was that it was taught by Bart Giamatti, a Renaissance scholar (Dante, Ariosto, Tasso, Petrarch), who went on to be University President. A lifetime, avid Red Sox fan, Bart gave up the Yale Presidency to, first, become President of the National League—each league had its own head in those days—and, then, Commissioner of Baseball.

Giamatti presided over the entire sorry Pete Rose affair. Here was the all-time MLB hits leader—surpassing even the legendary Ty Cobb—who was caught betting on the outcome of games, while at the same time managing the Cincinnati team. Which reminds me to boast that I retain quite a little bit about baseball history; I have a full shelf of books relating to the history of the game.

Although Rose denied wrongdoing until years later, he had been caught with his pants down, so to speak. Giamatti, having little recourse, banned Pete Rose from baseball for life. The whole drawn-out saga took its toll on Giamatti. A chronic chain smoker, he died a few weeks after passing judgment on Rose.

At the end of junior year, I took the MCATs without any special preparation and did well enough, although I cannot recall my scores. I was ready for senior year at Yale and ready to apply to medical schools. The question was, which ones.

One thing was for sure: I had determined not to apply to Yale Med. Not that it wasn't a good school. Not that I worried I might not get in. It was just that I enjoyed my time in New Haven, and I couldn't see another four years there, especially with no time to do anything else but grind. I wanted to remember Yale as a (mostly) happy and unique experience. I don't know of any other Yale pre-med from my class who categorically ruled out applying to Yale Med, as I did.

I took a summer job at a dialysis center at the Francis Delafield Hospital, loosely affiliated with the Medical Center, on Washington Heights in New York. The pay was marginally better than what I had received the previous summer, and the job looked good on my med school application.

And so we get to my last year at Yale. I had the opportunity to apply for a single room. I recall that there was a lottery of sorts, as there was only one small corridor with about six singles available. Underclassmen need not apply, of course. I hadn't had a room to myself since my second year at Hotchkiss. So it seemed like a great idea.

Actually, I wasn't exactly by myself. I had a cat, a Christmas gift from Amee, inappropriately named Scarlett O'Hara, considering its male gender. I like to think that I was decades ahead of the gender fluidity movement. I also once again was breaking the "no pets" rule, this time for most of the school year.

Scarlett didn't much care what I was studying, so long as I remembered to feed him and empty the cat box. Meanwhile, I continued to take the opposite tack from the Directed Studies approach and focused on one author per course, wherever possible. In addition to my studies in Spenser, Shakespeare, and Chaucer, I elected courses on Leonardo DaVinci, Wagner, and Goethe. All (well, excepting Spenser) remain favorites of mine to this day.

There were big changes on the Yale campus my senior year. Suddenly, there were all these female students around. Yale had gone co-ed, after serving as a bastion of male education for 269 years. A sign of the times? Better late than never? Admittedly, pun intended, there were plenty of women in the various graduate schools, but they were hardly in evidence around the undergrads, until this great leap forward.

It was a blast having women in class. Yale took in no seniors that first year of co-education, but the freshmen, sophomore and junior women were an awesome bunch. Smart? That would be an understatement. Quite a few of my male classmates had scored an 800 on the Verbal or the Math SAT, or perhaps on one of their Achievement tests. But Linda Kent, for example, had scored two 800s. And she was not the only female able to make that claim.

These new women at Yale would post letters to the "Yalie Daily," as we called our newspaper, complaining that no Yale men ever seemed to want to date them. Date them? We were afraid to talk to them!

Yet, how wonderful it was to have a woman take on a piece of poetry. I think women are wired differently, when it comes to critical thought and interpretation of verse. They bring a different perspective to the classroom discussion. The academic climate undoubtedly was enriched by our new co-eds—the social scene, at least for Yale men, not so much.

Now that I think of it, we had precious few women on the College faculty. All but one of my teachers were men. During the second semester of my junior year, I had taken a seminar on "The Age of Donne" taught by a nun (which rhymes), Sister Mary Paton Ryan. She was knowledgeable and tolerant of little *faux pas*, such as my falling asleep on a warm afternoon, while sitting right across the table from her, following an all-nighter cram for my Genetics mid-term. She acknowledged my nascent erudition and gave me a top grade in English.

So, when it came to the choice of an advisor for my last year, I naturally turned to Sister Mary Paton. I requested a reading project rather than a thesis, consistent with my one-author focus. She agreed, and together we embarked on an ambitious goal to read and discuss every piece of prose Herman Melville ever wrote. I read *Moby Dick* for the third time and enjoyed every page of it. I earned an Honors grade.

In my final semester, I took a fascinating seminar in Psychohistory. The course was taught by Robert Lifton, who was a psychiatrist and well-known author of *The Nazi Doctors: Medical Killing and the Psychology of Genocide*, not to be confused with light reading. He was also a disciple of Erik Erikson: *Youth and Identity* and *Gandhi's Truth*. In the meantime, the campus was in an uproar, in solidarity with the Black Panther Party and in protest over the escalation of the Vietnam War.

What a time that was! Abby Hoffman, who was founder of the Yippie (as opposed to the Yuppie) movement, and Jerry Rubin, a radical—later, a solidly pro-establishment traitor to the cause, but a big money-maker—were on campus. Local businesses boarded up doors and windows to prevent vandalism on May Day. The culmination was a general strike by the entire student body. During a mass rally at Ingalls Rink, we voted to refuse to take final exams. That was fine with Dr. Lifton, and it was fine by me. I had already been accepted to Columbia medical school.

We were so much a product of the '60s that even our class yearbook was a departure from tradition. It was published as three paperbacks in a case, a protest of sorts. The idea, I guess, was to emphasize that nothing under the sun is permanent.

Mom had a near-fatal illness that left me wrung out by the end of my time at Yale. Despite her years of alcohol abuse, she maintained her practice, ran the house, made it to all of Jonny's and my important functions, and continued to patronize the arts. And then the shit hit the fan. She came down with an infection in one of her heart valves: acute bacterial endocarditis, a late complication of childhood rheumatic fever. She was in fulminant heart failure from a leaking valve.

It was literally touch and go as to whether she could be stabilized enough to undergo valve-replacement open-heart surgery to replace the faulty valve. She spent several weeks in the ICU before, and another couple of weeks after, the surgery. Jonny came up from Venezuela and was a fixture at her bedside. I drove down to the City every chance I could get.

I remember sitting there, watching a tiny trickle of urine run down the catheter and into the collecting bag, each drop carrying with it the hope that she was about to turn the corner. With God's evident help, lots of prayers, and good fortune, Mom rallied, got through the surgery, and within a few months was back to work. She managed her practice and other activities—unfortunately, including alcohol consumption—well enough for another five and a half years, until her penultimate setback.

The 1970 Yale Commencement Exercises were, as always, held outdoors, come rain or come shine. Each residential college also had its own ceremony. Mom and Amee were on hand, beaming with pride, as I collected my diploma. Dad missed this graduation, too, but I knew he was proud of me all the same. I had worked hard, harder than I had at Buckley or Hotchkiss, to earn a coveted *cum laude* in English. Yale was a fabulous experience, but it was time to move on.

I loved my time in New Haven and was crestfallen when my class ring was stolen. The company that made it is long gone, and the newer designs just don't compare. By chance, the one day I looked for something similar on eBay, what popped up was a near-perfect match. All that was amiss was the date; 1973 might not work.

Well, I made it work. I bought the ring, which had mysteriously washed up on a beach in Tel Aviv, perhaps a gift from my Jewish ancestors. A crafty Seattle jeweler transformed the "3" into a "0," and there you have it!

I attended my Yale Fortieth Reunion. Neither Bob nor Steve was there. Rick, Charly, and John were, along with a number of other friends, including at least eight of the twelve of us who had gone on from Hotchkiss and four from Buckley. Reid Detchon and I represented both prior schools.

I led a sequence of yoga poses to an auditorium of classmates and significant others. They all grooved on chanting "Om" with me. It seemed to recreate, for a few shining moments, the Flower Power mood of 1970. It was a real trip down Memory Lane.

Our Fiftieth Reunion weekend was an online affair, as a result of the COVID-19 pandemic. My contribution was to initiate weekly Zoom "Boola Boola yoga" classes for classmates. At last count, only seven elected to participate, so I opened the classes up for all comers, even Harvard or Princeton grads. Even millennials.

MONIKERS

MEDICINE IN MY BLOOD

When we were young, Jonny and I often would call our mother Mumbles, for no particular reason. She hated it. Her reaction was always predictable, "...and don't call me Mumbles!" It was great fun. We made a point of taunting her with that pet name, especially when she already was annoyed. Our father called her Gouldie, and she called him Mortie. Cute.

Mathilde Mae Gould would never admit to this, but she was born in 1914, the same year as Dad. The older she got, the more years she shaved off her age. Near the end of her life, she was claiming to be eight years younger than her actual age. When she was admitted to a nursing home for terminal care, the doctor called, in an attempt to ascertain her true age. None of us knew. We didn't find out until we peeked at her driver's license after she died. You can bamboozle the family, but you daren't bullshit the Department of Motor Vehicles.

Mom gave us to believe that her mother was of Franco-Russian nobility, a White Russian *émigrée*. We would nod in seeming agreement to humor her, while shaking our heads behind her back. The truth is that sometime between 1910 and 1913 her parents, fleeing religious persecution, arrived on a boat, to be processed through Ellis Island, like millions of other ordinary immigrants to America. Grandpa took a job at a shoe factory and rented a small apartment in Manhattan's Lower East Side. He and Grandma moved on to South Norwalk, Connecticut, with little Mathilde Mae, when he became the foreman of the shoe factory there.

Dad's grandfather, Heinrich (he went by Henry), was, I believe, the youngest of the sibs, and the only one born in the U.S.A. The family came over from Germany, probably in the 1880s and settled in Brooklyn. Dad's father, Jacob (called Jake), served in the Army in World War I. Subsequently, he worked in a lumberyard in Brooklyn, which he eventually bought. He courted Sarah Neumann, who hailed from Czechoslovakia. Dad thought his mother the epitome of beauty. Somewhat biased, he always insisted that, "Czechoslovakian women are the most beautiful in the world."

Grandfather Jake succumbed to a heart attack in his mid-40s, probably occasioned by overwork. Sarah had a tiny pancreatic insulin-producing tumor, causing life-threatening hypoglycemia. The surgeon had to take an educated guess as to which half of the organ was most likely to contain the tumor, since he could not feel it. Imaging techniques such as CAT Scans and MRI were not yet invented—not by a long shot. Sadly, he guessed wrong. Dad told me that his mother died in an ambulance, while he, then a medical student, tried to resuscitate her. How traumatic that must have been! Mom never had a chance to meet Dad's parents.

Mortimer Wolf Weber (years ahead of Snerd) graduated with honors from NYU medical school at twenty-two, which is the age when most of us start med school. Not bad for a guy who claimed all his life to have been dyslexic, the result of having been converted at an early age to right-hand from left dominant.

My mother's father, Richard Gould, eventually bought the shoe factory in South Norwalk. In fact, at one time or another, he owned three factories, the one in Connecticut, and two in Pennsylvania—in Lititz and Kutztown. He made Lititz his headquarters and moved his family there a few years before my brother was born in 1940. Also, he again was renting an apartment in Manhattan. He and Grandma were moving up in life. Now they were on the gentrifying Upper West Side, Central Park West, to be exact.

As Mom tells it, her mother, Tamara Soliterov Gould, attended medical school at the Sorbonne in Paris. Just how she would have gotten there, considering she lived in Ukraine, is a matter of conjecture—I have my doubts. After Richard and Tamara emigrated to America, she apparently worked for a short time as a midwife. This much I can believe.

I know that Mom studied ballet at the Fokine School in New York. This was an impressive lineage. Michel Fokine and Vera Fokina were Russian *émigrés* and had been members of the Diaghilev *Ballets Russes*, which featured Nijinsky, the legendary dancer.

Not only did Mom benefit from years of ballet and classical piano training, but she also had a solid education and a Grand Tour of Europe after graduating from high school. It was on that trip that I surmise she became pregnant.

After the year away at the University of Wisconsin, when my half-sister was born and promptly put up for adoption, Mom returned to New York. She graduated from Barnard and, in turn, Columbia College of Physicians and Surgeons. P&S always has been in the vanguard of female medical education; a full one-sixth of the graduates in Mom's class of 1939 were women, which was remarkable for that time.

Mortie met Mae when he was a resident in pediatrics, and she was on her pediatric clerkship. He liked to tell the story of sneaking into the call room in the early morning and sprinkling cold water on Mom's feet to jolt her awake in time to make rounds. They made more than rounds together; they were married in the Ethical Culture sanctuary, on April Fools' Day, 1939. My brother, Jonny, was born a year later.

When America was pulled into the Second World War as a direct result of the Japanese attack on Pearl

Harbor, Dad was already in the Army Medical Corps. Whether he enlisted, or whether he had an obligation to serve based upon college and/or medical school tuition relief, is unclear.

Dad's training unit was shipped to England; that is, everyone except Dad. It seems that there was a colonel in the Philippines who was trying to recruit someone tall and athletic for his volleyball team. And guess who fit the bill? As a result, Dad spent the better part of two years in the jungle. He was proud to tell me that he was in the first group of US doctors to land in Occupied Japan at the war's end.

He rejoined the family in New York City after Armistice Day. By now, Mom had completed her residency in pediatrics and had opted for further training in allergy.

Dad joined the clinical faculty at New York University and continued to teach residents part time throughout his career, just as I was to do years later. He told me that his stipend as a resident in pediatrics just about paid his laundry bills. At least I received a living wage, even though the University of Washington pay scale was, and still is, about the lowest in the country. Like me, Dad voluntarily served for many years on the clinical faculty. Eventually, he rose to the position of Clinical Professor. I never quite got that far, peaking at Associate Clinical Professor. But then, I closed my practice at age sixty, whereas Dad continued to work until he was sixty-six.

He was appointed Director of Pediatrics at New York Eye and Ear and Beekman Hospitals. On more than one occasion, Jonny and I saw first-hand how much hospital personnel appreciated him, not only for his professional ability, but also for his kindness. His patients came from all over the city and from all walks of life. He also treated the children of some well-known people, including Jacqueline Kennedy Onassis and actor Jerry Orbach. He thought nothing of making house calls day and night, whenever he was needed.

Dad's patients loved him, and they stayed with him, often through several generations. After forty-five years of practice, he finally announced his retirement. Dozens of people sent him letters, all expressing their deepest thanks for his years of dedicated service. I deeply regret not saving these letters.

In what little leisure time Dad had, he would sit in his leatherette reclining chair in Jonny's old room, which he had commandeered, and would knock off *The New York Times* crossword puzzle every Sunday. This he did, invariably within an hour or so, while munching on pistachios—and always in ink. His many years working on crosswords made him a formidable Scrabble opponent, that is, until I finally managed to beat him. He refused to play me again. The occasional times I beat him in chess never made him quite that sore.

Mom continued her allergy practice for thirty years, until her alcoholism and other serious health issues got the better of her. She was in the forefront of desensitizing treatments for children and adults who were allergic to dust, molds, pollens, or pets. Many of her patients were well known, including banker David Rockefeller and his family, novelist John Steinbeck, and travel author John Gunther.

Along the way, she found the time to write a weekly newspaper column for *The Herald Tribune* called "You and Your Doctor," which ran for several years in the late '50s. She twice was awarded the Columbia University Meritorious Service Award for editing the P&S Alumni Magazine, which she did almost single-handedly for fifteen years. I remember her grumbling about how she couldn't count on her co-editors to write much of anything. As an editor of school newspapers and year-books, I certainly can relate to that.

She also wrote a play, probably when she was in medical school, entitled *A Contract Surgeon: A Play in Three Acts*. I have the unpublished manuscript, which sat on my desk for over thirty-five years, unread. I finally got to it. Although in no way is it redolent of Tennessee Williams or Eugene O'Neill, I must say it reads quite well. She once told me the work had been plagiarized by somebody or other and subsequently presented on stage. Who knows?

I believe I inherited the writing gene, if such a thing exists, from my mother.

Amazingly, she designed and decorated her dream vacation villa in the South of France while practicing medicine in New York City. She maintained a pretty good work-life balance, limiting her office hours to five or six hours, four days a week. She was very comfortable being called Mrs. Weber socially and Dr. Gould professionally. She would plan the menu each day and send the housekeeper off to the grocery store to buy whatever we needed.

Mind you, I only saw Mom cook one thing, and that was her mother's famous *boeuf bourguignon*. She gave me the recipe, and I've made it a few times myself, to mostly favorable reviews. The other thing she would do in the kitchen was inject the turkey subcutaneously with a significant amount of Chablis via a needle and syringe (always autoclaved first) that she brought from the office for this purpose. The white wine, she insisted, tenderized the bird. After I graduated from medical school, she let me do the honors, presumably because she felt that now I could be counted on to find the right tissue plane.

Mom's brother, W. James Gould, M.D. ("Big Jimmy," to differentiate himself from "Little Jimmy"—me) turned out pretty well for himself. He did his undergraduate work at Harvard, went on to New York University Medical School, like Dad, and opened an ear, nose, and throat practice.

The peculiar thing is that, unique among ENT specialists, he really didn't like to operate. Instead, he created a subspecialty in human voice disorders. He was invited to be ENT consultant to President Kennedy, and he removed some nasal polyps from President

Johnson. Considering the size of the man's nose, the polyps must have been whoppers. He finally burned out from Presidential ENT consulting with President Nixon. Watergate was the tipping point.

But, by then, he was a made man. He set up voice labs all over the country and became ENT consultant for opera stars like Maria Callas, pop singers such as Frank Sinatra and politicians, among them Bill Clinton. His office was filled with gold albums on the walls, Admiral Nelson memorabilia here and there, and Enrico Caruso's cribbage set.

Caruso I could understand, but Lord Nelson? Well... maybe because he had a voice like a foghorn.

Uncle Jimmy once promised to give me the cribbage set, but I never did get it. Then again, I never learned to play cribbage.

MISCHANCES

Mother's final illness was complicated, just like everything else about her. By this time, she and Dad were
living in Franklin Lakes, New Jersey, having sold the
Gramercy Park House and the villa in France. She and
I had no sooner returned to NJ, after dropping Dad off
at NYU Hospital for the first of his planned two-stage
ascending aortic aneurysm resection, when she collapsed. It was right back to NYU Hospital again.

She was admitted to the Intensive Care Unit, where
she gradually stabilized over the next week and a half.
However, the long-term prognosis remained grim, since
her liver was failing after all those years of alcohol abuse,
and her heart was failing from severe anemia. Once
again, she was in jeopardy of succumbing, as she had
been in 1970, when her mitral valve became infected.

The source of her anemia wasn't chronic disease,
but blood loss from a large tumor in her right colon. This
was surgically removed, and it turned out to be benign.
But little could be done for her end-stage liver.

My mother remained in the hospital throughout
Dad's stay from his first operation, his six-week convalescence, and his second aneurysm surgery. In all, for
something over two months.

I spent a good deal of time at NYU Hospital over
the course of Dad's two operations and Mom's long

hospitalization. All I can say is, no sane person in the Pacific Northwest would have tolerated the dinginess, inefficiency, and rudeness that was rife in this major New York City referral center. The floors were dirty and, when being "cleaned," were washed with black water. There were months' worth of old X-rays from previous patients stacked under the beds.

Families with loved ones in critical care might go almost a week without hearing from the physicians in charge. An intern, with no knowledge of the patients to whom the meds were being given, administered IV meds. There were cockroaches scurrying between the OR and the recovery room. I could go on.

In fact, I will. At that time, NYU had a one-room Emergency Room, with eight patient bays, separated by dirty curtains. One patient, a female Cardiology Fellow, ironically with an acute myocardial infarction (heart attack), was left in the ER for three days while they tried to find her a hospital bed. What a way to treat an MI! Lights on twenty-four hours a day, yelling and screaming, ambulance sirens blaring. It was unbelievable.

How people could tolerate such inefficiency amazes me. Yet a New Yorker can rationalize better than anyone else. Having waited all day for the doctor who never showed up, they will shrug their shoulders and say something like, "Well, what can you do? But he is the best."

You might even hear a complaint that the hospital

is dirty and overcrowded, quickly to be followed by a hopeful assurance that, "It has the best reputation." What would be the point of arguing with logic like this?

By this time, I was used to medical care in Seattle that was more sanitary, better run, more patient-friendly, and equally competent, not to get too far ahead of myself. Yet, I wonder if I would have had the same objections had I remained in New York City for my surgical career. I wouldn't have known any better.

When Mom finally became medically stable, she was transferred. First to her local hospital, and then to a nursing home in Wayne, NJ. She managed to rally enough to warrant discharge to return home.

Unfortunately, she deteriorated within a matter of a few weeks and was readmitted to the hospital in Wayne for her final days. She died at age seventy-three, in 1988, trying to convince her caretakers, right to the end, that she was only sixty-five.

After Mom died, while he was still able, Dad would drive down to the Flower Market in lower Manhattan every Tuesday morning, buy a dozen yellow roses, still tightly budded, and take them out to the beautifully landscaped, famous Woodlawn Cemetery in the Bronx. Mom was buried there, next to her parents—six family plots away from the gravesite of one of New York's best-known mayors, Fiorello LaGuardia. Dad would get down on his hands and knees with scissors and trim the grass.

He took me with him one time; I watched him do this. Tears came to my eyes. I offered to help, but he appeared to want to do it all himself. Devotion comes in many guises.

I never once heard him tell Mom that he loved her, or her him, for that matter. But obviously, he did. I asked him once why he stayed with her through all those years of alcohol abuse. He said, "It was for you kids."

Sadly, following Mom's death and two major operations on his thoracic aorta, Dad went into a long downhill spiral, remarried, and lost his mind. And what a mind it was to lose.

Early on, as he was sinking into dementia, he got lost while trying to drive his car home on a route he had driven dozens of times before. Not long afterwards, he got into a car accident. That was the end of his driving. No more crossword puzzles either.

Dad passed away at age eighty-four, ten years after Mom. The last time we saw him alive, he was in a hospital bed in his living room, with the side rails up. He was bed-bound and completely demented, although still quite sociable. It was so sad to see him like that.

We buried Dad next to Mom—actually, right on top of her.

MYSTERIOSO

Jon Gould Weber, the only non-doctor in the family and, arguably, the most accomplished of us all, was born in 1940. He has no memories of Dad prior to the end of World War II. Jonny's earliest memories are all centered on Mom, her parents and their home in Lititz, PA. The AJ Bedford shoe factory, which Grandpa owned and oversaw, was almost a second home. Jonny would go there with Grandpa, whom he idolized, five days a week. This likely fostered his lifelong affinity for business. And fine footwear.

The fact that I didn't make my entrance onto the scene until eight years and two months later qualifies me, at least statistically, as an only child; I believe the cut-off is seven years. By the time I was ten, in 1958, Jonny had matriculated at the University of North Carolina. He would come home for Christmas, but his rigorous schedule of swim training over the holidays kept him away much of the time. Ditto over the summers. Besides, I was either at Great Oaks Camp or at a cabin-building camp in Granby, Colorado. He moved out of the house for good in 1963.

Jonny, like Dad and me, loved baseball. We were fortunate to have the Yankee team doctor as a friend of the family. He generously provided us with two seats apiece for two World Series games, every year the team made it that far. And that was pretty much every year in the '50s.

In 1956, Jonny, being older, with more baseball savvy, carefully considered the options and kept what he thought were the primo game tickets for himself and Dad. He gave Mom and me the leftovers. As a result, he saw Whitey Ford, ace of the Yankee staff, pitch a so-so game. Mom and I got to see Don Larson, mediocre at best, throw the only perfect game in World Series History!

Not only that, but, after a game earlier that year, I had been invited into the clubhouse. Then-manager Casey Stengel gave me an autographed team ball, which I promptly forgot about. Dad found it in the basement and mailed it to me thirty years later, after it was appraised for $1,500. On eBay, you can buy one just like it today for as little as $3,599! But not from me. Mine is not for sale.

Unlike me, Jonny was not what you would call a diligent student. He claims that he really did not develop decent study habits until junior year in high school. He attended the Ethical Culture School for grades one through four, where he did little else but play. Middle school at Fieldston was more or less an extension of what went on at Ethical Culture, except that play became a bit more organized and rougher. Students were not pushed at all; as a result, Jonny is pretty sure that he learned nothing of any consequence.

He had no clue how to answer most of the questions on the Riverdale entrance exam for secondary school, but the admissions officer took pity on him and gave him the test as a take-home. Mom provided the answers, scoring higher than even the brightest kids who applied. They would have admitted Mom right into junior year!

The lengths parents will go to, to get their children into top schools, right? This kind of thing, and worse, has been going on, likely since the establishment of elite schools. The recent scandals hardly will put an end to the practice, I fear.

Fortunately, by his third year at Riverdale, Jonny was taking his studies more seriously. He placed in the top five percent in the National Merit examination. He was admitted to the University of North Carolina on a full athletic scholarship for swimming. He set conference records in all distance events, lettered in fencing, got a solid education, met Lucy Williams (his future wife), and skipped his graduation ceremony. Since Mom and Dad were not happy about the prospect of sitting around in all that heat, he saw little reason to hang around to pick up his diploma.

My brother was serious about his swimming. And he was damn good at it. While at Riverdale, he worked out with the Columbia swim team and, in summers, with the legendary Bob Kiphuth at Yale. Kiphuth regarded Jonny as an Olympian in the making. Unfortunately, a knee injury prevented him from participating in Olympic trials. This had to be devastating for him, since in 1960 he had posted the sixth-best time in the world in the 1650-yard freestyle (and third fastest in the United States).

Mom brought Jonny and me to the Rome Olympic games anyway, which for him was bittersweet; for me, it was way cool. Well, actually, brutally hot, but fun, nevertheless. We were able to get tickets to every event in the *Stadio del Nuoto*—the entire three-times-daily swimming competition that week, followed by another week of water polo.

In between events, we would wander around the Olympic Village, where my brother introduced me to many of the world's best swimmers, whom he knew from prior competitions. We traded Olympic pins with the athletes from other countries and amassed quite a collection. It seemed like the smaller the country, the more elaborate the pin. I wish I had saved mine. Still, it was an unforgettable time. And a great brother-bonding experience.

After Jonny's best shot at making the US Olympic swim squad ended disappointingly, the US Modern Pentathlon Team recruited him. He trained at Fort Sam Houston during the summers after his junior and senior years at UNC. His skills as a swimmer were what recommended him to the program directors, and he didn't disappoint them. In fact, he shattered the modern Pentathlon record for the 300-meter swim. In addition, he was a highly competent fencer and marksman. However, riding was not his forte, and he was distinctly average as a runner. So the experiment failed, although, while there, he made a few contacts with former intelligence officers at Fort Sam, which piqued his interest.

For a couple of years after college, my brother was only ten blocks away, living in an apartment with his wife, Lucy. Poor Lucy, who had to leave behind everything she knew and loved in North Carolina. Poor Lucy, forced to live under Mom's thumb, unable even to pick out her own furniture. Poor Lucy, not getting adequate support from Jonny when she tried to assert her rights over Mom, finally could take it no longer. She moved back to North Carolina, which was another devastating, life-altering event in my brother's life.

Jonny tried to drown his sorrows through eighteen months of graduate work in Foreign Service at Georgetown. He never completed his master's. Instead, he went to work for Moore McCormack Shipping Lines. They needed the position filled immediately and told him he could finish up his master's degree later. That never happened.

He spent nearly three years in Johannesburg, working for the shipping company. He gained experience, observing conditions in the neighboring countries and discussing his findings, more or less informally, with U.S.

Embassy officials. He knew more about what was going on in Rhodesia (now Zimbabwe) and the surrounding area than the so-called experts who were being paid to analyze the rapidly-evolving situation. This helped him land a better job: working part-time for the government.

Now single, he moved to Venezuela, where he met a studious Lebanese-Latina named Cristina. I visited Jonny in Caracas in the mid '70s—my only trip to South America—where I met the lady who was soon to become his wife.

Jonny now was working for IBEC, a company owned by Nelson Rockefeller. At the time, Rockefeller was keen on assisting South American countries in developing their own industries, primarily agriculture. Jonny got to know Rockefeller quite well, before he went on to be Governor of New York and Vice President for Gerald Ford. They travelled all over the continent together. Jonny met many Latin American leaders and generated helpful reports.

Jonny lived in Caracas for nearly ten years. He and Cristina married and produced a daughter, also named Cristina. (Not a lot of imagination went into this choice of names, but that was okay, because she turned out to be a beautiful, successful architect.) The family lived briefly in San Juan and Guatemala City, before moving back to New York for a few years. Jonny had been hired by Revlon, while also doing some consulting work for our government.

Jonny next took a job with Colgate-Palmolive and

moved his family to Hong Kong. He lived there for eight years and gained expertise in East Asian affairs, to complement his extensive awareness of conditions in various South African and Latin American countries. Through the years, he literally has travelled all over the world, save for Antarctica.

The Cristinas, *senora* and *senorita*, got tired of all this moving around. The grandmother, who I am pretty sure was not named Cristina, wasn't getting any younger, and mother and daughter moved back to Caracas to live with her. This was a sad time for Jonny, who was working for Colgate as he reported on conditions in the Far East. He had no one to offer him comfort or support, really no one in whom he could confide about his intel work.

He left Hong Kong and moved to Honolulu, where he met a Filipina named Alma. She needed his marketing expertise for her business. She designed and produced felt and Velcro educational products and toys, which were made in and exported from the Philippines. They formed a partnership, and the venture became quite successful. Jonny divorced Cristina and married Alma.

Jonny and Alma have been living in Carmel, California since 1992. With my work in surgery, swimming activities, and child-rearing, we did not have much opportunity to spend time together. Mom's illness and death reunited us, but then I had my own health problems, and we drifted apart again. Dad's dementia gave us reason to be back in closer contact.

Once Dad passed on, and we realized that we weren't getting any younger ourselves, we started to communicate more regularly. Jonny was a big help to me as I went through important life transitions. Before I knew it, we were back together as two long-lost brothers. We talked about his daughter and granddaughter, Alessia, his reverence for Grandpa, my kids, baseball, basketball, football, yoga, swimming, current events, and old times.

Not infrequently, he would ask my opinion about matters relating to his health. He has always been a bit of a hypochondriac; Mom and Dad were on to him and used to joke about that. Pretty soon, we were talking about politics, often stating opposing positions, but always respectfully. This transitioned into his opening up more about his professional career.

While I was staying at his house, my brother went into a back room and came out with a Distinguished Service Medal he wanted to show me. President Reagan had given it to him, with kind words of praise. How special is that? He also has been honored over forty times by the Department of Defense, by the Navy, and other organizations. More than a few missions were dangerous and could be fodder some day for a compelling novel, or maybe a television series.

When he isn't traveling, Jonny enjoys a nice life in Carmel. He continued to work two or three days a week until he turned 80. Prior to the pandemic, he worked out at the athletic club at Pebble Beach nearly every day. On a typical day he would swim fifty laps, take a sauna, have a drink with his buddies, among them Leon Panetta, and talk politics—tooling around in his fancy, spotless, baby-blue Jaguar that he won't let Alma or me drive, and watching Red Sox games, college basketball, or NFL football on his big-screen TV.

A few years ago, I asked him how much Mom and Dad knew about his secret work life. He had only recently begun to let me in on what he had been up to all these years. He had never said much of anything to Mom and only a little to Dad. Jonny was always somewhat reserved by nature, and, by necessity, his particular line of work made him even more so. I think he was very glad finally to be talking about some of it with me. He told me things that he never told Alma or either of the Cristinas. The more he opened up about it, the more relaxed he became.

We talked and talked for two weeks in Cabo during the two trips I took down there. I encouraged him to write a memoir and offered to help him in any way I could: editing, shaping the manuscript, and adding my two cents here and there. I was able to fill in some of the gaps in our family story—things that had happened after he had moved away. I also made some suggestions for the inclusion of anecdotes that he had shared with me.

His completed book, intended for immediate family only, is chock-full of fascinating stories, some very funny, some surprising. Jonny writes well, but not especially correctly. But what of it? That is where I come in. Editing his story for me was a labor of love. Besides, I was the one who cajoled him into writing it in the first place.

My brother has led a full and exciting life. He has worked as a part-time government consultant for half a century. He has been invited to sit in on important Republican Party councils, and has been well paid for his work. He generously donates his bonus money to the Alzheimer Research Fund in Dad's memory, even though Dad was unfailingly a Democrat.

Although he has done most of his consulting work for Republican presidents, he was asked by the Obama people to remain involved. To their credit, they recognized his almost uncanny predictive abilities. They even asked him to move beyond his areas of expertise in Latin America, Africa, and Asia—to get familiar with security matters affecting Eastern Europe.

Jonny wrote a letter to the Secretary of State with suggestions to affect some much-needed socioeconomic improvements in Venezuela. He has found it especially painful to countenance his daughter living in the midst of the steady downhill spiral of that formerly prosperous country at the hands of the chavistas. Much of his letter was adopted into a position paper and sent by the State Department to South American leaders.

The Senate Majority Leader's office solicited Jonny's perspective regarding how best to deal with the

Cubans, as the fifty-year trade embargo was lifted. At least three of the candidates for the 2016 Republican presidential nomination approached him with potential job offers. Somewhat reluctantly, he agreed to postpone his planned retirement in 2018 and pick up some responsibilities in the Middle East.

He only agreed to do so on condition that he be allowed to use the White House pool when the First Family was not in residence. The Trump people must have been desperate for Jonny's expertise, as they acquiesced, with the proviso that a Secret Service agent accompany him. Not necessarily lap for lap, but you get the idea. Imagine that! Who even knew that there is a pool in the White House?

Face it. Nearly fifty years is a long time to work in any field, especially while trying to keep abreast of volatile international political situations and traveling constantly. I never thought that he would quit, but he did. Finally. Six months later, he showed up for his annual fitness test, obviously no longer required. And passed, as usual, with flying colors.

Sadly, now that he is retired, the government has lost one of their very best consultants ever. He isn't lacking for projects. He is developing a series of lectures for the intel community. He serves on the board of the Hilton Hotels, Hawai'I, and has submitted a marketing proposal for Hilton worldwide.

In addition, he is promoting an enterprise to supply

more water to Jordan by pulling water molecules out of the air. Which sounds like a magic trick to me, although it should have significant humanitarian implications, water being so scarce in much of the Middle East. The Jordanians also have asked him to advise on ways to improve the shipping capabilities of their port city, Aqaba.

When the pandemic finally ends, time permitting, my hope is that he will begin training in earnest to break the 200-yard freestyle record for octogenarians.

I am quite sure that his decision to write his memoir inspired me to do the same. Hardly sibling rivalry. His life trajectory and political leanings have been considerably different from mine. His memoir reveals secrets for family eyes only. My life, with its gravitation towards new beginnings, is an open book. Otherwise, it would not be in your hands, would it?

MY SON, THE M.D.

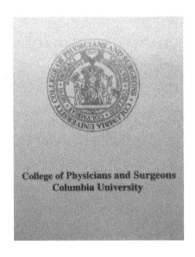

**College of Physicians and Surgeons
Columbia University**

*What if tomorrow bring
Sorrow or anything
Other than joy?
What if't be wintry chill,
Rain, storm, or summer's thrill?
Tomorrow's the future still;
This is today!*
From the school song

Before settling on Columbia medical school, I seriously considered a six-year, combined M.D./L.L.D. program at the University of Pennsylvania. Full of youthful idealism, I thought this training would put me at the vanguard for the reorganization of U. S. medical care delivery. I could see myself leading the charge of desperate consumers and frustrated doctors in the battle for an efficient and cost-effective health care system.

My admissions contacts at UPenn stuck a pin in this balloon, however. They suggested that I likely would end up as a malpractice lawyer, if I took this route. I had little interest in the law, and I had none whatsoever in litigation other than to promote my goal. So, it would be traditional medical school for me.

Columbia University College of Physicians and Surgeons, known by one and all as P&S, offered me early acceptance. I had a soft spot in my heart for Columbia, since that's where Mom achieved her medical degree. And I had spent a relatively pleasant summer taking Inorganic Chemistry at the Morningside Heights main campus, August heat and humidity notwithstanding. The admissions people were not a bit fazed that I was an English major and also had taken a number of art and music history courses. I liked that. They liked me. Maybe I had become a bit more attractive by then.

Even to this day, Columbia P&S leads the nation in merging the value of the arts with medicine. Students now are required to study art appreciation as a means to sharpen their powers of observation and listening.

Our medical school experience got off to a most unusual start in 1970. Due to an administrative mix-up, first-year students were told to arrive two days too early. Rather than send out a notice to correct the error, the school decided to put together a special trauma seminar for us. It was slapped together at the last minute, and it showed. None of the faculty seemed to have considered that the incoming medical students, mostly from non-medical families, wouldn't be accustomed to the gore associated with many medical emergencies. The presentations consisted of each trauma doc pulling out his or her worst horror-show slides and then describing the injuries—in gruesome detail.

Among the worst were x-rays of a head showing a nasogastric tube passed up into the brain rather than down the esophagus. But the corker was the ophthalmologist who presented two nasty sequences of eye injuries. One patient had been in a high-speed accident on the Autobahn and was found with his head stuck under the dashboard. One eyelid had been wedged open for a number of hours before he was extricated. You can only imagine what that eye looked like.

Even this paled in comparison with a series of photos of a man who had been hit in the eye with a spiked-heeled shoe by his irate wife. The first picture was a view of an empty eye socket taken from across the room. A progression of close-ups ended with a glimpse of a bit of an eye peeking up at a bizarre angle from the depths of the shattered socket.

At about this point, I recall six of my classmates leaving the room. Five of them went on to careers in psychiatry. The sixth dropped out of medical school altogether. But I stayed with the program all the way through, albeit with some regrets along the way. (Details on this will be provided, rest assured.)

After that gross-out introduction, medical school started in earnest with the pre-clinical sciences: Biochemistry, Histology, Microbiology, Physiology, and Gross Anatomy. Only the latter inspired any degree of creativity.

We were divided into groups of four, and each group had a cadaver to dissect. One group named their cadaver Abra. Get it? Our group named ours Ernest, although it was a female. (More incipient gender fluidity; we were way ahead of our time.) This was so, when asked by Fritz Abbott, the Anatomy prof, what we were doing—as he walked through the formalin-fumed room eating his cheese sandwich—we could honestly tell him that we were "working in dead Ernest." Abbott was, obviously, inured to the odor, but everyone else in the medical center would turn up their noses and make snide remarks when we entered the elevator after a day in his lab.

Fritz Abbott was a comparative anatomist, that is, one who looks for similarities and differences between species. One day, while slicing a piece of cheese with his pocketknife, he told us a story. His housekeeper had inadvertently knocked over and smashed his prize cat skull. On his way home a few days later, he noticed a dead cat on the side of the road. He hopped out of the taxi and decapitated it in order to replace the skull he lost. He told us this as his folded up his knife and put it back in his pocket. I asked him, "So, Dr. Abbott, is that the knife you used to chop the cat's head off?" He replied, "Sure. What of it?"

The morgue custodian was even weirder than Dr. Abbott. Think Igor from any of the Frankenstein movies. This man knew the story behind the procurement and death of every cadaver in the morgue and knew their names from memory. Reputedly, he talked to them at night, although this was unconfirmed. I do know that he often was seen muttering to himself. Or maybe it wasn't himself to whom he was muttering.

For some reason, Gross Anatomy (well named, by the way), which had historically been a full-year course, was pared down to an unbelievably bare (pun intended) eight weeks. We were left not knowing nearly enough before forging on to a crash course in Neuroanatomy.

There were, however, some benefits to the accelerated courses. We had thirteen months of electives at the end of our time at P&S. Those of us who were heading to surgical residencies were able to take an elective in Anatomy during the final year. We really needed more time to study the body.

It wasn't long before a sense of dissatisfaction with the medical education I was receiving started to creep in. All that seemed to be required at this level was rote memory without much thought. So uninspiring in comparison to my undergraduate studies. Fortunately, things started to pick up once we hit the wards, and decision-making became a factor; but this was six months down the road.

As I poured fact after fact into my brain, all I cared about was retaining enough to pass Part One of the National Boards. I simply could not abide the idea of having to retake it. I didn't care how well I did. I just wanted to pass and never have to think about the Krebs Cycle or static muscle potential again. Not that I had any idea at that point what I wanted to do with my M.D.

The best thing about Physiology was that I ended up with a new pet. We were assigned an experiment on frogs, at the end of which we were supposed to pith the poor creatures. Pithing is when you bend the frog's head forward and stick an awl into the spinal canal to sever connections with the brain. Well, my frog looked up at me so pitifully that I simply couldn't do the deed.

Instead, I tucked the frog into my pocket and legged it to the exit. I found a fishbowl somewhere, put some greens in it, plus a little sand and water. Presto! I had a frog spa. I named him Vmin because, at the time, we were studying something or other about whatever Vmin is.

I put Vmin on my bureau, and he (or she, or it) stayed with me all winter. Every day, I put Vmin on the floor and tried to get him (her, or it) to hop around a bit. I wanted him (generic) to stay in shape for his eventual release in the spring. Perhaps I was influenced by Mark Twain's, "The Jumping Frog of Calaveras County."

After the winter thaw, I took my little guy (or gal),

together with what had become a highly odoriferous spa, for a ride up to the Bronx River and dropped him (or her, or it) into a little tributary. At first, it seemed as though Vmin had no recollection of how to move or swim; he (maybe they?) just drifted. But then, to feelings of relief, mixed with sadness at our leave-taking, the legs started working. And off he (or whatever) went, a successful rehabilitation project.

Pathology was more interesting and a step up in relevance from Histology, but Introduction to the Patient was much better. We were allowed to put on short white lab coats, and we actually ventured forth onto the wards, admittedly with some trepidation.

The basic scenario was as follows. Working in pairs, we were brought to a patient's bedside, and our mentor gave a short introduction. We were left alone for what seemed like hours, but in reality, it was, perhaps, forty-five minutes. One of us would tentatively obtain the patient's history. The other would awkwardly attempt an examination, meticulously following a printed checklist. When the mentor reappeared, we would present the patient to him, as if it wasn't his (her, or their) patient. A short critique of the presentation followed.

The patients were generally free to kibitz. After all, they were the stars of the show, and many of them had something of value to add. I remember one veteran of the Columbia-Presbyterian (CPMC) wards, in particular: a middle-aged, outspoken African American woman. After she was questioned back and forth and examined up and down, the mentor came back to the bedside. Before he could open his mouth, the woman piped up, "Doc, I seen a lot of students around here over the years, and these two just ain't gonna make it!" What an intro to the patient! Maybe time to reassess career goals?

Ah, the wards at the old Presbyterian Hospital: twelve beds, six to a side, with sliding curtains. No air conditioning. Isolation techniques were rudimentary, and true isolation was reserved for very few patients. The Medical Center was huge—5,000 beds. In addition to Presbyterian Hospital and the College of Physicians and Surgeons, the complex included the Eye Institute, Babies' Hospital, the Psychiatric Institute, the Neurological Institute, the Hugo Black Research Building, the New York Public Health Building, Harkness Pavilion (for private patients), Atchley Pavilion (doctors' private offices), the School of Nursing, and Bard Hall (the medical school dorms). All of this was located over a 10-block area on Washington Heights, a half-mile south of the George Washington Bridge and three miles north of the main Columbia campus.

Three high-rise apartment houses were built during our first year to meet the crying need for safe, subsidized housing for students and residents. A seven-story extension was added to Babies' Hospital, even though there was no immediate need for this additional space.

Today, every inch of the building is in use. In later years, a huge library and research tower were added.

Cornell allied with Columbia in 1997 to form the New York-Presbyterian Hospital, while maintaining separate services at separate facilities. Or something like that. I suppose the main motivation was to create a "joint economy of scale."

Recently, a fourteen-story education building opened, complete with a simulation center. This will help students achieve a level of proficiency in dealing with patients before they ever have to deal with any live ones. Wow. Could we have used a simulation center in our day! That would have saved us a lot of embarrassment! When I think of all those patients we bruised and battered in our fledgling attempts to insert catheters into veins and arteries...

Incidentally, when I stopped by the hospital in 2015 for a nostalgic peek, it took something just short of an act of God to get me past the front door. Times had changed. Security had tightened. No more leaving kids in the lobby to make rounds on patients. We live in a different world today. Even more so since the pandemic.

In my day, Columbia had affiliations with Harlem Hospital, Roosevelt Hospital (near Lincoln Center), and Mary Imogene Bassett Hospital in Cooperstown, home of the Baseball Hall of Fame. Francis Delafield Hospital, where I had worked in the dialysis unit, was another. My Ob-Gyn rotation was at Roosevelt, and I went back there for my elective in Cardio-thoracic Surgery. The

Internal Medicine rotation was partly at Harlem Hospital. Urology was at Delafield. All of my other clinical rotations were at the Medical Center.

I had some really interesting classmates, several of whom had spent a number of years working in other fields. We had an army captain, a former professional dancer and a former teacher. And not just any former teacher, but the javelin-throwing son of my favorite teacher from Hotchkiss, Peter Beaumont!

During the first year, most of us lived in Bard Hall, as Mom had years before. The place likely had not changed much since then. Rooms were rather small and nowhere nearly so nice as those at Yale. But there was a ping-pong table and a gym in the basement. We got an active volleyball league going, which was quite competitive and lots of fun. I made some good friends through volleyball. And even more via the musical productions of the Bard Hall Players.

Amee graduated from Skidmore in May. Although we had a picture-book June wedding in the Englewood Episcopalian Church, I didn't have much enthusiasm about getting married, I'm embarrassed to say (for reasons that I will explain in a later chapter). Medical students only had one summer vacation, between the first and second years—which, I believe, still is the case. We took full advantage of it by heading off to Europe.

On return, we reclaimed Scarlett and moved into an apartment on the sixth floor of one of Columbia's new apartment buildings, where the rent was affordable. Amee took a job at the Psychiatric Institute, a rather weird place. Because it had been built into the side of a cliff, the building's entrance was on the tenth floor. If you had an appointment on the eighth floor, you would have to take the elevator down. I can imagine this was disconcerting for psych patients.

One of my classmates talked me into partnering with him in a *New York Times* newspaper-delivery business to help pay the rent. Our building was our route, and it had six apartments per floor. I developed a system of sliding the dailies out without having to hold the elevator door open. Shuffleboard at its finest. I could do all six apartments in the eight or nine seconds I had before the door closed.

The Sunday paper was a different story. Delivery required several shopping carts, rendering it a tedious process. I never had a paper route before, and I actually enjoyed it. In the words of my hero, Theodore Roosevelt, as he journeyed down an uncharted river in the Amazon Jungle: "It was my last chance to be a boy."

One of our paper customers, Donald Miller, was a Cardio-Thoracic Fellow at CPMC. Years later, he ended up at University Hospital in Seattle and was very active with the Seattle Opera. Often, we would see each other socially. Don never missed a chance to introduce me as his paperboy. It was a kind of standing joke.

Clinical rotations began in the second year and ran all the way through August of senior year. They were much more to my liking than the pre-clinical courses. I was at Presbyterian Hospital for one half of my Medicine rotation and at Harlem Hospital for the other. It was August and brutally hot and humid; sometimes the wards were almost fetid.

We would gather around a patient's bedside, and our attending would focus on whatever obscure disease was the flavor of the day. Whoever was assigned to that particular patient would lead off with the history and physical. Endless hours were spent on obscure diseases. Precious little time was devoted to common conditions like alcoholism, obesity, or back pain.

On one particular day—I am sure the topic must have been lupus; it almost always seemed to be—I was particularly tired, frankly exhausted. I had been on call the night before. Medical students were expected to draw blood, start IVs and obtain cultures at night. Supposedly, this was part of the learning curve. It also was a great savings for the Medical Center, since lab techs could go home at night. The labor of the med students was free and available at ungodly hours.

Well, picture me standing there in a semicircle of students, residents and attending staff, trying to stay awake. I nodded off and went into free fall. Fortunately, I bounced off a sturdy student on my right, woke up, and righted the ship, so to speak. Clearly, everyone had to have seen this. It was not what one would call a subtle move.

The attending carried on without missing a beat. Probably had seen something like this before. On the other hand, the patient, who was seriously ill, just wouldn't let it go. Every time I passed by his bed, I'd be greeted with something along the lines of, "Say, doc, I am feeling quite a bit better today. Tell you what; I'll get up and take a walk, and you can crawl into my bed here, and take a snooze!"

Internal Medicine at Harlem Hospital was mostly about getting into and out of Harlem safely. The CPMC bus would drop us off and pick us up right outside the hospital. Few of us dared to set foot outside the complex, especially after dark. Rudolph Giuliani had not yet arrived on the scene to clean up crime in New York, and this was about the roughest neighborhood in town.

My absolute worst experience there was the day I feared I would miss the last bus out. Rather than chancing the unreliable elevators, I raced down the twelve flights of stairs. As I reached the second floor, I realized to my horror that I had left behind important articles I needed for the next day's presentation.

I bounded back up the stairs two at a time, grabbed the papers and rushed back down. But after a few floors, my legs stopped obeying the commands of my motor neurons. I found myself slowing down more and more, almost to a crawl for the last four or five flights. It was like a nightmare when you are trying to run away from something evil, yet you can't move fast enough. I was in a sweat and totally panicked, afraid that I would miss the last bus. I didn't, or I might not be here now to write this.

I really enjoyed my OB-Gyn rotation at Roosevelt. We were treated pretty well by the staff and given a surprising amount of responsibility. I think I delivered sixteen babies that month. It was a bit nerve-wracking at first, but I got the routine down pretty well after the first few. Never dropped one, either. It would be another five years before I was unexpectedly called upon in the ER to catch another newborn.

My tour through the gamut of clinical specialties led me to the following observations:

- There is a continuum in medicine. It ranges from specialties that are almost all about diagnosis—with little to offer on the therapeutic side—to specialties where the diagnosis is apparent, and therapy is the main thrust. Neurology would be solidly at the "mostly diagnose then throw your hands up, as there is little that can be done" end of the spectrum. At the extreme opposite end would be Orthopedics, where the diagnosis is handed to you on an x-ray plate, the medical equivalent of a silver platter. All you have to do is put the pieces of bone back together, kind of like a shop project and using much the same kind of tools.

- Related to the above, Orthopedics is the happiest service in the hospital; Neurology is dismal.
- Nothing is more heartbreaking than to witness a child dying.
- Urology is an extremely gender-specific specialty. Why a woman would want to go into Urology is beyond me. Most men are squeamish about having their private parts inspected, much less handled, by a female with whom they are not on intimate terms.
- Surprisingly, Ob-Gyn is much less gender specific. Women must be more broad-minded. Or maybe they've had little choice in the gender of their doctor—until recent years.
- Gynecologists are inadequately trained to deal with many of the intra-operative complications they occasionally cause.
- Anesthesiology and Radiology are fields for physicians who like to keep their patients at a distance.
- Pathologists tend to have odd ideas about what constitutes humor, although they recognize a humerus when they see one. (Sorry about that.)
- Dermatologists think they are surgeons, but they aren't.
- Surgeons tend to be arrogant.
- Cardiac surgeons are surgeons on steroids.

- Psychiatrists can't stomach trauma cases.
- Male pediatricians have long eschewed the necktie in favor of the stethoscope. If only they would wear it more like the tie they abhor and not drape it around their shoulders...
- General surgeons ideally are like internists who know how to operate. In other words, they are trained to take care of the whole patient and not rely too much on consultants. Like internists and pediatricians, they are in the middle of that continuum between diagnosis and therapeusis.

And that is where I decided I wanted to go with my M.D. degree. Right smack in the middle, where neither figuring out what was wrong nor trying to do what was right would be primary goals, but rather doing both in equal measure.

I came to that conclusion after my Surgery rotation, which was toward the end of my third year. Dr. Barker, my mentor and a kindly, relatively approachable sort (for a surgeon) inspired me. I was also inspired by the somewhat unconventional Frank Gump. Ahead of the times, he was doing lumpectomies for breast cancer, when radical mastectomy, with increasing tendency toward modified mastectomy, was still the norm. He was blessed with a refreshing humility and a sense of humor. I would sit in their offices after OR work was done and groove on their wonderful anecdotes and experiences.

So, surgery it would be for me. Never mind that most of the other surgeons were obnoxious, egocentric, one-dimensional operating machines. I liked the challenge of arriving at the proper diagnosis and the potential to get in there (pun) and really fix the problem by planning and then performing the proper surgical intervention.

We had no surgeons in the family, unless you counted Uncle Jimmy, who, as I said before, was unique among ear, nose, and throat surgeons, in that he hated to operate. Dad, as a pediatrician, and Mom, an allergist, kept about as far away from the OR as a doctor could. I do remember Dad once proudly taking me to his office to watch him sew up a simple forehead laceration on a little boy. He would have had more sense than to attempt a wound closure on a girl's face.

Remember my childhood fixation about wanting to be a neurosurgeon? I mentioned that, right? Well, after watching a twenty-four-hour procedure, I dropped that idea. (Harvey Cushing must have had varicose veins. Perhaps this is mentioned somewhere in his biography. I wouldn't know.) Nope, it was going to be general surgery for me.

I had thirteen months of electives, and I used them to try my hand, as it were, in various surgical subspecialties. I also scoped out potential residencies in other parts of the country. I took full advantage of the time available. Coming as I did from a prestigious school like Columbia, it was simply a matter of a phone call, followed up by a letter, and doors opened.

I spent a month with C. Everett Koop at the Children's Hospital of Philadelphia, the oldest of its kind in the country. And it looked every bit of its age. They stuck me in some distant wing of the hospital—kind of a medieval garret, three floors up a curved staircase. Even the cockroaches wouldn't climb up that far, although I heard a bit of scurrying around in the walls more than once—or perhaps I dreamt it. Likely, I was sharing the third floor with rats.

Koop was the best-known pediatric surgeon in the country. I remember that he kept one fingernail long, which he said was to help him mobilize undescended testes during hernia repairs. He was a Quaker, wore a beard, and was an evangelical sort. And what a great teacher!

He went on to become the best-known Surgeon General in U.S. history. He kept his anti-abortion views to himself and devoted much of his time to inveighing against the cigarette industry. After this first sub-internship, I thought that pediatric surgery was the right path for me.

In retrospect, I believe I was temperamentally more cut out for a career in family medicine, yet I never considered that option until it was too late. If only I had taken the Myers-Briggs test, I might have saved myself from all the stress of a surgical career...

But I never had contemplated taking a personality test. I was committed to surgical training. I came back to New York and did a cardio-thoracic surgery rotation at Roosevelt. My Chief Resident was Donald Miller. Recall that I was merely a paperboy to him, which may have been what cured me of any temptation to become a cardiac surgeon. I always liked Don, but I did not like the attending chest surgeons. Too puffed up with their sense of self-importance. Too arrogant. All right, I will grant you that Dr. Oz does not come off that way. At least on TV.

I headed off to Dallas for a Trauma Surgery rotation at Parkland Hospital, a major trauma center. This is where JFK was taken after he was shot. Whew, talk about weekend Knife and Gun Clubs! We saw plenty of trauma at Columbia, but Parkland Hospital was a quantum leap above that, in terms of the volume of major trauma that came in.

The white folks in Dallas looked at Parkland as "the Negro hospital." They went to private Baylor Hospital, if at all possible. But, if one had suffered major trauma, Parkland was the best place to go. The plan was to stabilize and then transfer out to Baylor as soon as possible. That was considered optimal for those who could afford it.

As it turned out, my rotation at Parkland proved to be the key to why I ended up in Seattle. Shortly after my sub-internship ended, and while I was in my first year of residency at Presbyterian Hospital, I heard that the Parkland Chief of Surgery had left Dallas and moved to Seattle. He took with him an astonishing complement of eight surgeons and ten residents. It was beyond my comprehension how the University of Washington could accommodate such a large-scale transfer and how Parkland was able to recover from the unprecedented brain drain.

I was to find out more about what happened a few years later. In the meantime, I saw one heck of a lot of trauma and got a real sense of the seductively exciting career of a trauma surgeon. That is, if you like being called in on emergences at all hours of the night and testifying in court. Not my cup of tea.

Out of the blue, Uncle Jimmy called me one day while I was in Dallas. He wanted to know if I was planning to look at the surgery residency in Houston. I told him that I didn't think I wanted to be part of that scene. It was too heavily weighted toward cardiac surgery, and the general surgery program was not all that highly rated. Uncle told me that he knew Michael DeBakey, the world-famous heart surgeon, quite well, and he would make an introductory call on my behalf. I tried to say thanks, but no thanks, but he would not take no for an answer. So I thought, why not go and meet The Man?

I recalled my CPMC surgical mentor, Dr. Barker, telling me amazing stories about the brilliant Dr. DeBakey.

When DeBakey was invited to P&S as a visiting professor, Barker took him on a tour of the research labs. In each lab, the principal investigator gave DeBakey a short précis of what their research was about. In every case, after listening for ten minutes or so, DeBakey would ask questions and make suggestions. He not only had fully grasped what was being researched, but he appeared to have a better idea of what direction the work should take than the principal investigator.

I rented a car and drove to Houston to meet The Man. He had quite a set-up. He would see patients in his office until his assistant told him that he was due in one of the four operating rooms his teams had going simultaneously. The Man would walk up a private staircase directly to the scrub sink, wash, and step into one of his operating rooms.

It was perfectly choreographed. Every move. As he moved forward, the intern stepped back. The carotid artery would be exposed, clamped off or bypassed, and opened. The Man would clean out the plaque, sew the artery closed, and let his boys finish the job.

Then it was off to a second room, where the patient's heart was already on bypass, and he would sew an artificial valve in place. He would move on to yet a third room, where the patient's aorta was cross-clamped and the iliac arteries exposed, downstream from the aneurysm. Here, he would sew in the graft, or maybe just one end of the graft, leaving this crew to complete the job.

Room Four was a coronary bypass; the vein was already stripped from the leg and, again, the heart was on bypass. The Man would put on his operating magnifying glasses, and he would sew the vein in place above and below the blocked coronary artery. And leave.

Whenever there was a bit of a lull, he would duck out of his office and visit some of his twenty-odd patients in the Open-heart Recovery Room. At least once a day, more often twice, he would make rounds on the eighty or so patients he had in the Methodist Hospital. His Chief Resident was at his beck and call, with all pertinent information at hand.

The day I followed him around, he did the critical part of eleven operations. And that was a slower-than-average day. No exaggeration.

The general surgery residency at Baylor Medical Center required that first-year residents spend six months on the cardiac service: three months with The Man and the other three with the other four cardiac surgeons. For the DeBakey service, one choice was three months rounding on eighty patients twice a day at the Methodist Hospital. As soon as morning rounds ended, it was time to start evening rounds. Another option was to spend all day, six days a week, in the OR and be available for emergencies on Sunday.

But the most coveted option, a requisite for anyone hoping to go on to a Cardiac Surgery Fellowship with The Man, was to work in the Open-heart Recovery

Room. This was a 24/7 rotation. The resident (Read: slave) was forbidden to leave the premises. Conjugal visits were allowed once a week for fifteen minutes. Period.

I had a cup of coffee with a third-year surgical resident. He told me, "You really don't want to come here." Just like that. I didn't tell him that I had no intention of applying. He told me that he had opted for the Open-heart Recovery Room rotation, as he had wanted to secure the coveted Cardiac Fellowship upon completion of his five-year surgical residency. He told me that he had worked his ass off, yet not once had The Man spoken to him.

That is, until the day his mother died. On that day, DeBakey came out of nowhere, put his arm around him, called him by name—he was as shocked that Dr. DeBakey knew his name as he was at the news of his mother's passing—and told him to go home for a couple of days. The resident acknowledged this minimal act of compassion with tears of gratitude.

He came back from the funeral with a renewed faith in the Baylor program, only to receive the silent treatment again for the next two-and-a-half years. The poor guy couldn't wait to finish his residency and move on. As for me, I couldn't wait to get out of Houston.

Back to New York again for an orthopedic sub-internship to buoy my spirits. Not that I thought I wanted a career in ortho; it was just that it was so much fun to see all the healthy, albeit somewhat broken, patients smiling and busily healing. Admittedly, there were more than a few little old ladies with broken hips and amputees who weren't as happy as the others. Still, the ortho service was world-famous, and it was a pleasure to be a part of it, however small.

Next, I was off to San Francisco for a month of vascular surgery at the University's Moffitt Hospital. I was given a room for the duration of my stay—in the Haight-Ashbury section of town. It was nearby, yet far out. Stoned hippies were everywhere.

There was a triumvirate of vascular surgeons at Moffitt. The department head, Jack Wiley, was known internationally for his fine work, but locally he was known for a rather bizarre quirk. All visiting students and doctors were warned in advance not to cry out in horror when Dr. Wylie stepped back from the table immediately before opening the carotid artery, so the circulating nurse could remove his mask. He would then proceed to do the endarterectomy (plaque removal), step back again, and have his mask reattached.

Made no sense to me; in fact, it violated all tenets of sterile technique. But that was the way it was, and we were not to question the whys or wherefores. Anyway, San Francisco was fun, and I scrubbed in on enough vascular surgical cases to determine that vascular surgery was not for me. Too many revisions and too many poor outcomes that necessitated amputations.

And that was that for my fourth-year travels and sub-internships. I took an anatomy course intended for those who wanted to go on to surgical residencies. It was taught by Dr. Bhonsley, notable for having *hand sewn* the first aortic-bypass grafts out of cotton, which were then inserted into humans by Art Voorhees at CPMC. The image of Gandhi sewing his own homespun clothing comes to mind here. We were given opportunities to perform unnecessary operations on dogs. This was hard for me to accept—shades of my experience with Vmin.

I also took a month's elective to study alcoholism in depth. I wanted to supplement the scant amount we learned about alcohol addiction in medical school. I owed at least that much to Mom.

I spent the first two weeks at the Smithers Institute in New York City, run by Amee's distant cousin, Dr. LeClair Bissell, a pioneer in addiction treatment (daughter of the controversial Air Force General and known to the family as "Binkie"). While there, I set in motion a plan for Mom's rehabilitation. I hoped that she would eventually admit she was an alcoholic and be willing to sign herself in for a month of therapy.

I went from there to a "twitch farm," as the patients called the long-term, rather tony rehab facility, in New Jersey. I stayed there for two weeks, attended all the meetings, played softball, and ate with the patients. The only difference between the patients and me was that I stayed in the staff quarters. Well, that and the fact that I wasn't an alcoholic; I was a workaholic. Probably needed rehabilitation just as much.

Meanwhile, I went ahead and applied for a surgical residency position at CPMC, Roosevelt Hospital, and UPenn. Columbia-Presbyterian accepted me, which simplified life for Amee, Scarlett and me, as it meant we could stay right where we were, in the first residential tower.

Little did I know that I was soon to throw a big monkey wrench into the works by making a poor personal choice. I believe that things do have a way of working out for the best in the long term, but I have many regrets for mistakes I made along the way.

MUSIC MATTERS

A MAJOR MODULATION

More than almost anything else, the love of music has helped me weather life's storms. Mom occasionally remarked that, before I had much speech, I could sing children's songs, and in French at that. An inveterate Francophile, she loved to tell this possibly exaggerated tale, but it does suggest an early love of music.

Dad had a library of classical LPs. As a child, I would ask him to play Mozart's *Eine kleine Nachtmusik*, Schumann's *"Rhenish"* Symphony, and Beethoven's Seventh Symphony over and over. My parents took me to the New York Philharmonic children's concerts. I still remember my first exposure to Prokofiev's *Peter and the Wolf* and Britten's *Young Person's Guide to the Orchestra*.

They also took me to the opera at the Met. The first one I ever saw was *Carmen*. Both Mom and Dad enjoyed opera, but Dad drew the line at Wagner. To him, Wagner's operas were too long and too heavy. "Deadly," he called them.

Years later, after Mom had a series of serious health setbacks, I took her to the Met to see *Lohengrin*. Mom hadn't been well enough to attend an opera for years, and she was thrilled. She had an artificial heart valve by then, and it was audibly clicking at irregular intervals. She was getting "the look" from indignant people seated around her. I let them have it during the first intermission, while Mom was in the restroom. I understood their annoyance, but I wasn't going to allow anyone to spoil her last night at the opera. Especially not after the wonderful start she gave me, which turned into a lifetime of classical music appreciation.

Mom's interest in music went beyond simply sitting in the audience. She had a friend, Mickey Goldman, who was an "angel" (financial backer) for the famous Broadway producer, David Merrick. Mickey, a very flamboyant kind of guy, talked Mom into investing in a few Merrick shows. She made some money, and she lost some money.

Notable successes were *Fanny* and *Destry Rides Again*, and, best of all, *Butterflies are Free*, a solo production of Mickey's. There were losers, too, Losers including *Minnie... and the Boys* and *Take Me Along*. If reviews were dismal, Broadway shows would sometimes close after opening night.

Through the years, Jonny and I got to see dozens of musicals. Mickey infallibly would meet us during intermission with small containers of orange juice. The last of the big-time spenders.

Mom had had many years of classical piano train-ing and retained her Czerny exercise books, as well as Chopin, Bach, and Schubert scores in the piano bench. She would occasionally play a selection, but this became increasingly rare as her health declined. Her 1934 Steinway baby grand was the centerpiece in the living room.

I started piano lessons at about age seven with Bill Korff. He was a kindly, patient man who taught me to read music and play scales. I did not enjoy practicing one bit. Wish I had. Mostly, Bill would come over and play what I should have mastered. It always sounded lovely, but I just wasn't motivated.

Dad shipped the piano out to us after Mom died, and my daughters took piano lessons for a few years. The girls inherited my resistance to practice, despite our trying to browbeat them into it. Alas, another regret.

Singing was something else. I always enjoyed listen-ing to popular and folk music. I have been blessed with an accurate ear, a decent, untrained singing voice, and a good memory for lyrics. I know virtually all the lyrics and melodies of pop hits from 1957 or so until 1970, not to mention jingles and television theme music. After that, the grind of medical school kept me from keeping current with popular music. And off the boob tube.

Reading music never came easily. My useful singing range was limited to about an octave and a half, but I sang in the Brick Church Children's Choir and the Buckley

Glee Club, before and after my voice changed. Our beloved music teacher, Paul Rotella, who introduced us to Gilbert and Sullivan operettas, chose me for the choruses of *Mikado* and *Pinafore*. Bobby Camargo and I did a concert of Everly Brothers tunes during one Talent Assembly in seventh grade.

At summer camp, I did a lot of singing and, as a counselor, some mediocre guitar playing with my buddy, Phil Ruggiero. Phil was amazing from a musical perspective. He had a foghorn voice from years of screaming his head off about anything and everything, yet he was blessed with perfect pitch and a big range. And, oh boy, could he play the piano, or the guitar, or the trumpet. He played in the band all through high school, seemingly with the aim of driving the poor, beleaguered band teacher absolutely mad. Anyone else would have been so busted for throwing a jazz riff into a classical piece, as he often did. But not Phil, because he was so skilled.

Phil could hear a piece of music once and sit down and play it. If you didn't like the key he chose—for instance, if the top notes of "For Boston" were beyond your range—he would modulate down a second or a third and right in mid-phrase. This man's talent was truly awesome.

After two memorable summers as camp counselors, Phil and I remained friends and would see each other a few times a year. He would come to parties at the house, take off most or all of his clothes, drink a lot of beer, and pound on Mom's piano—not necessarily in that order.

Phil became a successful Wall Street trader and channeled his musical skills into conducting a barbershop chorus. I enjoyed an impromptu concert by his group in 1976 at the Bergen Mall in New Jersey. And he is still at it—even more so, now that he is retired. He also plays in a doo-wop band and arranges music. He recently sent me an mp3 of his complicated, eight-part arrangement of the song "I Thought About You," in which, incredibly, he sings all eight parts!

Nowhere nearly so musically gifted as Phil, at Hotchkiss, I soloed in the choir and ran the Bluenotes, which was an *a capella* group. There were eleven of us, plus Bob Small. He couldn't hold a tune, but he was more reliable in his attendance than anyone else. Anyone else, that is, except for Russ Walden and me. I was the music director, but really Russ was the key member. We simply would not have existed, were it not for him. His musical talents were on a par with Phil's. I am not sure about perfect pitch, but he sure could play the piano. And compose music. He was really, really good. Good enough to parlay his skills into a successful musical career.

We made a record in the school gym with rather crude recording equipment. We sold a fair number of copies, particularly to our friends and families. We played it during our Fiftieth Reunion dinner. Turned down low as background music, it sounded fine.

What we really liked best was to sit around jamming doo-wop tunes. We were pretty good at it, and we started sprinkling our concerts with more and more doo-wop and rock 'n' roll numbers. They went over far better than the staid and stale stuff, like "Stormy Weather."

It turned out that our experimenting by adding some contemporary Hit Parade songs to the repertoire became the genesis of Sha Na Na. A founding member, Scotty Powell, who was in the Bluenotes at Hotchkiss, went on to Columbia and joined one of their *a capella* singing groups. This group, too, began switching more and more to R 'n' R and doo-wop.

Pretty soon, they made a complete transition and were invited to the famous Woodstock music festival. They ended up with their own TV show, lots of concerts, and plenty of money. I think some of the group never bothered to graduate, although Scotty did. He, by the way, was one of the three guys wearing a gold lamé jacket and was the one who did the Elvis songs. Scotty grew up, went on to medical school, and now is an orthopedic surgeon.

But back to Russ. While at UConn, he visited Steve, Bob, and me at Yale during one football weekend, where he was last seen throwing up in the bushes. He pulled himself together and went on to be the piano accompanist and then music director, first for Mary Travers, of Peter, Paul, and Mary, and then for Judy Collins.

We remain good friends and see each other every time he has a gig in Seattle. Russ is now celebrating his twenty-ninth year with Ms. Collins, who, at 82, remains a vocal force to be reckoned with. They were putting on over 150 shows a year, pre-pandemic, and are cranking things back up and still making successful recordings as of this writing. Together, they have performed "Send in the Clowns" over 2,000 times!

I asked him recently how he manages to keep it fresh. He told me that it is a matter of the differing way he attacks the keyboard with his right fourth finger. That is what it boils down to. Seriously. Whatever it takes.

MELODIES AT THE ALMA MATER

At Yale, I joined the Freshman Glee Club and was selected for the Alley Cats, one of the best of the six *a capella* singing groups. We sang with twelve voices, some better than others, but even the weaker ones were still pretty good. Tryouts were competitive. At Yale, the singing-group scene is a very big deal.

There were some fine singers in the group; several went on to professional careers. We toured during spring vacation, road tripping for two weeks down the Atlantic Coast to Florida and back, mooning each other at tollbooths and performing other mature stunts as well as concerts. I was the business manager of the group, as if I knew anything about business, then or now.

Rick Peiser, our music director—better known as pitchpipe in singing group circles—was and still is a weird and wonderful man. Rick not only has perfect pitch, but he has a near-photographic memory. This just isn't fair. Fortunately, the rest of us mere mortals can console ourselves by noting that he has precious little common sense.

Rick forgot the name of the motel where the Yale Alley Cats were staying in Florida. This may not have seemed so bad, except that we stayed at the Del Rest Motel in Delray Beach every year, and this was our third year. He had gone out to play a round of golf and couldn't remember where he was staying, even after looking at the names of the six hotels and motels in the Delray phone book. He made his way back by remembering every street the cab had driven down on the three-mile route to the golf course, working backward in his mind!

He would do things like drink a lot of beer and then ask us to sing the "Hallelujah Chorus" on the beach. He'd stop, and tell us to start over at the 16th measure, as if any of us, except he, knew the score (which he was reading in his head). And he never missed a *Rocky and Bullwinkle* cartoon show.

Soupie—I called him Soupie, not sure why—could play the piano. He could sing, maybe not beautifully, but always on pitch, and he arranged a number of songs for the Yale Alley Cats. We sang in the Yale Glee Club together.

The Alley Cats got gigs here and there while school was in session. It was at one of those, a concert at the College of New Rochelle in the spring of 1969, that I met the great love of my life, Mary (who won't resurface until toward the end of this story).

By then, I was soloing in "Five Foot Two," "Aura Lee," wherein I took off my shirt (I know, TMI), and "All my Trials," which a musical, yet tone-deaf nerd whose name I forget, helped me arrange as my tryout for the Whiffenpoofs, Yale's elite senior singing group. It didn't do the trick. It was hopelessly complicated, although we got it right most of the time, including on our record.

Rick was selected for the Whiffenpoofs. A lot of people thought I was a shoo-in, and they were surprised when I wasn't picked. So was I; it was another major disappointment.

The blow was softened somewhat when I was elected president of the Yale Glee Club, beating out Bobby Camargo, my old friend from Buckley. The Yale Glee Club is the best-known organization of its type in the country.

We were privileged to have Fenno Heath as our Music Director. Fenno was a real inspiration, a marvelous composer and conductor—a worthy successor to the even better-known Marshall Bartholomew. The two covered a continuous span of over 70 years. It was a great honor to serve as Glee Club President.

It was traditional for the president to solo in "Eli Yale," which I did many times. It was also expected that the

Glee Club president would conduct the Yale Alma Mater, "Bright College Years," at concerts.

It also was customary for the incoming Glee Club president to follow his predecessor in joining one of Yale's storied secret societies. I broke that mold, obsessing about staying on track for a top medical school education—fearful of any further distractions. A girlfriend, Glee Club activities, and my studies were enough to handle.

We went on the Ed Sullivan Show that year, where we performed our Football Medley, fully orchestrated for the first time. Before, this had been done with nothing more than a simple piano accompaniment. We also were asked to sing the background for Lee Marvin performing "I Was Born under a Wand'rin' Star."

Picture 60 young dudes (Read: "city slickers"—its old-fashioned meaning) in tuxedos on the set of a quasi-Western ranch, with the star of the show, Marvin, meandering about the set. He walks off into a setting sun, while we hum the last verse. Kind of goofy? Well that was TV then. And it isn't much better today, either, if you ask me.

Unfortunately, Marvin showed up roaring drunk, with drink in hand, perhaps trying to recreate his role in *Cat Ballou*. He screwed up the takes on Saturday: flipped the bird, ducked under the boom camera, messed up the lyrics, and grossed us out with more foul language in less time than any of us ever had heard before. As a result, Ed Sullivan, who ordinarily stayed home on Saturday, was called in to read him the riot act. We had to go back early Sunday morning to try again, in advance of show time.

All music on TV in those days was pre-recorded and lip-synced. Some of it still is. At any rate, we finally made it through a decent "take," and the show went on the air. Consensus opinion was that our Glee Club sang well, but that Marvin looked pretty hung over!

About a month after Mr. Marvin's less-than-stellar performance, I was browsing through the mail in the Glee Club office, and I noticed a thick, hand-written letter. I opened it and read an apology of sorts from Lee Marvin. He claimed to be a sensitive artist, much misunderstood, and so on. Would that I had saved the letter. Sadly, disgusted with his antics, I tore it up. It would have commanded a pretty penny on eBay today.

What a thrill it was to perform Beethoven's Ninth at Carnegie Hall. It was conducted by Leopold Stokowski, in celebration of the maestro's ninetieth birthday. He requested a hundred voices, whereas we usually sang with sixty. This was easily remedied. We made up the difference by recruiting alumni, including William Sloane Coffin, then Yale Chaplain and a well-known figure throughout the protest years.

Senior year was also the year that the Yale Glee Club introduced a Women's Chorus (fully integrated into the YGC the following year). Several of these talented co-eds invited me to hold tryouts for the first Yale women's singing group, The New Blue. Like the Alley Cats, it's still going strong today. Amee helped me with the auditions, because her musical training was superior to mine. She was more facile at reading music, played the piano fairly well, and had a nice singing voice. To return the favor, I arranged the R 'n' R standard "Who put the Bomp?" for her *a capella* singing group at Skidmore.

At my daughter Katie's Yale graduation in 2003, I ran into a group of New Blue singers. I casually informed them that I was the one who had selected the original group, which was news to them, even though my contribution is acknowledged on their web site. It obviously meant little or nothing to them. Kids these days!

Camargo received a measure of vindication at our Fortieth Reunion when he was asked to join the '70 Whiffenpoofs as a replacement. Forty years late is better than never. And you know what? He was in better voice than anyone else in the group. Nobody was happier for Bob than I, except, possibly, his wife, Lucy.

Some years before that, Soupie assumed the role of pitchpipe for the 1970 Whiffs. For all of his lack of common sense, for all of his weirdness and wonderfulness, he has accomplished one heck of a lot. He went on to gain his masters at Harvard, a doctorate at Oxford in Urban Planning and taught for a while at Cambridge. Then he taught at USC, and now he is Professor of Urban Planning at Harvard. He has managed to remain friends with both Amee and me despite our divorce. His singing voice remains a work in progress. Oh well. But he keeps trying.

MAESTRO IN THE MAKING

At Columbia P&S, I directed a Christmas choir each year, with piano and flute accompaniment. We had a decent, sixteen-voice, four-part choir, anchored by stalwarts like Amee and Bo Riehle, another former Whiffenpoof. We performed choruses from *Messiah*, Bach cantatas, Christmas carols from France, England, and Germany—something different each year. We gave only one annual performance, which always was well attended.

The Bard Hall Players is an anomaly. Fifty years and still going strong, it is the only extracurricular medical student-run theater company in the country. I took the lead roles in two of The Bard Hall Players' musicals, *Anything Goes* and *Bells are Ringing*, even dancing a bit in both, believe it or not. We rehearsed for three months, made our own costumes, built the sets, and put on our shows for a single weekend only. We filled the house every night, mostly with friends and relatives. Regardless, a good time was had by all.

It was a blast, especially for an out-and-out eccentric like me. I suspect that the experience of absorbing these different stage personae and working to feel and communicate their different, varying emotions made me a better physician—indeed, a better person. Certainly, it was a great stress release from the daily grind of medical school.

A scene from "Anything Goes;"

How very fortunate to have an amazing amount of musical and artistic expertise in and around the Columbia-Presbyterian Medical Center. Consider that we had medical, nursing, dental, physical therapy, and occupational therapy students to choose from, in addition to the full medical, nursing, and ancillary support staffs (not to mention talented significant others like Amee). As a result, we were able to put together a full orchestra. Our sets were nothing to sneeze at, either.

I topped off my fledgling Washington Heights musical career by directing *Pirates of Penzance*, although I took no role in that one. Directing was a big enough challenge. A classmate, Rich Mattern, an excellent pianist, helped me with the rehearsals. We didn't have a full orchestra for that production; Rich played the piano score very well, and that sufficed.

Problem was, despite having good singers for all the other roles, including an excellent lead soprano, we lacked a decent tenor for the role of leading male. I had just the solution: Bob Camargo. He was doing a psychology internship in the Bronx and jumped at the opportunity. We were all set.

We invited Mr. Rotella to opening night. There he was, right in the front row, beaming with pride, watching two of his favorite Buckley boys, all grown up. I was conducting—in tails with white gloves, no less—while Bob was starring in a Gilbert and Sullivan operetta, to which Rotella had introduced us years before.

When the Dean of Students asked me to select music for our graduation processional, I selected my favorite tunes, recorded them all on a cassette, and carefully timed everything so I could march out to my favorite section of Handel's "Water Music." I stood by the door, stopwatch in hand, and told my classmates to walk faster or slower, in order to synchronize my entrance with the appointed music. Amee, Mom, and even Dad were there in the audience, proud as can be. Our boy, the doctor!

At graduation, the Dean awarded the Joseph Garrison Parker Award to me, for contributions to the cultural life of the medical school. I believe I earned—and treasure—that award more than any other I ever received.

SEMPER PRO MUSICA

I parlayed my interest in music into nearly six, somewhat disappointing years on the Board of Directors of the Seattle Symphony. Naively, I assumed my appointment was related to my having been a Music History minor, but I came to find out that it was all about raising money. Nonetheless, there were some benefits from the time I spent on the Symphony Board. I made friends with a number of the orchestra members and *The Seattle Times* music critic, Melinda Bargreen. The Maestro, Gerard Schwarz, and I were on a first-name basis; we even went to a few baseball and basketball games together.

Hans Lehman, a one-of-a-kind Seattle physician and arts patron, was responsible for getting me involved with the Symphony. Through him, I got to know the former Maestro, Milton Katims, and his wife, Virginia, quite well. Milton had been conductor of our Symphony for twenty-two years, before Gerry came to town. I especially appreciated the direct link to Arturo Toscanini, Dad's favorite conductor—Milton had played principal viola in Toscanini's NBC Orchestra.

The Katims and the Lehmans invited me to several musical soirées at their homes. I met some fascinating musicians and heard great stories. Lehman, Milton, and Virginia have since passed away, and Maestro Schwarz has moved on.

After my first heart attack, I was sorely disappointed when not a single person from the Symphony bothered to inquire how I was faring, especially considering that I had donated thousands of dollars. Although I only had a few months left in my second term on the Board, I just couldn't stomach sticking around. So I submitted a letter of resignation. There was not one peep from the Board thanking me for my efforts all those years. It was kind of like, "How dare you leave the Board before your term is up?"

Nevertheless, I have remained a loyal subscriber to the Seattle Symphony for nearly forty years. I just can't live without symphonic music. I have hundreds of CDs and drawers full of cassettes that should have been pitched years ago, especially now that streaming music services are so readily available. Although I could listen to recorded music all day, nothing can match the excitement of attending a live performance. For example, not long ago, I had the pleasure of seeing Jonathan Biss perform nine Beethoven sonatas in two successive evenings—all from memory!

Biographies of favorite composers enthrall me. Recently, I delved deeply into the lives of Haydn, Mozart, and Beethoven. However, I cannot bear to finish any of these books. I simply do not want them to die. I hope you can understand. Admittedly, it might be a bit of a reach.

I have maintained my subscription to the Seattle Opera for the same length of time. My particular, and peculiar, claim to fame is having sat through twenty-three complete *Ring of the Nibelung* cycles (four operas staged over one week). Mr. Bailey would be so proud. He was the one who got me hooked on Wagner. Or was it the oil paintings on the walls at Lüchow's?

Studying Wagner is a lifetime hobby. Amazingly, every time I sit through another seventeen-hour cycle of *Der Ring*, I feel thrilled, as if I were experiencing it for the first time.

The 1985 *Ring* afforded me the opportunity to meet John Macurdy. I remembered him as an outstanding soloist in the Brick Church Chorus and a leading *basso* at the Met after that. When he came to Seattle for several months of *Ring* rehearsals and performances, I was bold enough to invite him to my home in Edmonds for dinner. He accepted, and we became quite friendly.

My then wife Edie and I were invited to his home in Stamford, CT, and John was always helpful in obtaining tickets for us to Met performances. We went backstage, where, after a thrilling performance of *Othello*, he introduced us to Dame Kiri TeKanawa and Placido Domingo, among others. It was great fun.

In the mid-80s, Edie and I went to Santa Fe to see several operas. They were held outdoors, and the setting on a clear, starlit night was magical. One evening, we were in the back row, waiting for the start of Richard Strauss's *Ariadne auf Naxos*. All of a sudden, a woman seated in front of us put her hand up to her bouffant hairdo, and out flew a bat! There was some consternation, but it turned to laughter when I came out with my best one-liner of all time, loudly exclaiming, "No wonder the bat flew away; it's the wrong Strauss!" A reference to Johann Strauss's Der Fledermaus, or the Revenge of the Bat, for those who don't get it.

I have seen 140 different operas (The list is ongoing!), many of them several times. Particular favorites, aside from Der Ring, include Carmen, Don Giovanni, Salome, Faust, La Traviata, La bohème and Tristan und Isolde. Opera is grand entertainment—a fusion of acting, singing, orchestral music, and lavish sets and costumes.

Alas, the coronavirus pandemic has hampered, even curtailed, a multitude of live performances. Fortunately, opera on demand has filled much of that gap. In my case, it has afforded me the opportunity of seeing rarely performed works, thereby shortening my bucket list. And thank God for Spotify.

For three years at University Prep (the secondary school my girls attended) I taught an opera appreciation class. We focused on a single work and then went to see it performed. One year, it was The Barber of Seville; another, it was Tosca; and finally The Magic Flute. I hope the students who took the course will remain opera fans for life. Like me.

Admittedly, classical music has been my preference. That was what I tended to play in the operating room.

As we worked our way through any given procedure, Bach, Haydn, Mozart, Beethoven, Brahms, Strauss and others greatly helped relieve the stress.

Through the years, I had the circulating nurses keep a running list of musical pieces that I would not want to have played were I under the knife. The simple reason was that I was afraid that I would come out of the fog of the anesthetic, hearing such lovely music and thinking that I must have crossed over to the other side. They always thought I was kidding. No way.

We didn't always play classical music. One of my assistants, Dr. Ayengar, was Indian and persuaded me one day to play something of her choice. She proudly put on Ravi Shankar, which was fine by me. The thing was that my scrub tech started passing instruments to me with progressively harder snaps into my palm. At which time I realized that she couldn't take the sitar any longer, nor I the pain. We switched back to Mozart, and instruments were once again passed properly.

Occasionally we played jazz, folk, or even rock 'n' roll, often featuring some of the great groups I saw in concert: Smokey Robinson and the Miracles, the Temptations, Jefferson Airplane, the Bee Gees, the Rolling Stones, Simon and Garfunkel, and Peter, Paul, and Mary. As long as everything was going well, many of us in the room might have been seen now and then to be tapping our feet in time to the music.

My last public singing performances came a few years back while refereeing swim meets, of all things. On the first occasion, I stepped in for the swimmer who had been asked to sing the National Anthem and called in sick. I also sang "America the Beautiful" at the start of another meet, again in a pinch. But right on pitch.

My singing ability, such as it is, certainly did not derive from Mom, because she couldn't sing at all, even though she tried. I cannot remember Dad even trying. All Jonny ever sang in my presence were simple tunes with off-color lyrics. It must be a gift from God, and I certainly have tried to put it to use. I am grateful for whatever skill I have.

BATTLEGROUND

Hallucinating Picasso's *Guernica*

I dream'd I lay where flowers were springing
Gaily in the sunny beam;
List'ning to the wild birds singing,
By a falling crystal stream:
Straight the sky drew black and daring;
Thro' the woods the whirlwinds rave;
Trees with aged arms were warring,
O'er the swelling drumlie wave.

Such was my life's deceitful morning,
Such the pleasures I enjoyed:
But lang or noon, loud tempests storming
A' my flowery bliss destroyed.
Tho' fickle fortune has deceived me—
She promis'd fair, and perform'd but ill,
Of many a joy and hope bereav'd me—
I bear a heart shall support me still.

Robert Burns, "I Dream'd I Lay"

MOPING

Surgical residency started out well enough and then went downhill. Admission to the Columbia-Presbyterian Surgical Residency program was highly competitive; it was equally competitive to remain in it. Six were admitted, but only two would complete the five-year program. A single cut from six to two was announced at the end of the first year of internship.

With some entering groups of residents, the decision is made easier, because three or four will announce a preference to transfer, for example, to Radiology, Anesthesiology, or ENT—to name three common bail-out tracts. In my particular year, everyone wanted to go all the way through. I was told that the deliberations were lengthy for my group, as the determination of whom to cut and whom to keep was particularly difficult. Maybe they say that every year. Who knows?

At any rate, I was scheduled to be axed at the end of the second year, which made things tough. I felt like a lame duck of sorts. Fortunately, I was given plenty of notice, the time needed to look elsewhere, and excellent recommendations. I also had an entree to the

University of Washington through my sub-internship at Parkland in Dallas.

Professionally, I was all set. But my ego took a heavy blow. The idea of not being invited to finish the surgery program at CPMC was the second-worst thing that had happened to me at that point in my life. (The first will be revealed in due time.) Yet, I was determined to persevere in my surgical training, even if I had to cross a continent to do so. In the meantime, I learned a great deal on the wards at Presbyterian Hospital.

That first year was quite an experience. I assisted on a patient brought back to the OR for the tenth time to correct a recurrent right inguinal hernia. You would think that one of the many surgeons who had taken a crack at the job previously might have been able to seal the deal, so to speak. But no. In fact, the surgeon on this tenth go-round already had tried and failed four times.

Although I was just a simple, inexperienced surgical intern, it amazed me that no surgeon along the way had ever divided the spermatic cord in order to shore up the inguinal canal. This would have done the trick. Instead, here we were for a tenth try. And yet again, the surgeon refused to divide the cord. It was as if it were a matter of pride for him to jerry-rig another repair without taking this step; maybe he considered it too extreme. Mind you, the patient was in his late 70s. His right testicle would have been rendered non-functional had the spermatic cord been cut, but it was safe to say he had little use for it at his age. (At least, that's what I thought at age twenty-six.)

Not only that, but, to my amazement, and without consent from the patient other than the usual blanket disclaimer, the surgeon opened up the left side and managed to find a small recurrent hernia there, too. This marked the fifth go-round on the left side. I walked out of the OR after the procedure was over, muttering to myself in complete disbelief.

Early in my first year, two critically-injured parties were brought in at virtually the same time. It was a *Breaking Bad* type of scenario, if ever there was one. Separate trauma teams were summoned to the ER. Both patients had unstable vital signs.

O negative, i.e., uncrossmatched, Universal Donor blood was pumped into both, and off they were whisked to operating rooms. No names were as yet identified. The situation was only slightly less than completely chaotic.

While we were operating, we were told that the two men, now identified as Francisco and Moises, were related. My team had responsibility for Francisco. We couldn't save him; the knife had penetrated his aorta, and he essentially bled out. But we heard that his cousin was going to make it.

The chief resident told me to go out and talk to the family. Whew! Up to that point, I had never had to tell a family member about a death from any cause. I tried my best to empathize with the family. Yet, no amount of reading, even Charles Dickens, where unfortunate events abound, can prepare you for something like this.

I went out to face a room full of relatives. I let them know: "Francisco didn't survive, but Moises will be all right." Understandably, there were conflicted feelings. Profound misery about the one outcome, and joy over the other. I was pretty shaken. I promised to circle back to the Recovery Room, get the full story on Moises, and relay it back to the family.

Soon I was back in the Recovery Room filling out the paperwork on the deceased. Scut work like that always was the responsibility of the low man on the totem pole. A nurse came up to me and asked, "Are you the one who was sent out there to speak to the family?" I acknowledged that I was. "Well, you need to go back out there again. We got the names mixed up!"

You can imagine my horror.

So, I went back to the family and did what I could. Again. Picture the scene: the extended family, distraught about Francisco, yet happy about Moises, now had to deal with life and death information all over again, dry their tears for Francisco, and begin mourning for Moises. Or however they coped with it.

It would have been nice if somebody, anybody with empathy and experience, had taken the time in medical school to teach us how to be the bearer of bad news. Time spent learning compassion along with the signs and symptoms of diseases, kindness as well as diagnosis, and the value of apologizing when therapy went wrong would have been time well spent. Alas, we were expected somehow to know the right language to use in talking with our patients or their families. Many of us never did develop the skill, even after years in the field.

I hope I improved after this first sorry attempt. I certainly tried to. Believe me, I had plenty of opportunities.

These days, a number of institutions across the country are providing outlets for medical and postgraduate students, as well as residents, to tap into their emotional lives. For example, the Medical University of South Carolina annually publishes *Humanitas*: poems, short stories, photography and paintings by faculty and students. It is a privilege to retain several of these impressive collections on my bookshelves. What a wonderful venue for scientists to explore their artistic, compassionate side. Those of us who came before, having undergone extensive intellectual development with little or no attention to our inner life, can only wish that we had had similar encouragement.

On another night, the second-year surgical resident in charge of the ER told me to see a woman with a head laceration. This rather obese female had been cracked over the head with a beer bottle during a friendly discussion gone bad. As is often the case, the victim claimed she had no idea who the perpetrator was. She had a two-inch laceration above the hair-line—blood everywhere. There were two complicating factors: this patient was hypertensive, and I really didn't know what I was doing.

The nurse laid out the small trauma tray and left me to attend to another pressing issue. I gloved up, injected some lidocaine, and attempted to locate and clamp off the bleeders. The problem was that each time I clamped one off, two more would start up. I ran out of hemostats and requested more. Twice. I was getting nowhere. And not fast enough, either.

The second-year man was having a great time, surreptitiously watching me flailing away for God-only-knows-how long in the woman's scalp. After what seemed like an eternity of futility, he came over, feigning innocence, and asked, "Need any help?" He then took over, removed myriad hemostats, opened up some pretty large suture material, swedged on a big-assed needle, banged in four stitches, and cinched them down tight. Presto! No more bleeding. Chalk this up as another learning experience.

I had better success with a man who had tried to circumcise himself. He came in with his penis wrapped up in a towel and the foreskin three-quarters discon-nected. I asked him what was going on. It seemed like a reasonable question at the time.

He said he had pain after intercourse that would linger for as long as a week, and he was tired of it. Of course, he used language that was a good deal more colorful. He thought his problems must be related to "all that extra skin." He decided to take matters into his own hands, as it were. He got himself liquored up, took a razor and got right down to work. He said that he was making good progress until he hit something that began "pumping blood."

"What did you do next?" I asked. He said that he tried tying a shoestring around his member; he had heard something once about using a tourniquet to stop bleeding. When that didn't work, he tried squeezing Norman with his hands, Norman being the name he called his member. Don't ask; I didn't. Finally, he gave up and came in.

Well, what else could I do but finish the job? I had done one circumcision before, but it was on a newborn, and that was a simple matter. Actually, this was not terribly complicated, either. I found the offending artery, and this time clamping the vessel and tying it off worked. I was on a roll. And I finished the circumcision.

A few months later, I received a rather nice wristwatch in the mail along with a note: "From Peter, for the great help you gave to Norman and me." I wondered: *shouldn't the names have been reversed?*

I scrubbed in on more than a few open-heart procedures at Columbia. The two main attendings, Drs. Bowman and Malm, were marvelous technicians. And, like DeBakey and virtually all cardiac surgeons, they were anything but easy-going. Of course, I never saw them outside of the hospital. They may have been quiet and unassuming, for all I knew. But, from my vantage point, they were specialists in intimidation. They would do things like ask me to hold all of the sutures affixing the prosthetic aortic valve to the heart wall, spread out just so. Then they would say something like, "Now don't even think about moving a muscle. If you let up on the tension, the patient is going to die." Or words to that effect.

After one particular case, I was in the entourage rounding with Dr. Bowman in the Open-heart Recovery Room, when a patient, now awake, was asked how he was doing. He replied, "I'm OK now, but I can tell you, it was no picnic in there."

Bowman asked him what he meant. "I was awake most of the time, you know." My eyes were getting wider. "I remember that somebody washed my chest and covered most of it up with towels. Then I remember the anesthesiologist telling me, 'You're going to go to sleep now.' Except I didn't. Then he pried my eyes open, since I couldn't open them by myself anymore. I thought, *Now I'll be going to sleep.* Only I didn't."

"I was wide awake when you came into the room, Dr. Bowman. There was some talk, and movement of equipment. Then you asked for the knife, and you cut my chest. That hurt a lot. But that was nothing compared with the pain after you asked for the electric saw, or whatever you used to get down to my heart. I think I passed out after that."

Hearing this horror story, I think I almost passed out, but I had enough presence of mind to look over at Dr. Bowman. His face was purple with rage. I'm sure mine was ashen. CPMC had one less anesthesiologist the next day—passed right out the front door and never came back.

One day, my former nanny, Noreen, called me out of the blue. She was having extreme abdominal pain in the left upper quadrant. I had her admitted to the hospital, where the work up revealed a large tumor in her colon. I had to find the best man I could to be her surgeon.

Determining who is best is always fraught with difficulty. Surgeons are generally too biased and egocentric to have a dispassionate opinion. OR nurses favor the ones who yell less and refrain from throwing instruments, especially those who get the procedure done faster. Anesthesiologists know which surgeons do a better job preparing their patients for the ordeal of surgery. Referring doctors can tell you who promptly returns an improved patient. It may be common knowledge that Dr. So-and-So will take on the really tough cases. Yet, few can tell you who has learned when best not to operate, which I have come to believe is the real measure of the best surgeons. Asking other, more senior surgical residents seemed to be the safest bet.

No Yelp, back in 1975. However, Dr. Wiedel received the highest overall marks. He was a gentle man, and nobody questioned his skill or judgment. He was the right surgeon for Noreen. He did a great job on a locally extensive cancer. To get it out, he had to remove about half her colon, together with the spleen, the left kidney, and a loop of attached small intestine. This was a Herculean effort. She recovered uneventfully and lived another ten years, pain free and as ornery as ever.

I admitted a woman once whose chief complaint was that she was "feelin' poorly." And no wonder; she was severely anemic. The source of blood loss was a large cancer of the breast that was eroding through the skin—of which she appeared to be totally unaware. I wish I could say that I never again saw this level of denial, but I cannot.

There was a similar case some years later. This woman's husband had complained about an odor for many months, which she explained away as her "troublesome diarrhea." In all that time, he never noticed the stains on her shirts and bras, nor did he ever bother to look at his wife's body, where a large cancer had eaten away much of the skin. Worse than that was a woman who presented with a breast cancer that had spread almost halfway around her back.

None of these three appeared to recognize that they had breast cancer. Or, if they did, they smothered any awareness with layer upon layer of denial.

Interestingly, all became quite compliant, once they finally were willing to be examined. That is to say, they went along with all recommendations. Of course, it was far too late to be talking about cures.

Interns were allowed to perform some of the easier procedures. I performed quite a number of hernia repairs, appendectomies, and cholecystectomies (gallbladder excisions). Most of the time, a chief resident supervised me, with the attending surgeon occasionally popping in—to make sure that everything was going well.

Dr. Goodman, like most of the attending surgeons, usually operated on private patients, with residents assisting. He had a habit of eschewing surgical instruments whenever possible and dissecting with his fingers. We residents made fun of this practice, calling it "Goodmanizing." His considered opinion was that the finger was a more intelligent instrument than any piece of metal. Through the years, I came to recognize the validity of this point of view and never regretted learning the skill. Today's surgeons, increasingly trained in less invasive surgery via laparoscopy and robotics, have fewer opportunities to appreciate the judicious use of "Goodmanizing."

A month of orthopedic service was part of first-year General Surgery Residency. Ortho was arguably the strongest surgical specialty at CPMC. One Thursday evening, I received a call from the Department Chairman, Frank Stinchfield. I wondered why on earth he would be calling me, a lowly intern, whom he didn't know from Adam. He had bypassed the hierarchy, because he wanted whoever would be on call over the weekend to know that, "Miss Dietrich would be arriving at the Harkness Pavilion some time the following day."

Silence on my end. Then, "Sir, this would not be *the* Miss Dietrich, would it?"

"Yes, yes," said he, impatiently. "You'll be sure to let me know the minute she arrives, won't you?" I think I managed a yes between my ear-to-ear grin.

Friday came and went. No Marlene. Saturday, the same. I thought, *Dang it; my big chance to be famous, and the woman's a no-show*. When she did finally show on Sunday, she was not exactly ready for showtime. She made it from her Paris apartment to New York City, still in her housecoat and slip. She was disheveled and very much the worse for wear. *Boy*, I was thinking, *If any of her millions of fans could see her now!*

She had fallen in her Paris apartment and couldn't get up. Perhaps a bit too much *schnapps*? She called Michael DeBakey—a name that keeps popping up— because he had done (at least part of) an aorta bi-iliac bypass on her a few months before. DeBakey told her not to move, and he called Stinchfield.

A series of phone calls ensued between Stinchfield, Marlene, and a radiologist in Paris. The Paris radiologist had a portable X-ray machine brought to the apartment, whereby he determined that her left hip was broken. Then, more phone calls, which resulted in Marlene being told to fly to New York. As if there were no competent orthopedists in all of Paris.

And the saga continued. Pan Am was not able to accommodate a stretcher on a flight to New York. So Marlene called Howard Hughes, and a private plane was sent to Paris. And, *voilà*, Miss Dietrich made her entrance into Harkness Pavilion and, however briefly, into my life.

My job was to admit her, discreetly do a physical, and start an IV, which I accomplished on the first pass, thankfully. Despite the recent wear and tear and the years of alcohol, cigarette and who-knows-what-else abuse, not to mention (because I already did) her recent vascular surgery, Marlene still looked pretty good. To be sure, there were some wrinkles around the eyes, and her hands were veiny. And I am sure she had had more than a little plastic surgery. At seventy-two, she was no spring chicken. Oh God, a year younger than me, as I write this. And look at my hands!

Anyway, I dutifully reported directly to the Chief and semi-obsequiously slid into the background, as she underwent a successful hip repair. Marlene's daughter, a surprisingly frumpy Long Island housewife, showed up the next day while I was rounding on her mother. The two went after each other like cats and dogs. I was a bit embarrassed to witness the name-calling and sarcasm.

It was like being a child again, listening to Mom and Noreen going at it.

Some years later, the daughter wrote a tell-all biography of her famous parent. I leafed through the contents and, sure enough, there were a few paragraphs on the broken hip episode. Alas, no mention of yours truly, even though Miss Dietrich told me at the time that she liked me. I should have asked for an autograph when I had the chance.

Charles Revson, owner of Revlon, was one of Dr. Goodman's private patients. Mr. Revson had a rare form of pancreatic cancer and was nearly terminal when I met him. He hated the food at the Pavilion, although it looked pretty good to the residents. Expensive, too. Mr. Revson had his personal chef prepare a large pan of delicious lasagna every day, even though he hardly could eat a bite. Those of us in the know would endeavor to round on Mr. Revson during lunchtime. We would help him out with the food, so as not to disappoint his chef.

My brother was working for Revlon at the time, in a responsible managerial position. I thought it best not to mention this to Mr. Revson, as he was busy fighting for his life and not of a mind for chitchat. He did leave the hospital for a while. In fact, he almost took the hospital home with him. He hired nurses to care for him around the clock and paid a surgery resident to moonlight at his pad each night, just in case. I never took the job, but I heard there was a lot of partying going on. Lots of lasagna and plenty of booze. Charles Revson died August 25, 1975. No more free lunch.

I was devastated not to have been one of the two residents to make the cut, pun unintended and, anyway, not a laughing matter. My self-esteem was shattered. I was ashamed, embarrassed, and angry, all at once. I was in a frame of mind to chuck it all and make a fresh start. This adversely affected my marriage. As it was, I had entered into it more from force of habit after four years of dating than out of love.

I'm ashamed that I didn't put more effort into my marriage with Amee. She was a wonderful person and a good wife. Instead, I became involved with a woman who had been admitted to the private pavilion just as I was rotating off that service. I should have left it at that. I stopped by to chat a few times and, before I knew it, I was infatuated. I lost my bearings and began to look at this woman as Fresh Start Incarnate.

Callously, I separated from Amee, leaving her with Scarlett O'Hara, and moved in with Christine with little more than my clothes, medical books, and car. Christie had two adorable young children: a boy, aged five and a girl, aged six.

She came from an old, moneyed Philadelphia family and was living on a rented, eleven-acre estate in Irvington-on-Hudson, where she kept four horses and a goat. She had years of experience training horses for timber racing, a specialized type of helter-skelter stee-plechase through fields and streams, and over fixed wooden fences, popular in Mid-Atlantic states.

For the one year that it lasted, life with her was a completely different and quite liberating experience. She encouraged me to learn and practice Transcendental Meditation™, my first foray into Eastern spiritualism. With her help, I improved my dormant equestrian skills to the point of learning how to ride a flat-out gallop and even jump fences.

I commuted into the city and stayed overnight at the hospital when I was on call. Of course, I had to carry on with my duties as a second-year resident, despite the fact that my heart wasn't in it anymore.

Amee went back to school and earned her Master's in Social Work from Hunter College. She became a psychiatric social worker, specializing, ironically, in family therapy. After our divorce, she moved to Southern California and married a psychiatrist.

***

There were still some memorable experiences to be had at CPMC in that second year, before I was obliged to move on. Consider the case of the repeat jumper:

This fellow had jumped out of a fourth-floor window and fractured nearly half the bones in his body. ICUs and trauma teams being as competent as they are, he was patched up and discharged. A year later, he jumped again, this time from the fifth floor. This time, he managed to break perhaps three-quarters of his bones, and he also suffered some fairly grievous internal injuries. But, due to the wonders of modern medicine, he again survived.

I wasn't actually involved in his care until a year later. No, he didn't jump from the sixth floor this time. He was admitted through the ER because of a stab wound to the abdomen. He had an encounter with his sister in a stairwell, perhaps on his way to the sixth floor to jump. They argued, maybe about his poor judgment, and she stabbed him. For us, it was another opportunity to advance science. We operated, patched up his innards, fixed and, in several instances, refixed his broken bones and sent him home, presumably for another crack at jumping. I never heard how it went from there. Not well, I imagine.

One night, I did an emergency splenectomy on a man who had been kicked and beaten. Before he left the hospital, he insisted that I accept $1,000 for my efforts. I refused, telling him that I was on salary, if you could call $35,000 a year for 120-hour workweeks a salary. However, that was a lot more than Mom and Dad made in their day. He said he knew how underpaid we were and kept on insisting. Finally, I took the money and bought myself a fancy leather coat. Winters in New York City can get mighty cold.

In later years, I was to receive two more big tips. One was from the family of a centenarian, Hazel Morgan, on whom I had performed four unrelated operations over a decade. I was invited to her 100th birthday party. After she gobbled down a slice of cake, she stood up with a bit of help and said maybe a dozen words to the large gathering. It included five generations of family, her banker, her accountant, her lawyer, her primary-care doctor, and her surgeon (me). Hazel insisted that I accept $1,000, not in payment but as a gift. I donated the money to charity.

The third large tip came in the form of a gold ring with multiple diamonds. A woman who had a very complicated, recurrent bile-duct obstruction gave it to me. I worked very hard to fix this plumbing issue. I had definitely earned a bonus, although I tried to refuse it, as I had in the other cases. At a certain point, however, I feel that continuing to refuse a gift from a person who is adamant about giving it becomes insulting to the giver. Instinctively, I have always tended to be polite. So polite that I never objected when my ex-wife kept the ring after our divorce.

LES MISÉRABLES

I applied to the University of Washington program, mainly because I was enthralled with what I learned about Seattle in sixth-grade geography class. I also knew that, once I jogged his memory, the new Chief of Surgery there would remember me from my sub-internship at Parkland Hospital. UPenn offered me a spot in their program, but UPenn and I were never meant to be, I guess.

The Surgery Department of the University of Washington offered me a position which I eagerly accepted. Christie and I loaded up a medium-sized U-Haul truck with my car in tow and drove 3,000 miles away from everything we had known. She left the kids behind with her mother until we found a house and settled in. This three-bedroom home met her requirements, being around the corner from a highly-rated elementary school, while bordering on a horseback riding trail. For me, the location in Belleview was an easy commute into Seattle.

I don't know how the surgery program at UW was run prior to their bringing in Tom Shires from Parkland, along with his massive retinue of attendings and residents. I was familiar with the Parkland way of running things from my month there during senior year of medical school. It was an R3-oriented system, meaning more responsibility was thrown on the backs of the third-year residents than was the case at Columbia or other highly competitive programs.

Shires et. al. had made this unprecedented move in 1974, two years before I arrived at UW. Many of the pre-existing UW faculty didn't exactly cotton to having the Parkland way of doing things imposed on them. Shires was brought in as Chairman, and he made some sweeping moves right out of the chute. He canned the Chief of Surgery at Harborview and installed his own man. Ditto with the Burn, Transplant, and Vascular Surgery sub-sections. He expanded the residency and got rid of a few residents who couldn't meet his standards.

These changes created quite a bit of ill will, even to the extent of Shires's son receiving death threats. We're talking the Wild West here. The fallout was that the newly appointed Burn and Transplant Chiefs resigned within a year or so and left town. Then Shires himself moved on to head the Surgery Department at Cornell. His Vascular man, Mac Perry, stuck it out for one more year before following his Chief to New York City, so I did get a chance to work with him.

With all this brouhaha, it was no wonder that a space opened up at the R3 level. UW also took in a second resident at my level, David Cohen, plus a man from UCLA, who entered as an R4. All three of us had quite a bit of adjusting to do. We were more closely scrutinized and more frequently corrected (Read: humiliated) than the others for the way we presented cases at the weekly Morbidity and Mortality Conference. Clearly, there was a lot of pressure on all the R3s because of the way the work burden was apportioned. There was that much more pressure on the three of us, because we were viewed as outsiders.

I got off to a bad start during my first rotation. At Columbia, we were completely honest in our presentations, with no fear of recrimination. This was the way I presented my first few cases from the VA Hospital at the M&M conference. It wasn't done this way in Seattle, I soon found out. My Chief Resident, one of the Texas transplants, became furious at me for telling it like it was and, in the process, making myself and, more importantly, him look bad. He told me flat out that he didn't think I deserved to be part of the program and apparently voiced this opinion to all the other former Parkland residents and attendings.

For example, on my first day at Harborview Hospital two months later, I was in the ICU when the Chief Surgeon, Jim Carrico, another Texas transplant and soon to be Department Head, called me aside. Out of the blue, he said, "You know, Weber, jes' because you're from New York don' mean y'all cain't be trusted, an' jes' cuz' I'm from the South don' mean I'm dumb!" He smiled and walked away, just like that, leaving me wondering, *What the fuck was that all about?*

Not more than a week after that, Christie headed back East, intending to pick up her kids, who were staying with her mother in Nantucket. Next thing I knew, she changed her mind about returning to the Pacific Northwest, wanted me to ship her belongings back, and signed off on the house we had bought. That marked the abrupt end of what had the potential to be a long-term relationship.

It seemed like a conspiracy all around.

I was totally alone, really for the first time in my life. It was so dispiriting to be rattling around in a large, empty house, working my ass off in a program where I appeared to be unwanted. Too exhausted to utilize the meditation skills I had learned, which certainly could have been beneficial. It would be thirty years before my spiritual side re-emerged.

Not to suggest that it was easier for David Cohen or the R4 outsider. But David, at least, had a lovely wife and a couple of kids who gave him much needed love and commiseration. Professionally, none of us got the benefit of the doubt for anything, from anybody. In fact, the poor R4 transfer was canned at the end of the year.

David and I soldiered on and ultimately made it, in my case by the skin of my teeth. David went on to a successful career in cardiac surgery in Texas. We've kept in touch on and off. He recently contacted me to say that one of his sons was moving to Seattle, and he'd like to join me for a few beers to talk about the miserable old days. I must ask David whether he, too, has persistent nightmares, as I do, about the UW residency program.

Despite constantly being under the gun, I had some very interesting experiences. For starters, the Veterans Administration Hospital was an eye-opener: large wards, vets getting supplied with all the cigarettes they wanted (even for those who would inhale through their tracheostomies), vastly overworked nurses, and rampant inefficiency everywhere.

We were swamped with work all the time; there was always more to be done than there was time to do it. We continually had to remind ourselves to "Never miss a meal for a vet." Otherwise, we would have gone hungry nearly every day. Here, at least, we got free meals. Not so, at some of the other hospitals. Not even when the residents went on strike to protest.

Hub Radke, Chief of Surgery at the VA, was another weird and wonderful guy. Half-surgeon, half-philosopher, half-crazy—and the best man for getting out of a pickle in the OR I've ever encountered. In part, this was because he was a bit reckless and, as a result, had a lot of experience being in a pickle. He was super-critical of all his R3s, not just David and me. It seemed that everything an R3 did needed correction. And yet we would observe the Chief Resident do the very same thing and get heaps of praise.

The VA Anesthesia Department refused to be overworked and always was trying to cancel our cases or tell us that there wasn't enough time on the schedule. They would not allow us to start any non-emergent case that by their calculations might go past 3:00 p.m. An outdated list of average surgical times was their Bible. If we had a case that we wanted to start at noon and according to their list would take three hours and five minutes, they would refuse to let us do it. As a consequence, the length of stay for the patients was ridiculously long. And so was the waiting list to get an appointment in the clinic.

Mr. Magnusson needed a colostomy closure. In those days, bowel preparation for elective colon surgery was a five-day affair. Colostomy closure, according to Anesthesia, took three hours. So we booked the man for 11:30 a.m. That day, the case ahead of his ran over.

Turnover time between cases at the VA was notoriously slow. It was 12:15 p.m. when the nurses were ready to move the patient into the OR. Anesthesia balked and would not make an exception, even though Magnusson's bowel had been prepped and not even considering that the rooms were full for the following day.

So we moved Mr. Magnusson back to his room, ordered him a tray full of food, since he was famished, and started his bowel prep again the next day. And, just to be safe, we put him on the schedule for 10:30 a.m., five days later.

Well, wouldn't you know? There were complications again with the preceding case. And, once again, we couldn't get him into the OR before the noon witching hour. And Anesthesia blocked us again. And the schedule was full for the next day.

We residents couldn't take it anymore. We marched into Radke's office and demanded satisfaction for our patient, although he seemed not to mind another delay or another bowel prep—remember: free eats, free room, and free cigarettes.

Radke was no fool. He knew well that residents come and go, but Anesthesia abides. Therefore, he wouldn't buck the system.

Not to be deterred, we poured over the schedule until we found a rare day, almost two weeks away, when the Chief Resident had not yet co-opted the first slot. We made him promise not to bump Mr. Magnusson and then went to the patient and asked him if he wouldn't mind waiting another couple of weeks for that sure spot. He acted like he couldn't care less. He didn't want to go home. He was having the time of his life, chumming with the other vets, watching them come and go, even to the point of not really minding having his bowel prepped for a third time. This was the VA, and, from what I read in the newspapers, it has not changed much since then.

The Seattle VA had twelve-bed wards, reminiscent of the set-up at Presbyterian Hospital. At least in New York, we could get our orders followed. If we required vital signs on a four-hour basis, we could be sure they would be done and recorded. At the VA, no matter what we ordered, vital signs could not be obtained on the wards any more frequently than once a shift. So we made liberal use of the Surgical Intensive Care Unit for anyone who needed to be checked on more frequently.

The U.S. Public Health Service Hospital was a step below the VA, if you can imagine that. Here, where there were sixteen-bed wards, we couldn't be assured of getting vitals even once a shift. Or at all, after a single set on admission, in many cases. We felt obliged to put virtually all our operative cases, even simple hernia repairs, in the ICU, where the level of care approached adequate.

The UW surgical residency entailed working at seven different hospitals, each with its own, distinct patient demographic. The VA was virtually all male vets; females were rare. The Public Health Hospital had a lot of military wives, Coast Guard, both active and retired, and Native Americans. Harborview, the major trauma center, got the big trauma cases and many disaster dumps from outlying hospitals, which usually came in on Friday afternoons.

For example, the man whose entire pelvis had been raked through with a backhoe. The surgeon who first admitted him to a smaller hospital was unable to stop the steady bleeding from deep in his pelvis. We took the poor guy in transfer, since we were admonished never to refuse any referrals. He was losing a unit of blood every forty-five minutes, despite having had his pelvis packed with surgical pads. Our last-ditch attempt involved general surgery, orthopedics, and urology teams to stabilize his fractures, repair his groin, perform a colostomy, and stop the hemorrhage. Seven or eight hours of sustained effort. Until his heart gave out.

There were many complicated, multi-disciplinary cases like that at Harborview. The place also serves as a *de facto* charity hospital for the region, serving the lowest social demographic. I had the distinction of repairing a severe hand laceration on an Indigenous fellow named Charlie Everybodystalkingabout, who scored, and still holds, the highest blood-alcohol level on record. Amazingly, he managed to stagger into the ER under his own power. He was so inebriated that I was able to sew up his lacerated hand without any topical anesthesia. He didn't appear to feel a thing.

We rotated to Providence Hospital at the beginning of the fourth year. This was primarily a private hospital with a separate surgical residency. It had lost its accreditation, because it was too heavily weighted toward cardiac surgery. Why they got dinged for that, while the Baylor program did not, is beyond me, but that's medical politics for you. At any rate, the UW surgery program scarfed up Providence, and I was the first UW surgical resident to rotate there.

Providence had nurse anesthetists, unlike any of our other hospitals. They were perfectly adequate, in fact more reliable than a few of the Providence anesthesiologists. One anesthesiologist was accustomed to leaving the OR, often for as long as half the case. He would put the circulating nurse in charge at the head of the table and wander off for reasons unknown to us. We were appalled, but, as we were newcomers, we had to accept this behavior.

Even worse, there was an anesthesiologist who was researching the effects of ketamine, a narco-sedative, on himself and his wife, perhaps even while at work, for all we knew. His wife was a drug-cult princess of sorts. One day she just wandered off into the woods and never was heard from again. This doctor got his pink slip.

University Hospital took the complicated, non-trauma cases. The head of Vascular Surgery was rumored to have been the one who circulated the death threats against Shires's son, but that couldn't be proven. One of the cancer surgeons spent most of the time talking about his golf game and his private singing lessons and very little time teaching us anything. I must say that I was interested in his classical music training, and the fact that he was a good friend of the famous Metropolitan Opera *basso*, Jerome Hines. One of the cardiac surgeons was a trained artist and made beautiful drawings of all of his operations in advance of performing them. When on his service, I always made a point of asking to see the drawings. I doubt that any of my peers took that much interest.

The transplant surgeon was an outright manic-depressive. He was technically the best surgeon in the system, but incredibly difficult to deal with. He did not believe in using post-operative narcotics, claiming that he had a cousin who became addicted after a routine operation. He would tell his kidney donors and the transplant recipients not to expect intravenous pain medicine after surgery. We were horrified to see this bias imposed on every one of his cases. I will say this, however: his patients recovered faster than anyone else's. They had to.

Children's Hospital was part, although politically not really part, of the system. They had attending surgeons and pediatricians who were separate from the University system. We often were rounding on their service, as well as covering the University patients, which was politically tenuous at best.

And, again, this is where I saw the bias in the program against those of us who were not part of it from the onset. A fellow resident, considered a real star by the faculty, decided one day that he no longer was willing to make rounds with the non-University attendings at Children's. He said it was a waste of his time, because he wasn't learning anything. I had been summoned to Carrico's office that day. By then, the wise old man, John Schilling, who had been brought in as a sort of guru and assumed the Chairmanship after Shires left, had retired. Schilling actually appreciated my efforts and more or less defended me. But, alas, he was gone, and now Carrico was in charge.

Imagine me sitting there waiting and listening while Carrico lauds my fellow resident for eschewing rounds. I'm thinking, *Boy, if I ever pulled that stunt, I would be out of here so fast!* Carrico hangs up the phone, changes gear, and asks me whether I'd like to consider going into ENT. Or anything else, as far as he was concerned. I, of course, being a fighter—all right, a bulldog, if you like—declined.

The truth is, some of the attendings from Providence and Central Valley Hospital in Wenatchee, where we rotated as fourth-year residents, actually deviated from the prevailing culture of intimidation to tell me that I had done a good job on their service. Others would not have said anything positive had I walked on water, other than a grudging admission that I was a good mentor to the residents and medical students rotating with me.

Overall, I could see that the odds against me were building, and the handwriting was on the proverbial wall. So I pre-empted an impending disaster and asked to come before the faculty and defend my worthiness to finish the program. I fortified my position by getting a handful of attendings to back me up with letters of support.

This course of action was unprecedented. And let me tell you, it was no picnic, either. But I did what I had to do. Even though I beat the Texas "Mafia" at their own game, they didn't let up on me during my Chief Resident year. I wasn't out of the woods by a long shot, but I was still hanging in there. I was determined to finish.

In retrospect, perhaps that was a mistake. I am sure I would have had little, if any, trouble being accepted into the anesthesiology, orthopedic, or radiology residency. Or even ENT. But that would have meant failing in general surgery, something I would not allow, if I could do anything about it. Not after so many years of hard work, misery notwithstanding. Yes, there were signs along the way that I was not perfectly suited for a career in surgery, but I never found the time to pay attention to them. I was too busy just trying to get through each day to reflect. I spent my time reacting instead.

The pressure on me to get through the program was enormous. But that paled in comparison with the stress of just getting through each day. For the third and fourth years of residency, we were on call and generally expected to stay in the hospital every third night. Following an off-duty night, we were expected to have seen all our patients and to have gathered all pertinent information prior to 6:00 a.m. team rounds. Also, we were expected to have made a serious dent in the mound of surgical consultation requests that somehow seemed to keep growing despite our best efforts.

Consequently, we rarely got out of the hospital on our off-duty nights before 8:00 p.m.

During Chief Resident year, we were on call every other night. Although we were not required to stay in the hospital overnight, most nights we may as well have. Much more often than not, we were called back to supervise the junior residents.

We were expected to keep up with our homework. This amounted to wading through piles of articles from surgical journals, which were mailed to us eight times a year from Parkland Hospital. "Selected Readings in General Surgery" formed the basis of an extensive file system of articles we accumulated as we went through the program. By the time I finished, my collection took up three file cabinets. As the years went by, I filled another cabinet.

At Harborview, we were divided into two trauma teams. Today, by the way, there are four, with pretty much the same number of patients. Endocrinology studies have demonstrated an adverse effect upon patient care when residents put in more than eighty hours of work in a week, including night call. Mind you, we put in about 130 on average. Studies haven't been done to demonstrate the adverse health effects on the residents putting in these mega hours, especially since hours now are limited by law to less than two-thirds of what they were for us. Fact is that most surgical programs manage to get around this restriction in hours anyway. As a result, it is still true that:

- Surgeons tend to have a lower life expectancy than doctors in other fields. (I hope to be an exception to this rule.)
- Marriages during residency frequently are doomed to fail. Two of mine did. (So did my relationship with Christie, for that matter.)

One particular weekend during my last year, the Chief Resident for the other Harborview service asked to take an extended weekend off. This was frowned upon, as it put way too much of a burden on the remaining Chief, who then was required to cover both services. However, since the vacation-requesting Chief was that same favorite who was lauded for skipping rounds at Children's Hospital, and the overly-taxed Chief was yours truly, permission was granted. Net result: I never left the building, from 5 a.m. Thursday morning until 10 p.m. Monday night. Furthermore, during that span, I never made it to the cafeteria. Not once. I guzzled cans of Ensure during my rare spare moments. Yet, I survived that abuse as well. Thankfully, so did my patients.

I remember, with tremendous embarrassment, an occasion at Harborview when the fire alarms went off. All the fire doors closed, and firemen came pouring out of the elevator asking, "Where's the fire?" In a state of near-total exhaustion, I was leaning against the fire alarm. I was the one who triggered it. Fessing up was distinctly uncomfortable.

I did have other remarkable experiences along the way, some amusing, some amazing. Certainly not everything was dismal about my training in Seattle. Had it been so, I would have packed up my bags and moved on.

One time, the Assistant Chief of Surgery was demonstrating the use of the original surgical von Petz stapler, an ancient and unwieldy thing that was kept in a beautiful wooden box. He ordered it up and struggled to show us how to put it in place across the stomach, preparatory to dividing the organ to remove a bleeding ulcer. We were amused to see him sweat and strain to align the huge jaws of the von Petz. It must have weighed a good 10 pounds, and there were much smaller, more-effective stapling apparati readily available.

But this was University Hospital, the Mother Ship of the program, and he was affording us a direct link to the good old days. A teaching point was to be made: the original device was still useful. Stevenson finally lined the jaws up just right, and he proceeded to crank the wheel around and around to set the staples in place. He put surgical clamps above the von Petz and proceeded to divide the stomach.

He laboriously uncranked the wheel, whereupon the divided end of the stomach leaked large amounts of bloody stomach contents into the free abdominal cavity. And why would it not? It turned out that the scrub nurse had assumed the staples were already loaded and ready to go. They were not.

Stevenson was a very soft-spoken, mild-mannered man. But this was his breaking point. He took the von Petz out of the abdomen, let out a string of curses, and heaved it across the floor. He heaved it so hard that it went crashing out the open door of our operating room, across the common scrub area, into the adjoining room, across the floor, and smashed into the wall.

Meanwhile, open-heart surgery was in progress in the other room. Reportedly, the operating surgeon, who was in the process of sewing in a prosthetic heart valve, asked his assistant what that was about, without once looking up. Something along the lines of, "What the fuck was that?"

His assistant, who did lift his head, however briefly, casually remarked, "It's only the von Petz." And back to work they went.

During my fourth year, I had a great two-month rotation in central Washington with four surgeons. Two had come through the UW program prior to the advent of the Texas cadre, and one had trained at Columbia. These three were particularly sensitive to my plight and were generously supportive; I remain eternally grateful. I came to find out that there was no love lost between this group and Shires's men. This certainly worked to my advantage.

They let me operate up a storm. I believe I performed just under a hundred cases in those two months. My most memorable case was a young girl who survived a plane crash; her father was the pilot. The father survived, too, although both had serious internal injuries.

I also had to cover the ER for surgical emergencies, which seemed a fair trade. This was December and January, during which time my sole means of transportation was a bicycle. I can tell you that biking along Ridge Road in the dark and on snow was a unique experience.

I couldn't use my car, because I had remarried after a year of abject loneliness, and my wife, Sandy, an L.P.N., needed the Volvo in Seattle. Sandy was a kind soul, heavy into astrology and reading tea leaves. This I did not know when first we got together. That Christmas, she did my chart and informed me that the stars did not align properly for a permanent relationship. I scoffed at this, only to find out how true it turned out to be.

The fourth of the central Washington surgeons had trained at the University of Iowa, where the Department Chairman, Ed Mason, had introduced his seminal work on stomach stapling for morbid obesity. We had a few discussions about bariatric surgery, then in its infancy and not yet performed anywhere in Washington State. This radical new approach piqued my interest. Little did I know then how it was to transform my surgical practice.

In the fourth year, there was a rotation that was supposed to encompass both the Harborview Burn Unit and Surgical Pathology. Surgery Boards at that time included pathology questions. I was the first in my group to be on this rotation. I also turned out to be the last.

The Burn Unit was overwhelmingly busy. We were inundated with burn patients, both adults and children. Some of the cases were so very sad: child abuse, child neglect, industrial explosions, fires, and more. Oftentimes, the outcome was a fatality. I got to know the Medical Examiner on a first name basis, because I was in that office checking on post-mortem results so frequently.

I would have to say that the Burn Unit was the most depressing of all the rotations in my surgical training. I will never forget the three children who were playing with matches and lit their playhouse on fire. The oldest, being nine, made it out the door first and was the least burned. The six-year girl suffered second and third degree burns over two-thirds of her body, including her face, arms, and torso. She survived after a lengthy hospitalization involving multiple grafting procedures and treatment for sepsis. Her three year-old sister was not so fortunate, having nearly the entirety of her little body burned.

Because the Burn Unit did not have a plastic surgeon at that time, I got to do dozens of skin grafts, even on faces. We finally did recruit a plastic surgeon. He stopped me once in the hall, six months after I had finished the rotation. He told me that I had done far more facial grafting procedures than he had in his plastic surgical fellowship. His praise of my efforts was a welcome relief from the litany of criticisms I had to endure. His kind words reverberated and helped me get through many a long night. To this day, I continue to pay it forward by never hesitating to give praise where deserved.

I recall a man, totally lucid despite burns over ninety percent of his body, to whom I had to say, "This is a hopeless situation. Nobody can survive a burn to this extent. All we can offer you are comfort measures," meaning increasing doses of analgesics. And that was what we did. The Burn Unit surely was a depressing place to work.

An elderly gentleman was brought in with eight percent of his body burned. I had never seen a fatality with burns of this limited extent. I scoffed at the formula that stated: "Age plus percent burns equals mortality." I told the skeptical Burn Unit Director that I would get this ninety-two-year-old man through his ordeal. I was given the go-ahead to give it my best shot. I failed. We could not stave off fatal infection.

Now, back to Surgical Pathology. I was so busy on the Burn Unit that I never made it down to their laboratory until week three of the rotation. I walked in, apologized profusely, whereupon the nattily attired professor told me that they had saved an amputated leg for me to examine and document the arterial obstruction that caused gangrene. I took it out of the refrigerator, where it had been decomposing all this time. Most of the tissue had liquefied, and there was a naked shinbone sticking up from an attached, more or less intact, grey foot.

I put my gloves on, opened the bag, tried not to smell the contents, and lifted out the leg, while the professor stood there impassively, his Pathology residents smirking at their workstations. The liquefied contents of the bag slipped off the table and splattered all over Dr. Wang's suit pants. Mercifully, he accepted my apology. One only can imagine what he really was thinking. I dissected out a couple of clogged arteries, wrote up my findings, and got out of there as fast as I could. I never found the time to go back.

That fiasco marked the last time a surgical resident rotated onto the Surgical Pathology service. Surgeons were no longer to be examined in pathology as part of the board certification process. I wonder whether my fiasco had influenced that decision.

The burn nurses, recognizing the long hours I had put in on the Burn Unit, gave me a going-away present. It was a bright red Tee shirt emblazoned with the words "NO CODE."

We come to the Chief Resident year—the light at the end of the long, dark tunnel. Question is, will the Seeker after Truth (in this case, me, a bit idealized) have the energy to complete the Quest? Exhausted, spiritually bereft, friendless... Can he complete the journey? And to what purpose? To be able to exult in having beaten the odds, perhaps?

He is at odds with his peers. He carries deep resentments like heavy bags of medical waste on its way to the incinerator, in hopes that by loosening his burden he will lighten his load. It is not to happen for another three decades, but how can he know it at the time? He just slogs on.

Is it courage? Is it stubbornness? Inertia? Is it for the love of humankind? Or is it for want of something better to do?

I made it back to the VA as Chief Resident. The same things I did as a third year in the OR—for which I had been criticized, as all third-year residents were (only more so, because I was like a junior-college transfer to the college team)—were now routinely lauded. "Atta boys" resounded, for the first time in months. Radke now accepted me, even shared his philosophy of life with me in odd moments.

Picture this scene:

I am in the OR finishing up a primo vascular case (oh boy!), a carotid artery endarterectomy (clean-out). I can hear Radke yelling at a third-year resident in a nearby room. I am so glad to be done with that stuff. He says, "Go on, Galbraith. Be bold." Then, "Go on. Keep dissecting." And then, "Yes! Cut through there."

I can't hear Galbraith saying much of anything, but Radke keeps egging him on. And yells, "Cut the god-damn thing." And then, total silence, followed by, "Tim (I didn't know Radke even knew his first name), you cut the fucking duct!" Sure enough, the resident, pushed recklessly, had cut the common bile duct in two!

Repair of the common bile duct is a job for the chief resident, so I am summoned to the other room to repair the mess. Galbraith is red in what little of his face I can see. Radke is subdued, in a pickle again, and I get some more praise for helping him get out of it.

I shifted over to the antiquated Public Health Hospital, where the attending surgeons pretty much left chief residents unsupervised. They spent their time filling out billing slips, so they could collect whatever minimal payment was forthcoming from the government. These days, attendings have to show their faces in the OR for at least part of the operation, even if they opt not to scrub in. It's the law.

Picture me again, this time assisting the R3 on an appendectomy:

I have devised an ingenious way to hook one end of the double-armed retractor over the sterile gown and into the band of my scrub pants. This way I can retract tissue, while putting both of my hands to better use. A really neat trick, and one I am quite proud of. The problem is that, at the end of the case, when I pull off the sterile outer gown, my pants fall down. Right there in the OR, in front of the whole crew! Now I'm the one who is red in the face.

Back to Harborview, where we repaired a self-inflicted stomach laceration on Pin Wow, a prisoner—anything to get out of jail for a while. We quickly patched him up and sent him back to the Big House, only to have this self-same Pin Wow come back a few days later. He had removed all the skin stitches and was caught reaching deep inside his abdomen, trying to remove the sutures in his stomach. This time, after re-repairing him, we opted for a total body cast to completely im-mobilize the guy and prevent further self-tampering. Then sent him back to prison.

Protocol at Harborview for blunt trauma cases was to lavage the abdominal cavity (meaning to pour in fluid and drain it out again) through a needle, looking for evidence of free blood, which mandated a trip to the OR for open abdominal exploration. However, with potential penetrating trauma, the policy was to openly explore the abdomen if local exploration of the wound revealed signs of penetration of the fascial layer. It was not uncommon to end up finding nothing to repair. These days, simply peeking in with a laparoscope has reduced dramatically the need for open exploration.

But this was back in the good old days, and I was su-pervising the third-year resident during an open explo-ration. We found absolutely nothing to repair. The knife had gone through the outer layer of fascia, but it had not penetrated the inner layer at all. This was a Friday night, and the Knife and Gun Club was going strong. We had two more trauma cases waiting in line for the next available OR, and we clearly were anticipating an all-nighter. I told the R3 we would go for the Harborview record for the quickest abdominal exploration.

However, we cheated a bit in setting the record. I made the R3 run the fascial closure, rather than using the preferred method of interrupted sutures. In other words, tying one knot at the top and sewing the length of the incision closed with one long suture, knotted again at the bottom. This was the technique used routinely by private surgeons in central Washington and at Providence, where time was money, and rapid OR turnover was honed to a fine art. All of us who had seen this practice were impressed and hoping to adopt the technique at Harborview and University Hospitals. However, the attending staff was dead set against it. That particular night the attending was at home in bed, so I seized the moment.

My R3, totally inculcated with the party line, tried to resist. But I assured him it would be okay and that by running the fascia, we would set a record. This convinced him. After all, a record is a record. Ten-and-a-half minutes, skin to skin. Hear that, folks at Guinness?

Aiming for relative immortality, we ended up in absolute ignominy. We closed up this case, and we were well into the next, when we heard unusually loud hollering and coughing coming from the Recovery Room. The patient had popped open his continuous closing suture—tersely called "dehisced"—right there in the RR. So back he went into the OR, where we closed him up again, and this time with interrupted sutures. Of course we got the "What did we tell you?" look at the next Mortality and Morbidity Conference.

Another black mark against me, but no real harm was done. Since a precedent for continuous closure suturing already had been set by others at the outlying hospitals, I came away relatively unscathed. By the way, I went back to the technique of running closure for the majority of my straightforward cases in private practice and never saw another dehiscence.

Harborview had no Ob-Gyn residents in-house, and one evening a woman came in through the ER in labor and about to deliver. I was there supervising one of the R3s, when the head nurse came and told me. I said, "Go call the Obstetrics service." She said, "You don't understand. This woman is about to pop that kid out."

I asked her what I was supposed to do about that. She said it was my job to deliver the baby, as I was the senior resident on hand. I told her that I hadn't delivered a baby in five years. She took me by the hand and said, "Don't worry; I'll tell you what to do."

It was the woman's thirteenth baby. She gave a little cough, and out it dropped into my waiting and slightly trembling hands! Slippery little thing, but I held on to it.

As another example of the bizarre cases at Harborview, imagine this:

There is a man with excruciating abdominal pain who very likely has a perforation somewhere in his bowel. We obtain his consent, and transport delivers him to the OR. There he is on the OR table, alone with the anesthesiology resident. Because it is Saturday night, all hell is breaking loose in the ER. A combative patient in the Recovery Room requires restraint—Code Strong, we call it. Everyone peels out of the OR to help the RR nurses.

Everyone except the patient and the anesthesiology resident, that is. The guy looks up at the resident and asks, "Say, man, I ain't gotta have this surgery, right?" The resident, already thinking about the next two or three cases he would have to do before breakfast—meaning no shut-eye—looks down, says, "No, I guess not," packs up his briefcase, and leaves the room. The guy, buck naked, gets off the OR table, walks down the corridor dragging his IV bottle, takes the elevator to the lobby, and demands that the astonished lady at the switchboard call him a cab and tell his girlfriend that he is coming home.

She has the good sense to alert the surgery team. I send my R3 to straighten out the mess. The cab comes, but the R3 demands that they wait right there until the guy's girlfriend shows up. Someone throws him a towel, she arrives, and they argue for a while. Finally, she wins, we put him on a stretcher, practically anesthetize him right in the lobby, and we take him back to the OR.

Being a lefty wasn't too much of a problem, even though all the commonly-used surgical clamps are set up for righties. They can palm the instruments and open and shut the ratchets that lock the clamps in place easily. Those of us who are of a more sinister bent have to learn to bias the instruments in an almost counter-intuitive way to make them work. That is, unless we switch to specialized left-handed instruments. I tried these once on one case, but found that I had been so inured to compensating with the usual tools that I felt awkward. Awkwardness is not a good thing in a surgeon. So I told the crew to ditch the southpaw stuff.

Then there was that ten-hour operation at Harborview. The poor patient had the worst type of pancreatic inflammation. Pancreatic fluid, a strong base every bit as corrosive as acid, leaked out into the surrounding tissues and started to dissolve them. We operated in order to debride (cleanse) the upper abdomen, and, subsequently, we had to go back and debride some more. The mega surgery was occasioned by his developing a bleeding ulcer, which we could not control without recourse to removing the lower half of his stomach.

The problem was that, because the abdomen had been opened for a third time in just over two weeks, all the tissue planes were disrupted and plastered together. It was well-nigh impossible to distinguish the interior belly wall from the stomach, colon, or small bowel. Forget trying to identify the edge of the liver and the bile duct. Everything looked the same!

So, we literally chiseled our way down to what seemed to be the stomach and eventually managed to get the job done. I exhausted two interns, two medical students, two anesthesiologists, heaven knows how many nurses, my R3, and the staff man, who begged out as soon as he realized that the case would take all night.

He said to me, "Jim, I leave this to you. I know you can do the job. Good luck!" And he took off to deal with a half-severed arm in the ER—faster than you could say Mickey Mantle. He ended up in the room next door, reattaching the arm, happy as a pig in slops, while I was in surgical Purgatory. He was right though; I did get the job done. Eventually. For that whole time, I never left the room even to urinate or eat, while the rest of the team rotated in and out with reckless abandon!

On another occasion, I had a young girl survive open-heart Emergency Room resuscitation at Harborview. As a result of blunt trauma, she had a partial tear in her superior vena cava, which is the big vein that enters the right side of the heart from above. Closed-chest CPR was not working, and signs pointed to blood in the sac around the heart. This we relieved with needle aspiration, but her heart stopped. We opened her chest in the ER.

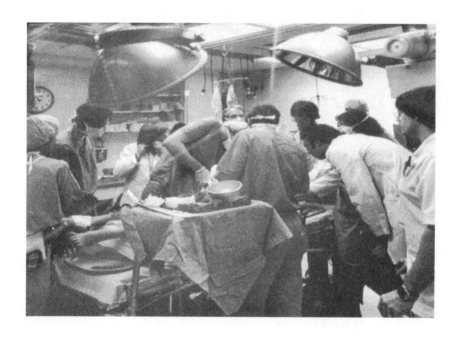

Surgery in the ER. I am in the white coat, supervising
—no mask, no scrubs (no time).

Next, we took the girl to the OR, keeping her alive by gently compressing the tear and replacing the massive blood loss until the cardiac surgeon arrived to repair the vein. She was discharged from the hospital four days later, almost as if nothing had ever happened!

At University Hospital, I was the first resident to perform a stomach-stapling procedure. I went on to do two more that year, one at the Public Health Hospital. Feelings of empathy for morbidly obese patients welled up inside me. These patients were not well accepted by the rest of the medical community. Perhaps I felt a kinship, since I was not well accepted, either. On one occasion, the director of Vascular Surgery moved his patients to the other team when I rotated there, just so he would not have to work with me. Can you imagine how that felt?

Early in my residency training, I harbored thoughts of going into pediatric surgery. I had been heavily influenced by my sub-internship in Philly with the wonderful Dr. Koop and by my first-year resident rotation on the pediatric surgical service at Babies' in New York City. I felt that this field would be a nice fit for me and would show Dad how much I respected his lifetime devotion to the care of children.

At the beginning of my chief resident year, I sent out feelers to the programs in Seattle, New York City, Philadelphia, Cleveland, Cincinnati and Buffalo—six of the then nine accredited programs in the states. I got back a series of lukewarm responses. Clearly, each program director had checked in with Carrico, who, obviously, had damned me with faint praise.

Exceedingly discouraged, I nevertheless proceeded to set up some interviews. I felt that I could sell myself well enough in person to overcome any less-than-stellar recommendations from the surgeons in Seattle. Considering the pressure I was under, I was hardly in the best frame of mind going into these interviews.

Seattle Children's Hospital told me outright that I would not be accepted into its program. It was the old

"We have so many qualified applicants" routine. Philly and New York City responses were similar.

I took the train to Buffalo, feeling very down about my prospects with the other three programs. Getting off the train in Buffalo, I stepped into a three-foot snowbank and decided then and there not even to bother to show up for the interview. I did interview in Cleveland and Cincinnati, but heard pretty much the same story.

It became clear that I would have to abandon my hopes of a career in pediatric surgery and make do with general surgery. So, back I went to Seattle to finish.

During my last rotation at the VA, I was giving a talk on something or other. Nursing students from the Bellevue Community College were on hand. One in particular caught my eye. She and I turned out to have a patient in common.

Edie was in the last throes of a moribund marriage, and I was in a marriage that had never gone anywhere in the first place. My then wife, Sandy, had her life, her friends, and her career. I had no friends in Seattle, just my ongoing struggle to get through the nightmare residency. Her joining forces with me was more like moving in with a new roommate. As I mentioned, she already knew, and had told me, that our marriage wouldn't last. This self-fulfilling prophecy soon came to pass. She remained in Seattle, moving up from L.P.N. to R.N. I ended up leaving Sandy for Edie.

Edie was like a breath of fresh air. She appeared at

the time when I was starting to see the light at the end of the tunnel. I was finishing up my training in Seattle and was looking to move on as soon as possible. She offered me the opportunity of making a clean break, and I knew that I needed to take her up on it.

Before residency was over, Carrico managed to get to me two more times. During my last rotation at Harborview as Chief Resident, I had a patient who required a major liver resection. Carrico and I talked about the case. I put it on the schedule, assuming that I would be doing the surgery with his supervision, only to find out in the OR that he had decided to do the case himself with another attending as his assistant. I was "welcomed" to stay and watch and even to scrub in, if I were so inclined. I managed to manufacture enough of a crisis to justify leaving the OR—humiliated, yet still retaining some measure of my wounded self-esteem.

The last slap in the face I received from Carrico came at the year-end Residency Banquet. He informed me that he was not going to sign off on my residency certification papers until he heard that I was doing a good job from the surgeon whose practice I was going to join in Astoria, OR. He said that he wouldn't make inquiries for at least six months. This meant that I wouldn't be able to sit for my Surgery Board Examination for a full year.

Clearly, the Texas "Mafia" did their darndest to keep

as much pressure on me as possible, for as long as they could. I thought *Whatever; I will soon be rid of the whole pack of them*, reminiscent of what Alice said about the Queen of Hearts and her court in *Alice in Wonderland*.

Except that the "Mafia" still plagues me in nightmares from time to time. Yet, blessedly, less and less frequently.

MAELSTROM

In 1979, I jumped out of the frying pan of a terribly difficult situation in Seattle and right into the fire of small-town medical politics in Astoria. Not Astoria, Queens, which is where my East Coast friends thought I was heading. Oh no. I am talking about Astoria, Oregon, a city of some 10,000 in the northwest corner of the state whose name is consistently mispronounced on the Atlantic seaboard.

On the surface, the proposed opportunity sounded quite good. Dr. Tim Patrick had contacted the U.W. Surgery Department and inquired whether anyone might be interested in joining him. Carrico grudgingly passed the request on to me, only because all of my co-residents had already locked up positions. I suspect he preferred the idea of my practicing surgery in a different state.

The Astoria opening sounded promising enough. Hell, after what I went through at UW, anything looked good. Patrick made me what sounded like a generous offer. His extensive practice took him to three hospitals, although the bulk of his work was at the Columbia

Memorial Hospital, the largest in the area and right across the street from his offices. The catchment area surgeons in Astoria served, including surrounding towns, was a respectable 40,000 people. That suggested that there would be plenty of cases for the four general surgeons in that neck of the woods.

I already knew one of the other two surgeons from his short stint a few years previous at the Seattle Public Health Hospital. Bob Wayne was a somewhat eccentric, at times a bit hyper, but harmless, apolitical guy. He proved to be of considerable help to me in later years. The other surgeon, Richard Harris, was a rather stiff, former military doctor. He had taken Patrick's place at the Astoria Clinic, after Patrick had pulled out under less than amicable circumstances.

I knew going in that there was something of an "us against them" mindset. About three quarters of the physicians in town were affiliated with the Astoria Clinic, making it something of a 600-pound gorilla in the marketplace. They referred exclusively to Harris, who was serving as Chief of Surgery at Columbia Memorial. Wayne confined his activities to the Seaside Hospital, a smaller facility. Patrick had established a good referral base among independent practitioners not aligned with the Astoria Clinic.

Patrick offered me a rather scary two-year contract, in that there was a non-compete covenant, should I ever want to terminate my association with him. I was advised that the geographic and temporal restrictions in the covenant were unenforceable, so I went ahead and signed on. Frankly, it was the only egg in my basket at that time. Overall, it looked to be a decent deal. Certainly, there was more money offered than I had ever seen as a resident.

Edie and I, starting our new life together and soon to be married, moved to Astoria. Talk about culture shock! There was no live theatre, and there were precious few interesting academic offerings from the community college, which was more like a trade school. And there were plenty of jacked-up four-wheel drive vehicles. On the other hand, there were lots of gorgeous Victorian homes, many with fabulous views of the Columbia River and the opposing shores of southern WA.

Astoria, the oldest city in the Pacific Northwest, was founded as a fur-trading colony in 1811, just six years after the Lewis and Clarke expedition ended nearby, at what became Seaside. Washington Irving's book, *Astoria*, written in 1849, introduced thousands of Americans to the Pacific Northwest—although he never visited the region himself.

We rented the upstairs of a duplex, and I rolled up my sleeves and prepared to go to work. Except that, compared with my residency, there was not that much to do. I kept thinking there must be something I should be doing, as I seemed to be idle so much of the time. Edie was up in Seattle three to five days a week in nursing school, so I busied myself making the rounds of the independent docs in town, emphasizing the "Three

As." Availability, Affability and Ability—not necessarily in that order.

I had gotten off to a good start, making contacts and doing a few tough cases, when one of the nursing supervisors complained about something minor I had said or done. The complaint got to Dr. Harris, who spoke to me about it. I told him what happened, and he took my side. However, he warned me, "When you lay down with dogs, you get fleas." I began to sense some serious trouble.

I mentioned a case of Harris's to Patrick, which I thought should have been handled differently. I meant my comments to be within the context of collegiality, the way residents discussed alternative approaches to getting a job done in those rare collegial moments at UW. Patrick's reaction shocked me. He went to a locked safe and brought out a list to which he added this case. He wanted particulars: names, dates, details. He wrote everything down and then locked up his notes again.

It turned out that Patrick was on a vendetta with the intent of bringing the Astoria Clinic to its knees. I did not share his agenda. I just wanted to take care of sick folks, make a living, and recover from the trauma of the preceding years of training.

Things came to a boil when Patrick operated on what he thought was a case of acute appendicitis. He subsequently re-operated for persistent symptoms. At no point had he ever examined the groin of the patient.

This fifteen-year-old boy turned out to have a large testicular cancer. Patrick cavalierly told the boy's parents the devastating news and took off for Hawaii an hour later, leaving his patient in my care.

In retrospect, neither abdominal operation should have been performed. I opted to consult a urologist, who should have been involved in the first place. I had made plans months previously to attend the College of Surgeons meetings in Chicago, which I told Patrick about immediately. He never mentioned any conflict with his trip to Hawaii. I left the boy in the competent hands of the urologist, who removed the cancerous testicle and made things right.

Dr. Harris informed his colleagues at the Astoria Clinic about this fiasco. They had their own shit list going of Patrick's transgressions and made a case for patient abandonment. Along with thirteen other cases, they took it to the Oregon Board of Medical Examiners, which, in their opinion, proved that Patrick was incompetent.

Harris was correct; I was flea-bitten by this association. The Board came down with a reprimand for Patrick, and I was thrown in for good measure. Patrick hired a big-shot Portland lawyer who got us off the hook with a total reversal of their adverse findings. Little effort was required in my case, but I am sure he had to pull a few tricks out of his bag to clear Patrick, who by then had lost his hospital privileges as a result of numerous cases of potential surgical mismanagement.

Ah, but there is more. This same lawyer proceeded to sue both the Astoria Clinic, which was owned by twelve physicians, and the hospital for conspiracy and restraint of trade under the Sherman Anti-trust Act. This he was able to do, since patients came from two different states.

I had had enough by this time. Only one year into my two-year contract, I wanted out. I was released from the non-compete covenant and was able to stay in the community by agreeing to cover for Patrick. Harris certainly would never help him out. I got my free pass.

Edie and I really did not want to leave town. We were sort of getting used to the roar of the four-wheel drives and had made a few friends. Besides, we were three by then. Our daughter Emily had been born on Independence Day—a sign to start my own practice? She arrived just a month and a half after Mount St. Helens blew its top, ninety miles away.

Since Dr. Patrick was pretty much in disgrace and, obviously, now biased against me for leaving his practice, I couldn't ask him for the requisite recommendation to Carrico for approval to take the Surgery Boards. But I had done a few cases in Seaside and had assisted Bob Wayne on a few more. He generously wrote a strong letter of recommendation, and that did the trick. That and the fact that Harris had nothing to criticize about my work in Astoria. I took the Boards and was certified.

A few words about the surgery board certification process are warranted. It's a two-step process, the first being a written or qualifying exam. It is a four- or five-hour comprehensive test. I believe the failure rate in those days was thirty percent. A failing candidate could retake the exam the following year and up to five times. After passing, it was on to the orals.

Orals were a grueling affair. They were conducted in a hotel room, with the candidate sitting on the hot seat in front of two examiners. One would be a well-known surgeon, whose articles were likely in the candidate's file cabinet. The other examiner would be a local surgeon. The older, renowned surgeon tended to be more even-handed in his or her questioning; it was the local person one had to watch out for. This type typically would be trying to trip up the poor candidate, leading him down the garden path into a trap. His hidden agenda was to impress the senior examiner. Meanwhile, the poor examinee would be left squirming.

The failure rate for orals was twenty-five percent. A person could retake orals up to three times. Failure at that point necessitated repeating Chief Resident year before taking another crack at it. Thankfully, I got through unscathed. (Furthermore, I passed recer-tifying examinations on the first try every ten years thereafter.)

The next level was Fellowship in the College of Surgeons, but that required a three-year period of post-residency practice in one location. Since I had left Tim Patrick's clinic and set up on my own, this meant my first year wouldn't count. This made little difference to me. After making it past more than a few obstacles, I finally was on my way to a successful career in surgery.

The nasty lawsuit between Patrick and the Astoria Clinic exploded into a case with national implications, which ended up going all the way to the Supreme Court. Medical peer review, and what was thought to be immunity from prosecution, was really what was at issue. The case went on for the next five years.

Fortunately, as an independent practitioner, I was not a party to the suit. I was deposed briefly, and that was it. The local court found in favor of Patrick and against the Astoria Clinic. The hospital, which also had been sued, got off lightly. The clinic, on the other hand, was fined nearly two million dollars.

Although the Appellate Court overturned the verdict, the Supreme Court unanimously found for the original decision and against the American Medical Association and the Joint Committee for Accreditation of Hospitals, both by now parties to the defense. The final decision sent shock waves throughout the national medical establishment.

The Supreme Court's decision bankrupted the Astoria Clinic. It also financially ruined twelve doctors, who were decent, hard-working fellows, sadly without adequate insurance coverage for this sort of case. All of them left town. For years, it was hard to find doctors willing to practice in Astoria. Most of the medical business went to Portland or Longview, Washington.

Patrick, a really sub-par surgeon, in my opinion, and a nasty man besides, became very rich, although a *persona non grata* in Astoria. He relocated to Pennsylvania, leaving a toxic residue in his wake that took years to clear. Most people, including me, were glad to see him go. He didn't need to work anymore, which probably was best for all concerned.

But he still was capable of making trouble. Years later, when I moved back to Seattle, he tried to stir up a hornet's nest at the Ballard Hospital. Gratuitously, he told the Chief of the Medical Staff that I had been put on probation in Astoria. What he didn't say was that this probation was the direct result of his leaving me in the lurch with that testicular cancer case, instead of honoring my request for a few days off to attend the College of Surgeons meeting. He also neglected to mention that my probation was lifted as soon as I left his practice, and soon thereafter I was appointed Chief of Surgery.

The Ballard Chief of Staff asked me about this unsolicited call. I told him what really happened, and he sent a surgeon down to Astoria to verify the facts. I felt obliged to hire a kick-ass, personal libel attorney, who wrote one very strong letter to Patrick and his attorney. The letter served as fair warning that any further interference from either would result in an immediate lawsuit. That put an end to that. But I was seething about this uncalled-for piece of vindictiveness.

I bumped into Tim Patrick for the last time at a College of Surgeons meeting many years later. I could see he was trying to get my attention. I walked past him without so much as a word, overcoming my first impulse to deck the SOB with a stiff left hook. Years later, in 2002, he and his wife, Sandi, died when their Cessna crashed in a snowstorm. It is a well-known fact that doctors make bad pilots. Perhaps bad doctors are even worse pilots. R.I.P.

But back to 1981. I really was enjoying being out on my own, immune from the brewing legal storm between Patrick, the hospital, and the Astoria Clinic. Blissfully un-aware of the sweeping negative implications of the ultimate outcome. Our second daughter, Katie, was on the way.

Since things from our perspective were looking up, it seemed to be the right time to buy a house. We found a nice place near the Community College and a short walk to the hospital. It was an attractive Dutch Colonial with more room than we needed at the time and a yard for our basset hound, Use Guise. We had a view of the Columbia River and the WA shoreline. All this for $65,000!

One of the local orthopedists owned two houses a few blocks away, one of which he rented to me. It was a beautiful Victorian. Edie was instrumental in helping me get things organized. We put the office upstairs with a consultation and break room. Below, there was a lovely waiting room and three exam rooms. We couldn't have asked for a nicer set-up.

We hired a capable front-office person named Myrna, who substituted as a baby-sitter when all the usual ones were unavailable. Our office nurse, Christie (a different Christie—the first one was long gone), worked part-time in the county jail, where she dealt with near-constant verbal harassment. I would like to think that working with us helped her preserve a measure of sanity.

***

There were, however, some memorable surgical cases in my four years' stay in Astoria. Two of the most interesting concerned Russians. The first of these was an able-bodied seaman who had to be evacuated off a giant tanker due to peritonitis. He had a perforated ulcer, which I fixed by patching up the hole with surrounding tissue. But this was only a temporizing maneuver. He had a fifteen-year history of ulcers and clearly needed a more definitive operation. Permission had to be granted by the Russian authorities. The Russian Embassy put me in touch with one of their surgeons, who gave me approval to proceed.

While all this negotiating was going on, the seaman was having a wonderful time. He was particularly enthralled with indoor plumbing, which he had never seen before. We invited him over to dinner one night. He found our home fascinating, especially our closets and several bedrooms. He never had seen such splendor in his hometown of Novosibirsk, a city of over two million people in central Siberia.

He was considerably less pleased by the way another Russian, who happened to be in our small hospital at the same time with appendicitis, totally shunned him. Apparently, this was because the other Russian patient was a member of the Communist Party. Commissars evidently did not mix with simple seamen under any circumstances.

His ship took off without him, and the Embassy had to arrange to fly the man home. He cried when he left and sent me a postcard a few months later.

Another Russian patient of mine was part of an ethnic woodcutting enclave. One day, he had slipped up on his chain saw, slicing the left side of his face. The cut ran from the side of his cheek through the edges of his upper and lower lips and on down to his chin, through a thick, black beard.

I obtained his consent for repair under general anesthesia, as the laceration was far too complicated to repair under local anesthesia in the ER. He pleaded with me not to remove any part of his beard. Due to his Orthodox religious beliefs, it had never been shaved.

I reluctantly agreed to honor his wishes, wondering how to find the skin edges through all that hair. I began by putting in a vast number of sutures along the course of the long laceration. Pretty soon, it became more expeditious to tie beard hair from one side of the open wound to beard hair from the other side. Overall, I utilized more beard hair than suture material. And the re-approximation was good, not that my work ever would be seen through all that hair.

One of my patients had a run-in with a plate glass window. This particular fellow loved hanging out at the Desdemona Club, reputedly the dingiest dive in town. For reasons known only to him, he decided to punch his hand through a window. The glass shattered, puncturing his arm with dozens of shards. In he came to the ER, more or less under his own steam, covered in blood. The ER doc took one look and knew he was over his head. He called me in. I repaired dozens of lacerations to his arm, shoulder, and chest under general anesthesia.

There was a piece of glass deep in his wrist that I could tell had severed the median nerve. This required neurosurgical repair using a microscope. Astoria had neither a neurosurgeon nor an operating microscope. The neurosurgeon who ostensibly covered our hospital was in Portland, two hours away. I called him from the OR. He told me to leave that area alone, including the imbedded piece of glass, and send the man to Portland for delayed nerve repair after the inflammation had subsided.

A year or so later, I was sued for negligence for having left a shard of glass in this man's wrist. My lawyer could hardly keep himself from laughing at the frivolity of this case. Especially since the plaintiff had asked for my services again when he next appeared in the ER, this time having been stabbed nineteen times by his girlfriend.

On the appointed day in court, the plaintiff's lawyer notified the judge that his client was unavailable to testify, because he was incarcerated in the city jail, more than likely throwing wisecracks at Christie. The lawyer missed his chance to take a crack at me, as the case was thrown out.

Astoria was woefully deficient in a number of other medical specialties. Amazingly, we had no anesthesiologists, although a lot of surgery was performed. We had four nurse anesthetists.

I had worked with certified nurse anesthetists (CRNAs) before at the Public Health Hospital, where they had in-house anesthesiology supervision. The supervision for our Astoria crew came from Olympia, two and a half hours away. That horrified me at first. Yet, after seeing them at work, I was impressed with their capabilities and became more comfortable with the arrangement. To this day, anesthesia in Astoria remains the purview of the CRNAs.

The one time the system failed was during a major catastrophe in Ilwaco, WA, site of what has to be one of America's smallest hospitals. I was at home when the call came that they had a man in their ER with a pulsating abdominal mass and perilously low blood pressure. Suspecting a leaking abdominal aortic aneurysm, I made a quick call to the Astoria operating room and told them to pack up all their vascular instruments.

I zoomed over to grab the stuff, told them to alert the police that I was going to speed across the big bridge that spanned the mouth of the Columbia River, and that I needed an escort. I drove across at speeds upwards of ninety mph, at one point passing a string of nine vehicles. There was abject terror on the faces of those I zoomed past. The police were waiting on the other side. The road had been cleared, and a convoy of squad cars escorted me to Ilwaco Hospital, in no time flat.

By now, the man's blood pressure was unrecordable, and he was unresponsive. There was no time to administer anesthesia. We cut off his clothes and quickly splashed some Betadine solution on his chest and abdomen. I opened his abdomen with one swipe of the knife, swept the contents aside and compressed his aorta against his spine to stop the blood loss from the tear in the vessel wall below. This took perhaps three minutes. The plan was to put the patient to sleep, now that his bleeding was contained, and his blood pressure was beginning to rise. So far, so good.

Problem was, he was a big guy with a short, thick neck, and the CRNA couldn't get the breathing tube into his airway. No tube, no anesthesia, and no anesthesiologist. Meanwhile, the man was starting to come to.

I had an osteopathic general practitioner assisting

me (more like standing there, aghast). I placed his hand where mine had been, told him to hold tight, moved up to the head of the table and performed a tracheotomy, again without anesthesia. Bull neck or not, I had that tube in within another five minutes. It wasn't pretty, but it was working. The CRNA was now able to put the man under. His pressure was normalizing.

I took a few breaths, went back to the belly and proceeded with the operation. In that tiny hospital, I successfully managed the repair of his ruptured aneurysm. As we were closing up, I asked the nurse to check pulses in the feet. The left foot had no pulse and was cold; the right was fine.

I surmised that some plaque debris from the aneurysm had become dislodged during the compression phase of the surgery and had blocked blood flow to the leg. This would require opening up the groin, which could wait until I could get the patient transferred to Astoria. At least there I would have a fully-equipped OR, with an ICU for post-op care.

So, back we rushed across the bridge with another police escort and the patient still under anesthesia. In Astoria's vastly better OR, I opened the artery in his left groin, fished the errant plug out of the main artery below, and restored full circulation to his left leg.

Exhausted, I accompanied the man into the ICU. His blood pressure was normal, he had normal peripheral circulation, and he was nodding appropriately in response to simple questions. We set the ventilator on assist mode to give him a rest overnight. The nurses gave his tracheostomy a proper dressing, I wrote detailed orders and went home for a few hours' sleep. I felt great about this save in the face of extremely adverse conditions.

I had only been asleep an hour or two, when I received a call that my patient had coded, and he was not responding to resuscitative attempts. I rushed back to find him flatline on the EKG, with his neck massively swollen.

His tracheostomy tube had dislodged when the nurses turned him to one side to tidy him up. I had left sutures on either side of his tracheal opening, which I attached to clamps just in case such a thing might happen. The idea was to pull on these sutures, thereby enlarging the opening so that the tube readily could be reinserted.

Sadly, in all the confusion of the code, the nurses forgot about the sutures and simply connected the dislodged trach tube to a hand-operated oxygen delivery bag. Essentially, they pumped oxygen into the soft tissues of his neck, but none found its way into his lungs. Despite the heroic measures to save this poor man's life, he died an unnecessary and preventable death. I was in tears. All my efforts had come to naught. So tragic. And frustrating.

No doubt Ilwaco Hospital, with all of a dozen beds and no ICU, was a low-budget affair. On another occasion,

I was operating on a patient there with what looked on the x-ray to be an abdominal mass. It turned out to be a retained rubber dam, inadvertently left behind from a previous operation performed elsewhere. I pulled out this darkly stained foreign body and passed it off.

To my amazement, some months later when I asked for a rubber dam to facilitate closing a belly, I was handed the very same one I had pulled out from the first patient. The nurses had washed it off, re-sterilized it, stained as it was, and put it on the shelf. I politely insisted that they provide me with an unused rubber dam, which they did, reluctantly...

One of the most curious situations I ever encountered involved a woman with a large mass in her left breast. It was suspicious on examination and equally suspicious on mammography. Certainly, she needed an excisional biopsy, to which she readily agreed. However, she called the next day to tell me that she would have to cancel, because she was going to the Philippines to see the faith healers. I asked her why, and she told me that they previously had cured her hemorrhoids.

I had heard of these faith healers before; they lurk in the jungle, where they prey (pun) on people's naïveté and fear of doctors. I asked her to have the specimen sent to a licensed pathologist in Manila and to see me when she got back. I made her promise that, if the mass was still there upon her return, she would let me operate. She agreed to all this.

A month or two later, she showed up in the office—with seventy-two photos of the faith healers in action. Wearing wide-sleeved shirts, they were leaning over her. They then presented her with a mass of what looked to me like chicken fat, and that was that. Of course, no incision. That was the point.

While she was gone, I had done a little research and had found the following posted on the Web:

Faith Healing Involves More Chicken Guts than You'd Think:

We did something called psychic surgery. We'd have someone lay on a table, and beneath the table would be a bowl of chicken gizzards and livers mixed with blood.

We'd lift the person's shirt up and act as if we were going to take out a tumor or an infected gall-bladder or, like, a possessed kidney or something. We'd pretend to cut the stomach open, putting a hand in front of our fingers to hide it, then pull out the gizzards and the liver, calling them cancer or "Yendik, the Kidney Demon." Applause and donations would follow.

I asked her, "What did the Manila pathologist tell you about this 'mass'?"

"Oh, I never told the faith healers that I wanted to take the mass with me to the city. I couldn't insult them like that."

"Well, what did they say this thing was?"

"They said that it was not cancer, although it was on its way to becoming a cancer."

"Okay; fair enough. Now, you remember, you said I could re-examine you. Right?" She did, and so I did. I put her hand up to her breast. "Do you feel that?"

"Yes, I do, doctor."

"Now, you also remember that you agreed to let me operate if the mass was still present when you returned from the Philippines. Right?" She did, and I put her back on the schedule. She asked me to remove a few lumps and bumps here and there while I had her in the OR. I sighed and agreed to what is called in the trade a "Blue Plate Special."

I took out the breast mass. It turned out to be a large chronic abscess. No cancer. I am sure that the faith healers convinced the patient that they saved her from cancer by whatever they did. Who am I to say otherwise?

The largest mansion in town is the Flavel House, today owned and operated by the Astoria Historical Society. Captain Flavel was a bar pilot who made a fortune guiding big ships across the notoriously treacherous Columbia River bar. It's known as the graveyard of the Northwest because of the plethora of sunken ships in the immediate vicinity. Bar pilots were, and still are, the elite of the elite in Astoria.

I operated on the wife of one of the bar pilots four times. Ellen Gibson had a bowel obstruction, which caused necrosis of three-quarters of her small bowel by the time I had been consulted and opened her abdomen. I removed the dead bowel and left her with an ileostomy, which subsequently required revision. She required caloric support intravenously for years, until her remaining bowel adapted a bit.

The goal was to close the ileostomy and re-establish continuity with the colon, so that she would be able to get off the IV supplementation. To accomplish this, I tried an experimental procedure, reversing ten precious centimeters of what remained of her small bowel. This had been done on a handful of patients, with mixed success. When the procedure worked, the reversed direction of peristalsis in the short segment would slow gut transit down enough to allow for more absorption. When it didn't, it would function as a partial obstruction of flow and require undoing, typically with loss of a few more centimeters.

It worked for Ellen. She was a real trooper. Unfortunately, she received very little emotional support from her husband, the bar pilot. He was nice enough to her when she was his healthy trophy wife. But not after her health turned south, as we say. When she finally got her health back, she divorced him.

Once I was out on my own, I developed a practice in weight-loss surgery. I attended an instructional course in Iowa City given by Ed Mason, the godfather of bariatric surgery. I soon determined that the final iteration of his evolving approach to stomach stapling was the most promising. Although I continued to use this technique for the rest of my long career in bariatrics, I tended to gravitate increasingly toward gastric bypass—also pioneered and refined by Mason—as a better operation.

My first bariatric case in Astoria turned out to be the only one where serious complications ensued. Intra-abdominal infection necessitated removal of the reinforcing mesh band, and the patient's long-term result was poor. Undeterred, I forged ahead with more cases. After that initial failure, my success rate was excellent.

I especially recall another of my early bariatric patients. Her surgery was uneventful, at least from my perspective. From a legal standpoint, however, there were complications. She went to jail for two years, convicted of embezzlement—I wonder if my fees were paid out of "hot" money. Periodically, I would get questions from the jail physician about what she could or couldn't eat or drink. While in jail, she lost half of her preoperative weight, which completely changed her appearance. She was able to return to her hometown without having to suffer the shame of being recognized as an ex-con.

In the process of stapling the stomach of another morbidly obese woman, I found two asymptomatic large ovarian tumors, one the size of a football and the other more like a softball. They had not been noted on my preoperative physical exam, which had included a pelvic exam. The woman simply was too heavy for the tumors to be detected. So, I extended my incision and took them out.

Meanwhile, the messy lawsuit between Patrick and the Astoria Clinic was still ongoing. It hardly affected me, but considering that and the limitations of small-town life, I felt that it was time to consider a move. I sent some feelers out to Seattle and discovered that Dr. Lowell Eddy was looking to bring in a young surgeon and ultimately wind down his practice.

I gave him a call and soon discovered, to my absolute delight, that he and Mom had been classmates at P&S! Well, I took that as a clear sign and jumped at the opportunity to move back to Seattle in 1983. Edie was delighted as well.

We had no luck in our attempts to sell the house. The only serious offers, if you can call them that, were to swap the place for a large RV (in significant disrepair) or a share of the Astoria plywood mill (a struggling enterprise). We opted to surrender our equity and head north to greener pastures.

MANUMISSION

MYSELF

Lowell Eddy was everything that Tim Patrick was not. He was kindly, collegial and supportive, beloved by all. A lot like my Dad.

Walking to work was no longer an option. Dr. Eddy's practice was in Seattle's North End. His main office and hospital were in a neighborhood called Ballard. He also shared part-time office space with a general practitioner, Alan Dahl, in the city of Edmonds and had a secondary referral base at nearby Stevens Hospital.

We bought a home in Edmonds from an orthopedist who was downsizing. We needed a large house, what with two children, a dog and 21,000 pounds of furniture and overflow office contents, the vast majority of which we accumulated during our four years in Astoria. The house was near a grade school with a huge playfield. Charming hanging flower baskets decorated the Edmonds town center. I especially appreciated the five minutes' commute to Stevens and the twenty minutes to Ballard.

From the get-go, the Ballard and Stevens surgeons provided me with much-appreciated collegial support. Interestingly, one of them formerly had been with the Astoria Clinic, prior to the advent of the infamous Dr. Patrick. He was delighted to have "gotten out of Dodge." Sound familiar?

There was one exception, whom I first met in the Ballard Hospital doctors' lounge. I doubt that he was unaware that I was now on the staff—news travels fast through hospital corridors. As if feigning ignorance, he handed me the business card of some surgeon in Tacoma, and told me that I should call him because he was looking for a partner. Somehow, he and I never did seem to develop much of a working relationship after that opening gambit.

Dr. Eddy and Mom were delighted to get together for an informal forty-fifth year medical school reunion, and Dad tagged along. Lowell pulled out a dog-eared class list and read out the names one by one. He and Mom would share what, if anything, they knew about "old so and so." Dad would kibitz occasionally with any information he might have. I had a ball just sitting there and taking it all in. What a charming occasion!

Lowell asked me to take care of him one day. He had self-diagnosed a ruptured diverticulum (perforated colon) and told me he needed emergency surgery. He was literally writhing in pain, although not tender to deep palpation. I told him that I wasn't convinced he needed surgery. At least he was a compliant patient. I sent him home on mild pain medicine and told him to come back twelve hours later for a re-evaluation, or sooner, if needed. He reported in the next morning that he had erupted in blisters across the left lower quadrant of his abdomen. Turned out it had been a case of herpes zoster (shingles) mimicking a surgical emergency.

Lowell called it quits about four or five months after he brought me in and introduced me to his patients and referring docs. He had a very nice practice, mostly surgery, although quite a number of his patients thought of him as their primary-care doctor, and he also did annual physicals for them. I certainly didn't want to shut my door on these wonderful folks, but I gradually wound down this part of the practice, focusing on surgery, the specialty for which I had been trained.

His office assistant stayed with me for a few more months, until I was able to find a suitable replacement. After a few disappointing hires, Edie, who continued to serve capably as my Office Manager, found us a suitable, experienced front office person in Betty Williams and a no-nonsense, former military nurse, Gloria Fitzgerald, for the back office. This team stayed intact for a decade. First Gloria retired—the commute to and from Whidbey Island was getting too much for her—but Betty lasted another five or six years, until health concerns rendered her no longer able to handle the job.

We hired medical assistants to replace Gloria. The

first, Summer Williamson, was careful and deliberate in the extreme. She never made a single mistake, because she made sure she fully understood what it was I needed done before doing it. This often required repeating or paraphrasing myself more than a few times, which sometimes bordered on the frustrating, especially when the OR was after me to come over as soon as possible.

The second, Lisa McGinness, had worked up from the ground floor. Indeed, she had begun, at age ten, as our babysitter. By the time she was in high school and had a driver's license, we trained her to keep the files in order. Next, she learned to pinch hit for Betty in the front office. Finally, she shared the back office work. Lisa was the opposite of Summer. I only had to tell her something once to have it done, and often the task was done before I asked for it. A few slip ups, but an A+ for efficiency.

Over the last fifteen years, the front office was capably attended to, first by Joanne Marshall, who shifted focus to become a highly successful wedding officiant—not for me—and later by Pam Persky, who stayed with me until the practice closed.

Working between front and back, for a pre-medical school learning experience, was Jonathan Watling—a Yale grad, looking to get back into the academic grind after nine years of a different grind on the U.S. Olympic Rowing team. Which he did, with distinction: moving on from my office, to Columbia P&S, to an orthopedic residency at Presbyterian, to a successful practice in Maine.

In the mid-'80s, I brought in another surgeon. For a brief time, I shared office space with Deborah Goller, who had trained at UCal, San Diego. She came with strong recommendations, and she did not disappoint. Ultimately, she decided to relocate her practice to nearby Everett, Washington, where her husband, an anesthesiologist, was employed.

A few years later, Tom Jurich wrote me from Ed Mason's program in Iowa City to see whether I might be willing to bring him into my practice. Tom's recommendations were just a bit qualified, but I liked him. Mason assured me that Tom would make a capable surgeon, given a bit more seasoning. I thought I heard echoes of what Carrico might have told Tim Patrick about me. I was sympathetic, so I encouraged Tom to come aboard.

Indeed, Tom proved to be a perfectly capable surgeon. He stayed with me for several years, until he married a young woman from his church, bought a home in Edmonds, and decided to join a surgical group there. I think the idea of having patients in two different hospitals didn't appeal to him. In retrospect, who can blame him?

In truth, my position was a bit odd in that the people at Stevens considered me more as a Ballard doc, whereas those at Ballard looked at me as a Stevens doc.

Whatever. I had a solid referral base at both places, and many of my referrals came from former patients. Every time I got to worrying because it seemed that I was not busy enough, it soon seemed that I was nearly overwhelmed with cases. I also maintained operating and staff privileges at Northwest Hospital, but rarely had cause to go there.

In the early years of private practice in Seattle, I would see my Stevens patients, as Lowell had done before me, at Allen Dahl's general practice office. This man was so kind to me. He charged me minimal rent, in fact, nothing at all until my practice was better established. After he retired, I rented office space in a group clinic building, but because I wasn't a partner (Partnership made no sense for me, given that so much of my work was in Ballard.), I was kicked about from space to space.

I shared offices in turn with a pulmonologist, an orthopedist, a surgeon, and the gastroenterology group. For the remainder of my time in the clinic, I landed with a physiatrist (a rehab doctor). You might call me peripatetic (derived from the Greek, meaning "to amble about," presumably while discoursing with someone like Socrates). Finally, in my last years of practice, I asked Stevens patients to travel the whole nine miles down to the Ballard office. That certainly made things simpler, no longer having to transport charts and equipment back and forth.

I met a Romanian family one evening at a dinner party given by one of the Ballard anesthesiologists. She had worked at the VA when I was a resident and, therefore, as I explained before, had a very different take from my own on allowing elective cases in the afternoon. Yet, by this time we had made our peace. The Romanian man had been a trauma surgeon in the old country, and his wife was a post-doctoral researcher. She was able to find a decent job at the UW, but he was relegated to driving a pizza truck.

Several weeks later, I was called to the ER to see a woman who had been shot accidentally in her home—by this very same Romanian ex-trauma surgeon! It seems that he and his son had been taking a guided tour of the house after dinner, whereupon they noted a rifle in the back of a closet and pulled it out. The trauma surgeon pulled the trigger, assuming the rifle wasn't loaded. Wrong. The bullet hit the hostess right in the hip and exited on the opposite side.

The only injury I could find, aside from the entrance and exit wounds and two neat holes in the pelvis on x-ray, was a track across the top of her vagina that was bleeding minimally. I packed her vagina, watched her overnight, and discharged her the next morning. Who knows why this crazy incident happened? Maybe the dinner was overcooked. Even so, there are more polite ways of showing dissatisfaction than shooting the hostess. Especially when one is in the United States on a visa. The hostess never pressed charges. Just a freak accident.

Stevens Hospital had the third-busiest ER in the state. Harborview's was and still is the busiest. Even so, I saw some serious trauma at Stevens. One memorable case was a young man who blew off most of his hand, trying to chuck a cherry bomb out the window while driving—in my opinion, much worse than texting while driving. The cherry bomb never made it out of the window, but bounced back, landing in the driver's lap. With a car full of kids and his wife on board, he had to think fast. So, he grabbed the incendiary device, shoving it between his back and the seat.

I don't know what his coat or the seat looked like. Nor do I know how he was able to drive without causing an accident. I was the first surgeon to see his hand, and there was little left to salvage, only his little finger. For the next decade, the newspapers ran a photo of that mangled hand as a warning about fireworks to all the idiots out there.

At least, that guy survived. I cannot forget the tragic case of an eighteen-year-old who was on his bike on the freeway, when he was hit by a car going well over seventy mph. This poor kid was attempting to ride his bike, unaccompanied, from Alaska to Pennsylvania—to raise money for the American Cancer Society. He took a wrong turn and was trying to backtrack when he was hit. Since the teen responded to ongoing CPR in the ambulance, we took him to the OR in a desperate attempt to save him.

His belly was full of blood, but I was able to

determine that the source was the inferior vena cava (the big vein that returns blood to the right side of the heart). It's in an almost totally inaccessible place behind the liver. I knew what to do from my trauma experience at Parkland and Harborview. I already had clamped off the blood supply to and from the liver. Now I had to crack, i.e., open, his chest, access the heart, insert a big chest tube through the opened right side of his heart past the tear in the inferior vena cava, and let anesthesia catch up on the massive blood loss. This maneuver successfully stopped the hemorrhage, but he arrested several more times and finally flatlined. God only knows what the condition of his brain was after being hit. We never had the opportunity to find out.

Just as was the case with the woman in Astoria, I had to remove over three-quarters of a patient's obstructed small bowel, leaving her with an ileostomy and not nearly enough remaining gut to sustain life without supplemental IV calories. The difference here was that this girl was twenty, whereas the woman in Astoria was in her late fifties.

To my amazement, her need for extra calories started decreasing, to the point where I was able to stop the infusions completely. When I took her back to restore intestinal continuity with her colon, I found that her remaining small bowel literally had tripled in length. I had measured bowel length carefully at the time of both operations. It reminded me of salamanders, who re-grow their tails when severed.

Let me not forget the 102-year-old woman with acute inflammation of the gallbladder. Now, a case is a case, and I enjoyed removing gallbladders as much as the next guy. Lowell was incorrect when he told me, "Jim, I am sorry to tell you that there are no more gall-bladders in Ballard; I took out all of them." In fact, I know for a fact he had left quite a few behind. Besides, Ballard's demographic was changing. More and more young families were moving in, so there were plenty of gallbladders waiting to be removed.

Removing a gallbladder on a 102-year old was overly aggressive, I thought. And the family-medicine resident working with me couldn't have agreed more. So I simply gave the dear lady local anesthesia, made a one-and-a-half-inch incision, located the tip of the inflamed gallbladder, opened it up and scooped out the stones. I closed the opening around a drainage tube that I was able to remove in the office three weeks later. Her recovery was rapid and uneventful. She nearly made it to 104.

I utilized local anesthesia for major surgery on two other similar occasions. In one case, it was to remove the right side of the colon; in the other to remove a cancerous breast. Both patients, although elderly and frail, tolerated the surgery remarkably.

Through the years, I performed quite a bit of cancer surgery. Several of my patients developed more than one cancer. Most memorable was Mary Rhoades, a talented pianist, composer, and conductor. She had an early-stage breast cancer that I removed. In the process of surveillance for possible recurrence, I found laboratory evidence for a possible second tumor of the intestinal tract. It was confirmed, and out came an early-stage colon cancer.

I often ran into Mary at the Symphony during inter-mission, where she had seats in the front row center, as close as possible to the conductor. She invariably would introduce me to her friends as "the man who had saved her life. Twice." As if I needed any more motivation to give it my all as a surgeon.

Two breasts I didn't get to operate on were obvious cancers. Yet the patients refused to have anything done about them, surgically or medically. Neither woman would accept my argument that: with surgery, there was a reasonable chance of long-term survival, possi-bly even a cure; without it, death was virtually certain from metastatic spread. Sadly, one of them came back to me a year or so later for terminal care.

Then there was the biker-babe breast surgery. She brought in a magazine that showed her posing with a Harley, her affected breast in all its former glory proudly emblazoned on the cover. She asked me to be particu-larly careful in removing the mass to give her a good cos-metic result, in case the editors might offer her another gig.

Only once in my career did a patient attack me. I was attempting to remove another breast mass. Anesthesia sedated the patient, and the nurses put her right arm out on a table extension, strapped down. Somehow, she managed to pull her arm free while I was operating, She threw a right hook, which I dodged, but the hand ended up right in the wound.

We sedated her more heavily, re-prepped and re-draped, and on I went with the surgery. Amazingly, despite better arm restraint, out came the arm again, and along came another right hook. This one was a bit slower, but fast enough to escape the circulating nurse's desperate attempts to stop it. Once more, the hand fell into the wound. That was quite enough for me. I finished the case with her completely snowed, under general anesthesia.

It turned out that the woman's ex-husband was a prizefighter! She and he had duked it out numerous times before she finally dumped him. I found this out, not from the woman who had tried to coldcock me, but from another patient, the fighter's second wife, who had been subjected to similar sparring matches.

One day, I was in the operating room at Stevens Hospital doing a gastric bypass, when I overheard the nurses gossiping about the case next door. Kindly Dr. Stan Silberman was opening a man's stomach for a second time to remove a handful of coins he had swallowed. Apparently, this man had done the same thing a few years before. Somewhat facetiously, I told my scrub nurse to let Stan know that I was a numismatist, and I would appreciate his giving me any Indian head pennies he found in the stomach.

Stan was completely floored to find exactly what I had wished for! So in came the penny from his OR room to mine, along with an 1878 trade dollar—as a kind of bonus. Both were a bit blackish from stomach acid, but they were well preserved and cleaned up quite well. The trade dollar is worth $150. Technically, of course, it should have been given back to the patient. Or to the pathologist. On the other hand, there are plenty more, less valuable, coins around for him to swallow next time.

MENTORING

Clemens Fischmeister, an Austrian, had a great talent, which I've never seen duplicated. Wiggling one's ears is, I think, genetically inherited. Dad could do it; so can my daughter, Katie. But Clemens could wiggle one at a time! Amazing control. He could have made a lot of money with this trick. Instead, he chose medical school.

I was contacted by UW and asked whether I would mentor this young man. Dr. Jurich was with me at the time, and we ended up having a terrific time working with Clemens. We gave him a really good clerkship experience. For his final exam in surgery, Clemens had to sing "Take Me Out to the Ball Game" to my father, in perfect English. He succeeded, whereupon Tom and I gave him an American flag sweatshirt as a going-away present. Between the two of us, we cured Clemens of any further thoughts of a career in surgery. He returned to his homeland to finish medical school and ultimately opted for homeopathy.

We reunited twenty-five years later in Vienna, where I went in celebration of what I prefer to call my second thirty-fifth birthday. He gave me a repeat performance of his sequential ear wiggling. He politely declined when asked to reprise "Take Me Out to the Ball Game," being out of practice.

I cured another young man of his dreams of becoming a surgeon. Sam Sherrar, manifestly unlike me, was a favored son in the UW Surgical Residency and had been doing a year of research. This was encouraged at the time and was distinctly different from my day. During the time he was in the lab, the further away he got from the drudgery of night call and all-night stands in the OR, the more he thought he would be better off switching to some other specialty. Surreptitiously, he had approached the Anesthesiology Department, and they showed strong interest in snatching him away from Surgery.

I recently had mentored Sam's wife, and he said he wanted to shadow me for three days, to see what the private practice of surgery was really like. After the first day, he called to say that he wouldn't be back. He had seen quite enough. He joined the anesthesiology program, and he has been happy ever since. I feel I made a difference in his life.

Sam had the courage and foresight to switch careers in mid-residency. By contrast, I was too focused on surmounting the obstacles I faced in my training to even consider taking similar action. I acknowledged my accomplishments, yet I did not feel fulfilled. As a result, happiness wasn't to be mine until much later.

Lynn Oliver, Sam's wife, was in the Family Medicine Residency and stayed on as an attending. In 1984, her colleague, Nancy Stevens, a former medical student who had rotated through my surgical team, invited me to teach the family-practice docs during their second year. This request came out of the blue and just when I was considering volunteering to teach at Harborview for one month a year.

I longed to be teaching again; I had had few opportunities to teach in Astoria. I was proud that Dad had taught pediatric residents for much of his career, and I wanted to be on the clinical faculty, as he had been. However, I had qualms about joining a trauma team for a month, being subject to any number of all-nighters and having the regular staff collect the fees for my work.

Before I became the Surgical Liaison, the family medicine residents were rotated in with the general surgery residents at University Hospital. Obviously, the family docs were given all the scut (Read: drudge) work, while the surgery residents got to do cases, or at least assist in the OR. If a family doc ever made it to the OR, it was just to hold the surgical retractors.

The idea was for second-year residents to come to me instead and work for a month learning surgical principles, doing consults, working up patients, assisting me in the OR, and seeing post-ops in the office. I taught them how to assist in surgery, sew up lacerations, remove small lumps and bumps, and do needle biopsies of breast masses. The rotation with me began as an elective, and, soon enough, the majority of the residents elected to rotate with me.

The Family Medicine Department caught a lot of flak from the Surgery Department, which was smarting from the loss of warm bodies to do their scut work. The Surgery Department promised to make things better if the family docs would come back. They did, but for political reasons more than anything else. Not surprisingly, it wasn't long before the family docs were back doing the dirty work and learning next to nothing. Soon after, the Family Medicine Department invited me to resume teaching their residents, this time as a required rotation.

I was now teaching a full six months each year. My faculty appointment was through the Surgery Department. I moved up through the ranks and eventually became an Associate Clinical Professor. Best of all, I never had to attend a single faculty meeting.

In all, I worked with the family-medicine residents for 25 years and was twice honored for my teaching. I never was paid a penny for this. This work was a privilege. I learned a lot about medicine from the residents, and they eagerly absorbed the precepts I put forth about surgery. I always found time to throw in a bit of my philosophy of life. Shades of Dr. Radke from the V.A. I even provided lessons in parallel parking for one resident. He had come from Zimbabwe and bought a brand new car without knowing how to park it.

The residents learned some memorable teaching points. One day, I received a call from an eleven-year-old girl who was putting together a science project and wanted to know, "What do you do with the things you take out of the body?" This struck a sensitive chord in my heart, since I had for some time been bemoaning the fact that I was always removing parts of the body and hardly ever getting to put anything in. Oh, I put in my share of intravenous chemotherapy ports and even a few pacemakers. But those operations were few and far between, compared with the vast number of gallbladders, appendices, thyroids, colons, and breast masses I excised.

I took the young girl at her word that she was genuinely interested. I called our pathologist, Jim Bellamy, who was possessed of absolutely no discernible sense of humor, as is the wont of most pathologists. I asked him if I could take the kid and my resident on a little tour of his neck of the woods. "This is highly irregular," he said. Yet, he consented. He set up a little exhibit for the two of them and graciously demonstrated how he made stained slides from tissue samples and what tissues looked like under the microscope.

The girl listened patiently. When Bellamy had finished, he asked her whether she had any questions. She said, without hesitation, "What do you do with the things you take out of the body?"

Bellamy rolled his eyes, as if to say, *What do you think I have been showing you these past twenty minutes, you little twerp?* He was totally nonplussed. But I now realized where she was going with this.

I turned to the pathologist, and I said, "She is asking you what you do with the things we take out of the body." I thought he was going to hit me over the head with his tray of slides, but he restrained himself. I turned to the girl and said, simply, "Oh, we throw them into a special bag and burn them." She said, "Thank you." That really was all she wanted to know in the first place! The rest of it was TMI. My resident laughed about this all the way back to the University Hospital.

Sometimes surgery requires a certain artistry. There was a guy moaning in the ER, doubled over with peritonitis. What was most concerning to him, though, was the Road Runner tattooed in the middle of his abdomen, right where I needed to make the incision. The surgical repair of his perforated ulcer was easy enough, but the skin closure took quite a while. I made a concerted effort to line up all the tattoo lines and reconstruct the Road Runner. My resident opined that he was a bit on the skinny side when I was done—not the patient, the Road Runner. Just the same, even if he wasn't exactly the same, he was still recognizable.

Another man came in with a perforated ulcer, generally considered a surgical emergency. Yet he refused surgery. At first I was okay with that. I explained to my resident that the British have long experience treating perforated ulcers with nasogastric tube suction and antibiotics. Those who show no signs of improvement are taken to the "operating theatre," as they call it. Well, this man fell into that category, but he still wouldn't let me operate—until he was at death's door. By then, it was far too late to intervene.

I couldn't save every emergency case that came my way. The saddest loss of all was a beautiful nine-year-old girl who died from a ruptured appendix. The appendix is not always located in the right lower quadrant. I have seen it in the upper abdomen, on the left side (in a patient with complete reversal of organ location), and in the pelvis, where it lurked in this poor girl's case. She had been complaining of lower abdominal pain for three days, but, because she wasn't hurting on the lower right side, the nurse practitioners—who fielded daily calls from the concerned parents— never considered appendicitis.

She appeared to improve for a few hours and then collapsed in pain. Her heart had stopped at home by the time the EMTs arrived. They resuscitated her and brought her in to the ER. We took her directly down to the OR, where we found a pelvis full of pus secondary to a ruptured appendix. There was little problem in removing the causative focus, but she kept arresting.

Even though I opened her pericardium (the heart sac) for open chest massage and restored the heart to function four or five times, the heart finally stiffened, and she expired on the table. Many of us were in tears, myself and my resident included.

Thank goodness, my other appendectomies were successes. The funniest of these involved a sixteen-year-old boy who had become afflicted two days before the finals of the national high school car-mechanic contest. He pleaded with me to let him fly to Indiana the day after his appendectomy. He told me he had been preparing for this event for two years. When he reassured me that there would be minimal lifting involved, I relented and let him go.

Would you believe it? He won, and the prize was $10,000, plus guaranteed car-mechanic jobs virtually anywhere. He told me the surgery might have slowed him up a few seconds, but that it was really no sweat.

One of the oddest appendectomies I ever did was the one that presented itself through an opened inguinal hernia sac. The kid was pretty skinny, and there was the tip of the appendix, looking right at me. I tugged gently, and out popped the whole thing. Obviously, we had not obtained consent for an "incidental appendectomy" as part of a hernia repair. The boy was underage, and his father was out in the waiting room. So I sent the resident out to explain that, if it were my kid, I would want the appendix removed. Also, to mention that, statistically, he had a five-to-ten percent chance of developing appendicitis over the course of the rest of his life. And I threw it in, or rather, took it out, as a freebie, since insurance would never have paid for this add-on anyway.

One night, the Ballard ER called me about a severed penis, which had been found by a janitor in a cup behind one of the public toilets. My third-year resident had seen a lot, but she had never seen anything like this. We put it on ice, waiting to see if the rest of the person would show up looking for it. He never did. We sent the penis to Harborview, figuring that they might know what to do with it. Meanwhile, we administered to the janitor, who had fainted. I was reminded of the botched circumcision I cleaned up years before.

I started what I thought was a routine gallbladder operation. In x-raying the connection between the gallbladder and the bile duct, I found a doubled duct at the bottom of the gallbladder. Furthermore, the bile ducts from the right and left side of the liver each were doubled. And to top it off, there were two gallbladders inside one envelope—each containing stones. This was something for *Ripley's Believe It or Not*.

Hospitals require that all surgical specimens go to Pathology for analysis and documentation. Slides are made, and the remainder of the specimen is incinerated, as we explained (finally) to the 11-year old girl. But there was no way I was going to relinquish this unique specimen.

I allowed the pathologist, again Jim Bellamy, to photograph the double gallbladder. Then, I browbeat him into giving it back to me. I put it in a jar in formalin and kept it right by my desk for two decades, so I could show all the residents a curiosity they likely never would see again.

After I closed my practice I brought the prized specimen home. My wife wasn't keen on having it around, although she didn't try to make me discard it. I tried the argument that beauty is in the eye of the beholder, without much success. She compromised by having me keep it out of sight. I pull it out of hiding every so often. Just to marvel at it.

I saw a patient once with a nasty, enormous keloid scar. He got it years before in the Borneo jungle, during WWII. He came upon a Japanese infantryman, and the two went at it, hand-to-hand, with bayonets. As the vet told me, "He got me right here, right in the middle of my chest. But I got the better of him!" You should have seen my wide-eyed resident.

He went on to explain that he laid there for a while, bleeding and moaning, until an intrepid Bornean farmer found him. The farmer took him back to his hut, washed the wound, packed it with seaweed, and sewed it closed with a shoestring, no less.

Unsurprisingly, the wound became infected, whereupon the farmer cut and removed the shoestring, opened the wound, cleansed it, and left it open for a few days. He then popped in some more seaweed, took up another shoestring, and sewed the wound shut again. Persistent fellow.

Again with the wound infection. Again with the

cleanout, again with leaving the wound open for a few days. And once again with the seaweed and shoestring closure. Only this time, the wound healed.

Sort of. The keloid was rather prominent, to say the least. I excised the nasty scar right in the office under local anesthesia and gave the man a decent closure, which healed uneventfully. End of saga. Fifty years, skin to skin. Not a record.

One Christmas Eve, I began a case with some trepidation. My goal was to relieve a bowel obstruction in a man who previously had undergone nine abdominal operations, although none by me. I laboriously dissected my way down, finding nothing but dense scar tissue from all the previous surgical interventions. I began, literally chiseling my way around the abdomen, millimeter by millimeter. I sent word home for the family not to expect to see me before Christmas Day. Indeed, the surgery took a full ten hours. I sent my resident home after five. The patient did well enough, but I was exhausted, having equaled that marathon case from my residency. "Déjà vu, all over again," as Yogi Berra said.

In 1990, after Tom Jurich moved out of the office space we shared, the Swedish Hospital surgical training program recommended Chris Wilke. After completing his residency, he joined my practice and stayed with me for about three years. He was industrious, reliable, and competent. He just wasn't all that comfortable covering the bariatric side of my practice. Nobody was, really. There were the usual, often subconscious biases against giving "fat people with no willpower" an "easy way out." Moreover, there was the recognition that bariatric surgery is high-risk for complications and therefore potentially litigious. Made me feel like the proverbial voice crying in the wilderness.

MALADIES

In 1982, Dad needed major prostate surgery. I flew back to New York to lend a hand with the household chores. Mom had suffered a stroke in 1978 and had fallen and broken her hip, which required surgical repair. This was followed by an unsuccessful twenty-eight day stay at the Smithers Institute. Breaking through her tenacious defenses had required that she be transferred to a long-term rehab unit in New Jersey—the facility where I elected to study alcoholism as a med student.

She had returned home, never to drink again, yet pretty much incapacitated, either unable or unwilling to leave her room, except for twice-weekly physical therapy. Her affect had become flat. Oh, how I missed that singular vibrancy of hers—that I never was to witness again.

Yet, Mom was one brilliant, tough woman, who somehow rallied enough to travel in early 1983. She and Dad flew out to Hawaii to visit Jonny, who was living in Honolulu at the time. On the way back, they stopped in Astoria for a few days.

We took them on a shopping trip to Portland, because Mom had outgrown her clothes, the result of nearly five years of inactivity. It was hard to see her like that, walking with a cane and fifty pounds overweight. Edie took her to Portland's most fashionable store, I. Magnin's. Mom sat there like the *grande dame* she always believed she was, while a personal shopper presented outfit after outfit. She bought most of them without trying anything on.

Around 1984, we flew back East with Emily and Katie to visit Mom and Dad at their new house in Franklin Lakes, NJ. It seemed odd for my parents now to be living in New Jersey, especially after complaining for so many years about the stink around Secaucus and how terrible the Jersey drivers were. But times change, and living in the house at Gramercy Park had become burdensome. It had too many stairs for Mom, who never walked well after her hip surgery. There was also the hassle with parking, and, besides, Dad was now retired.

They got a good price for the house, just under a million dollars. A good return on a thirty-year-old $75,000 investment. Recently, it sold for over six million, whereupon it was completely renovated, to the tune of another two million. I was privileged to have a look inside and could hardly recognize any traces of the way the place used to be. So it goes.

My parents found a lovely home in a lovely town. Forget Secaucus; New Jersey is not called the Garden State for nothing. The house sat on about an acre, but it was too large for two elderly people. Several years later, they moved to a smaller townhouse in Wayne.

When my third daughter, Betsy, was born, in 1986, we asked my former nanny, Noreen, if she would like to move to Edmonds to help us out. She traveled with us to Chicago for my induction into the American College of Surgeons and from there to Seattle. Having her live with us was a mixed blessing, at best. For me, it was nostalgic, but for Edie it was a nightmare. Noreen was over eighty and getting pretty frail.

She insisted upon sneaking smokes in her room, even though we asked her to smoke outside. And she pulled the same stunt with Emily and Katie that she had done with Jonny years before. She regarded baby Betsy as her charge, but she was no longer quite up to the job. Noreen strove mightily to shield Betsy from pernicious influences like Emily, who took offense, and Katie, who really didn't know any better. Emily and Katie would tell on her for smoking in her room. Fair is fair, after all.

Little did I know at the time how sick Noreen was. It was not just that she was getting old; she was riddled with cancer. Since this was thirteen years after her huge abdominal surgery, I presumed that this was not related to her bowel, but more likely originating in the lungs, as a result of her many years of smoking. She had multiple lesions in lung, bone and brain. She was sent to Calvary, a terminal-care hospital in the Bronx. Edie and I saw her one more time in the hospital a few weeks before she died. She was like an emaciated little bird. She no longer knew who I was.

After she died, I got a nice note from her niece. She sent a Polaroid of Noreen's gravestone, a check for $5,000, and a jade ring my mother had given her years before. I believe that Noreen remembered me in her will because she always regarded me as the child she never had. Because she loved me, although she, like my parents, never told me so.

Edie had her hands full with the children. She also was caring, in turn, for Noreen, her mother, who suffered from depression, and, later, my Dad. We brought him out after the second of his two thoracic aortic aneurysm operations. Mom had died by then.

Although Dad was physically weak and emotionally bereft, we couldn't keep Dad with us long term, even if he had wanted to stay. Our fourth daughter, Joey, was born just ten days after Mom died. We now had four children and a dog. We were one busy household.

I did try to lessen the burden on Edie by taking one or another of my daughters with me on weekend rounds. But unlike Dad, I didn't leave my children in the hospital lobby. I took them to the nurse's station. The nurses seemed okay with it, and all went well.

Except for the day when Emily, age five, pointed to me as I was charting. "See that man there?" The nurses nodded. "Well, he's not really a doctor." The nurses tried to remonstrate. "And you know what else? He's not really my dad." Embarrassment all around, except for Emily, who cheerfully continued to scribble on Progress Note paper.

In the early '90s, Stevens Hospital started a Take Your Daughter to Work Day tradition. Emily and Katie were getting too old and far too sophisticated to participate.

But Betsy, now seven, was just the right age. So I took her with me on the appointed day. The nurses had a hard time finding a small enough scrub suit, and, even with that, they had to roll up the sleeves and cuffs. Betsy looked like a homeless waif, but she made it into the OR.

I was doing a hernia repair. The nurses had her sit in the corner while they prepped and I draped the patient. Then, they allowed her to come a little closer. She had never seen, or even imagined, anything like this before. There was her daddy cutting into a patient; there was blood, needles, and more. Surprisingly, she was very curious and came closer and closer. Pretty soon, she was on three stacked step platforms, looking over my shoulder.

Betsy did a repeat performance the following year. Thereafter, it was Joey's turn. She got to watch a gastric bypass and a breast excisional biopsy. The next year it was gallbladder surgery. By then, I was doing almost all my gallbladder cases laparoscopically. Which meant looking at a monitor. Just like TV. Really cool for kids.

During one operation, Joey was watching the screen while I was working away. Next thing I knew, there were a dozen kids in my OR watching TV. It was like I was running a weird kind of day care. Of course, I loved every minute of it. So did the nurses and scrub techs, as many of their kids were among the group in my OR. It was one big, happy family.

Before bedtime, Joey loved watching the video I had made of a laparoscopic gallbladder operation.

We couldn't see any harm in that, and it seemed to calm her down.

Because I was active-staff status at both Stevens and Ballard Hospitals, I had to take call, covering the ER for surgical consults at both places. It was every fifth night and every fifth weekend at Stevens, and every third night and every third weekend at Ballard. Fortunately, we had fewer hits to the ER at Ballard. Still, that worked out to a whole lot of being on call. Let's not forget that I usually had patients at both hospitals and had offices near each. I was always going back and forth for surgery and rounds. I tried to coordinate my schedule as much as possible, but, oftentimes, things just didn't work out as smoothly as I would have liked.

Between my busy surgical practice, resident teaching, child raising—with all its ancillary activities, not the least of which was swimming—board activities for the Seattle Symphony and Bathhouse Theater, and tickets to the Seahawks, Mariners, Sonics, half a dozen other theater organizations, the Opera, and the Symphony, I was running myself ragged. If I wasn't dashing off somewhere or other, I was off riding my bicycle.

A colleague once remarked that he had never seen anyone go to as many events as I did. I would rush home from a long day in the OR, plus/ minus office hours, scarf down a meal (often in the car), and we would be off to another event. As I think back to those hectic days, I am amazed that I was able to pack in so much.

Partly, I think it was like being a kid in a candy store after being deprived of sweets for several years. Let's face it: Astoria was a cultural dustbin. Or, perhaps, being that busy kept my demons at bay. Maybe, had I been less on the go, I would have reflected upon the fact that I really wasn't suited for the work that I was doing. That I could have been a pediatric surgeon. Or I should have been in a primary-care specialty. Or even a full-time teacher.

Nobody can keep up a schedule like mine for very long. In 1990, I had the first of four heart attacks. It was a partial myocardial wall infarct, and it came without warning while I was riding my bike. I was able to pack up the bike and drive myself to Ballard Hospital. They kept me there for three days, and I pretty much fully recovered. Within a few weeks, I was back on my crazy schedule. I maintained it for another five years, including training for and completing the Seattle-to-Portland bicycle race.

From 1990 through 1991, I served as Chief of Staff at Ballard, having previously been Chief of Surgery. It was during my tenure as Chief of Staff that Ballard merged with Swedish Hospital, on the recommendation of the hospital CEO. He convinced the Ballard Medical Executive Board that the hospital was about to go into debt for the first time in its history.

I fought the idea of merger as long as I could. I knew that in merging with another hospital four-and-a-half times larger, Ballard would get swallowed up.

And, as feared, this came to pass. Prior to the merger, Ballard had the highest ratio of nurses-to-patients in the city. Effective immediately after the merger, the ratio dropped to exactly what it was at Swedish. The patients noticed and complained, but nothing could be done. The die was cast.

In 1995, I had a second myocardial infarction, again while biking. This time I stayed down, at the edge of the trail. Several people walked right by without offering to help. One man wagged his finger and told me that I should carry nitros in my pocket, just in case. And then he walked off! Wasn't his problem.

Finally, a Good Samaritan called 911. I was carted off to Evergreen Hospital, where a balloon dilatation of my right coronary artery was performed. Edie got me a referral to a psychologist who, like me, had had a heart attack at an early age. I met with him for a few months, tried to come to grips with my disease, which I felt was mostly due to genetics, and resumed most of my previous activities. I did stop taking call to the two ERs, other than the occasional weekend, to help out. Of course, I continued to take call for my own patients.

Bike riding was getting tough on my knees and es-pecially my wrists and neck, so I began running. I never had been much of a runner beyond what little I did at Hotchkiss. I took up running, I think, because I was unhappy with the turn my life had taken. After nearly twenty years, my marriage to Edie was unraveling. I made another poor choice and became involved with another woman.

Perhaps, in part, as an act of penance, I ran, sometimes as much as fifteen miles a day, eventually hitting fifty miles a week. I would run on the road in the dark of night. I went through a pair of running shoes every three months. I stopped, because I realized that endorphins were controlling my life and not making things any better. Sort of like Forrest Gump, I guess.

I had another coronary hit in 2001, while at work in the OR. Fortunately for the patient, I was just completing the skin closure after a mastectomy. At that time, my first diagonal and right coronary arteries were stented. I bounced back pretty well this time, too, and began on high-dose statin therapy to get my cholesterol levels as low as possible.

In 2005, a few months after reconnecting with my now-wife, Mary, after almost half a lifetime apart, I had another cardiac event. The left anterior descending artery was tightly narrowed. I was told that it probably could not be opened without surgery.

I requested that two interventional cardiologists work together. One of them was an expert with the Rotoblade technique, which I suspected might make a LAD stent placement possible. I was afraid that, even with both men working on me, they might give up too quickly, so I requested no sedation. I wanted to be wide-awake and able to urge the cardiologists to press on if necessary. I knew that this was not going to be a simple matter.

Poor Mary was alone in the waiting room, terrified. She was told the procedure would take an hour and a half. It took close to six hours. The whole time she was out there, she was deep in prayer. Her prayers, plus my exhortations, plus getting the second cardiologist involved, resulted in success.

Several years ago, I had some angina and was found to have narrowed the blood flow through the LAD stent. Placement of a new stent inside the older, narrowed one fixed the problem. By this time, I had given up my practice entirely and had switched over to teaching yoga. But I am getting ahead of myself.

MEMBERSHIPS

MAKING WAVES

From 1991 until around 2005, I was an active member of United States Swimming, which gave me great enjoyment. Officiating at swim meets became more like a second job, albeit a non-paying one, for most of those years. I also served as secretary on the board of Pacific Northwest Swimming (PNS), an association of fifty-four Western Washington swim clubs, for five years. I was president of the Cascade Swim Club in the late 90s, during which time I researched and wrote the early history of the club, a fun project.

When Emily and Katie decided to make the move from summer league into year-round swimming with Cascade, I made a major commitment to the sport. The year-round program consisted of daily practices, with swim meets every month or two. Edie would drive the girls to their daily practices. My job was to take them to the weekend meets.

I started to think seriously about training to become

an official. It felt like a good way to pay something back to the sport that had meant so much to my brother, quite a bit to me, despite my limited involvement, and now was becoming a big part of the children's lives. Besides, it was boring to sit around for four hours just to watch a few short races. Far better to be down on the deck, where the action was.

My mentors inspired me throughout the rigorous training. In short order, I became a Stroke and Turn judge, first on the local level and then on the championship level, since Katie was regularly qualifying for championship meets. I soon took training to become a Starter and then became a Referee, also at the championship level. This process took about four years. By then, Betsy and Joey also were swimming year-round.

Logistics were getting complicated. The older girls, now swimming with the seniors, were too young to drive. The Age Group (younger swimmers') pool was nearby, while the Senior Group used a different pool two miles farther south. Seniors were expected to train twice a day and, over Christmas break, often three times daily. Edie logged a lot of chauffeuring miles.

At most local meets the Age Group events were held in the morning and the senior competition in the afternoon. And most meets were Saturday/Sunday affairs. This meant that I was working all day, all weekend. On top of my surgery practice.

As I think back and to my credit and amazement, I rarely missed any of the kids' races, even if it meant getting up at 5:00 a.m. to make hospital rounds before heading off to meets and rounding again at 8:00 p.m.

Ever the teacher, it was a joy to mentor the newly-accredited judges and trainees who worked under me. My reputation among the officials in our swim community was solid, and I remain proud of that. With the swimmers, I was semi-affectionately known as "Doctor DQ." I was a bit of a stickler for correct form in starts, relay take-offs, strokes and turns, although I always did my best to be fair and gave swimmers every reasonable advantage in disqualification disputes.

When I took over as president of Cascade, the club was considered by Pacific Northwest Swimming, the parent organization, to be a renegade. Cascade, founded in the late 60s, had a long and distinguished history as an elite club in the Pacific Northwest. Jonny was familiar with the club, as some of its swimmers were Olympians and held world records. At this time, however, Cascade had been opting out of regular attendance at PNS meetings, while objecting to this and that policy change. For too many years since the club's heyday, only a handful of its swimmers had qualified for Nationals, and none for Olympic trials.

Clearly, the club needed to go mainstream again to re-establish a modicum of respect. Only then would better swimmers come back and elect to stay. To that end, I joined the Pacific Northwest Swimming Board, first as an at-large member and then as secretary. During my tenure, Katie became Swim Representative, and after that our club treasurer, Jody Woodruff, became PNS Treasurer.

Cascade experienced a complete turn-around as a result. The census has doubled, and nearly every year swimmers go to Nationals. We had a few move on to Olympic trials as well, and Cascade has re-established its prominence in the PNS record book. Emily contributed to this excellence in no small way as an entry-level Age Group coach. She introduced to competitive swimming several swimmers who eventually became PNS record holders.

In 1997, Pacific Northwest Swimming submitted a successful bid to host the Spring Junior National Swimming Championships at the world-class Weyerhauser venue in Federal Way, WA. The only problem was that nobody wanted to step up and serve as meet director. Furthermore, none of the bigger clubs were interested in running yet another championship meet. I volunteered myself and my club, knowing full well that Cascade was too small at that time to take on full responsibility.

But I had an idea. I believed that several clubs could be persuaded to work together to carry the load, split up the work, and share in the profits. This turned out to be a massive undertaking: a full six months in the planning; coordinating six different swim clubs; supervising 600 volunteers; and hosting 800 swimmers. I lavished praise on all the workers and went out of my way at every opportunity to thank everybody. Just as I did every day in my surgery practice.

As I think back, this was by far the biggest project I ever have undertaken, much bigger than the musicals at Bard Hall, the Hotchkiss yearbook, serving as Chief of Surgery in Astoria or Seattle, developing a Bariatric Surgical Program for Northwest Hospital (more about this to come), writing this or my other books, or editing my brother's work.

For the record, the meet was a huge success, although it marked the beginning of the end of a hitherto successful marriage—for which I take my full share of responsibility. I was way over-extended, vulnerable, and consequently feeling unlovable—deservedly mired in the Slough of Despond, until rescued by a fortuitous phone call.

MONUMENTAL

Theodore Roosevelt is my hero of heroes. An abiding interest in him has been a major bright light in my life. It began the day I saw his likeness carved in granite on Mt. Rushmore. That was back in 1976, when I was on my way cross-country. I had the usual background in American History through my years at Hotchkiss, but I took no history courses at Yale other than Art and Music History.

The first book I read about Theodore Roosevelt was David McCullough's *Mornings on Horseback*. I was hooked. I read about his early years, how he overcame his physical limitations, and how he rose "like a meteor" in politics, to use his own words.

I read numerous biographies dealing with his adult life. His boxing adventures at Harvard were amusing. The loss, both of his first wife, Alice, and his mother, Mittie, on Valentine's Day, 1883, was sad beyond words. The solace he found as a neophyte cattle rancher in the still-somewhat-open American frontier was gratifying. I thrilled to the tales of TR making midnight rounds in the Bowery as president of the New York Board of Police Commissioners. His work to reform the NYPD and later the Civil Service was exemplary.

But even these legendary adventures paled in comparison with the way he recruited, trained, and led his Volunteer Cavalry in the Spanish-American War. The youngest President in our history, he is considered to be the father of the modern Navy, the first President to make full use of the press to his advantage, and the first American recipient of the Nobel Peace Prize, despite his advocacy of Big Stick diplomacy. He also made possible the building of the Panama Canal and was, far and away, the greatest conservationist of all our Presidents.

This was a man with a photographic memory, a voracious reader—estimates vary from one to two books *per day*—and he was a prodigious letter writer (more than 150,000). In addition, he was a formidable ornithologist, an accomplished taxidermist, a big-game hunter without equal, an explorer who co-led an expedition in the Amazon jungle, mapping 600 miles of a previously uncharted river, and the author of over forty books. I have left off some of his other major accomplishments, but space does not permit. Rudyard Kipling aptly described TR as "more phenomenal than Niagara Falls."

I collected early editions, including some firsts, of his books, a twenty-two-volume set of all of his works, each with an introduction by someone famous, such as President Taft. I also acquired books about his predecessors and successors in the Presidency, books about the navy, about the carving of Mt. Rushmore, books focusing on different aspects of his career, books about authors who wrote about TR, books about the

Spanish-American War, and books by his children and even his valet. Over 300 books, filling more than four bookcases!

I purchased a Presidential Appointment document, dated 1901, and signed by TR and Elihu Root (then Secretary of War—ultimately Secretary of State). I also procured a beautiful, oversized print of a photograph of TR taken toward the end of his Presidency by the celebrated "Photographer of Men," Ian Pirie MacDonald. He stated that, of the 70,000 subjects he photographed in his long career, from the early part of the twentieth century until his death in 1942, TR was his most difficult subject.

TR was a favorite subject for cartoonists, with his oversized teeth, the Big Stick, his big-game hunting, his Bull Moose Party and split from the Republican mainstream as popular subjects. Three period magazine cartoons occupied pride of place above my desk.

Ultimately, I donated my entire TR collection to Dickinson State University in North Dakota. I know and respect the key people there, who have embarked on the ambitious project of digitizing everything by, or about, or even peripherally related to TR, some four million items. They helped initiate a drive to create a Presidential Library for TR.

Although Springfield has an ersatz Lincoln Library, the U.S. government did not authorize Presidential Libraries prior to the one created for Herbert Hoover.

This means that funding will have to come from the State of North Dakota and private donations such as mine. Plans are coming to fruition, and the library is scheduled for grand opening on July 4, 2025. God willing, I hope to be there to witness this.

For years, I have been a proud member of the Theodore Roosevelt Association. To date, I have attended five of their annual conferences. Linda Milano, the TRA Associate Director, took me on a private tour of TR's home, Sagamore Hill, in Oyster Bay, Long Island. What a thrill it was to walk into rooms that had once resounded with his engaging laughter and scintillating conversation, to look at his personal library, his collection of artwork, photographs, and trophies.

Katie's decision to become a history major at Yale pleased me no end, especially when she took my advice regarding the subject matter for her senior thesis. She wrote a scholarly and very complete account of TR's involvement with the Simplified Spelling Movement.

What was that, you ask? TR had issued a Presidential Proclamation (pejoratively referred to as a "ukase," as if he were a czar), while Congress was in recess. It stated that some 300 words would be simplified thereafter in all Executive Branch publications, according to the recommendations of the Simplified Spelling Board. These included: *dropt, thoro,* and others. He was excoriated for this, both by the U.S. and the British press. Cartoonists had a field day. But TR was a pragmatist; he knew how to cut his losses, *altho* he continued to employ simplified spelling words in his own letters. Truth be told, he was paving the way for untold legions of texters to follow in our day.

Little did I know, as I immersed myself in Theodore Roosevelt's history, that one day, like TR, I would cut my own losses, making a dramatic move that would change the course of my life.

MOTIVATION

MORBID OBESITY

Weight loss surgery began to capture my attention during the last year of surgery training at UW. I carried that involvement forward into my practice in Astoria and from there to Seattle and Edmonds. What started out as a side interest, rapidly became a major one and, ultimately, the mainstay of my surgical practice.

Obesity had become an epidemic, starting in the mid-80s. In general, the medical establishment, reflecting then-prevalent negative societal biases, all too often undertreated this unfortunate group of people. It wasn't until 2013 that morbid obesity finally earned disease-classification status from the American Medical Association. This slow recognition seemed a repeat of the way alcoholism was treated until the late 70s. Like obesity, alcoholism was long considered a condition, secondary to lack of willpower, not a true disease, and therefore not worthy of mainstream medical attention. Perhaps this linkage between my mother's suffering and the plight of the morbidly obese is what triggered my abiding commitment to the surgical amelioration of massive overweight.

When I was establishing my *bona fides* in this area, I had precious little competition in the north end of Seattle. Two surgeons in the area were doing occasional gastroplasties, but neither was on staff at Ballard or Stevens. Except for me, nobody else was dedicated to this line of work. This may have been because earlier enthusiasm for radical intestinal bypass as a weight-losing intervention—although technically a rather simple procedure—had been fraught with an unacceptable risk of complications, including an alarming number of cases of liver failure, usually fatal. This led the general surgical establishment to look askance at efforts to find effective and safer approaches to weight loss surgery (WLS).

Many prospective patients simply were not suitable for WLS. Some were not able to cope with the rigors of proper preparation for the surgery, or the requirements for dietary adjustments and vitamin supplementation afterwards. Some had inadequate family support. Many were not really motivated to get thinner. It was my practice to have everyone potentially interested in WLS undergo a thorough psychological evaluation, in part to give them insight into their disease, and in part to help me screen out poor candidates.

Not surprisingly, competent psychologists with much interest in or knowledge about morbid obesity were very scarce. So scarce that, early on, I had to make do with a speech pathologist from Ohio State University, who was researching similarities between stuttering and morbid obesity, of all things. After much searching, I found a local psychologist who was enthusiastic about helping me. Vic Hayes became my go-to guy. He was grateful for referrals and did his homework on the issues affecting this population.

However, when my practice in the field grew to the point where I was doing 125 bariatric procedures a year, Vic became totally inundated and finally begged my indulgence. He no longer was finding sufficient time to deal with his first love, adolescent psychology. He asked me how I would feel about his selecting five or six psychologists and personally training them to take on some of the load. That wasn't a pun, but you get the picture. I ended up with a cadre of competent psychologists, and the arrangement worked for everyone.

Quite a few of my referrals came from other patients. I don't mean to sound disparaging, but every obese person has ten obese friends. Otherwise stated, "Like seeks like." Sure, I got some referrals from other M.D.s, frequently orthopedists and urologists who had patients they wanted to operate on, but not until they lost a hundred pounds or more. They would ship the patients off to me when they were at the highest risk for surgery, have me do the heavy work of getting them fit for more surgery, do their thing, and then bill for two and three times what I had charged.

Let's face it: WLS is fraught with complications. Medical co-morbidities abound, as most patients wait too long before seeking surgical intervention. The surgery is technically challenging. Complications are much more common in those who are massively overweight.

Unfortunately, some do not survive. I lament each of my fatalities, yet I am proud to say that, at a time when the prevailing mortality rate was in the range of two percent, my fatalities were much rarer. National norms are now closer to the extremely low mortality rate I achieved in my series of more than 2,000 of these procedures.

I want to make it perfectly clear that I never took credit for taking weight off anybody. Rather, I merely provided the patients with a tool to help them take the weight off on their own, by greatly reducing the reservoir capacity of their stomachs. The surgery gave them a real sense of satiety, typically for the first time in their lives. In addition, with bypass of a portion of their small bowel, capacity to absorb what little they now could eat was decreased.

I never rushed anyone to the operating room. Oftentimes, we would ask patients to wait six weeks or more, in order to make essential lifestyle changes before performing the surgery. During this waiting period, he, or more likely she, as ninety percent of my patients were females, would undergo tests to rule out hormonal disorders (which I never found, by the way). They'd also have consultations with appropriate specialists to optimize their medications. They were instructed to begin a moderate exercise and dietary-restriction program. The goal was to achieve a ten percent weight reduction before the surgery. Those who did ended up with better results.

Educating these patients was, for me, a moral imperative. They were taught how to read food labels and learn the optimal approach to stretching and exercise. I emphasized the lifelong need for vitamin supplementation. I provided follow-up for as long as they cared to follow up with me and never charged for these visits.

I smoothed the road for them. But do not think for a minute that their journey was easy. They had to say goodbye to their "best friend"—eating to their heart's content. Mind you, their best friend was killing them.

All patients were required to attend an introductory seminar. They were encouraged to attend one of the four support groups we started, so they could talk to patients who either had undergone the surgery or were contemplating it.

The uniqueness of my service couldn't last. Other surgeons were bound to enter the field. In the early years, really until the late 80s, there were fewer than 300 bariatric (derived from the Greek: *baros*, or fat and *iatros*, or physician) surgeons nationwide. But then, word got out that there was an epidemic in the works and that newer techniques were effective and safer. Also, with advancements in technique and equipment, the surgery could be done with multiple small incisions through a laparoscope, rather than through a single larger incision, making it a more attractive option.

Truth be told, I became so proficient at gastroplasty (simple restrictive stapling of the stomach down to a tiny reservoir capacity) and gastric bypass (restrictive stapling, plus partial intestinal bypass) that I could do the surgery through a three-and-a-half-inch incision. In many cases, the surgical scar eventually shrunk down to just over two inches. Compare that with the six up-to-one-inch incisions used with the laparoscopic approach, and you can see why my patients were perfectly happy to go the open route, in my experienced hands.

Before we knew it, there were almost 2,000 self-styled bariatric surgeons in the registry—and likely hundreds more who were undocumented. The American College of Surgeons became concerned about the lack of experience among the new breed of surgeons. Certainly, they were trained in laparoscopic techniques, but they lacked expertise in dealing with the myriad medical conditions and psychiatric issues besetting the morbidly obese. They were unlikely to pick up on the early signs of complications, and they were unpracticed in the optimal ways to deal with them. The American Society for Bariatric Surgery, to which I belonged from its onset, also became alarmed at the situation.

Both Societies set up their own commissions to determine the best way to handle the influx of new, often inadequately-trained bariatric surgeons. Ultimately, the ACS gave way and let ASBS establish training guidelines for surgeons and hospitals. The concept of Centers of Excellence was developed. The criteria for inclusion very nearly matched what I had independently established years before. The problem for both Ballard and Stevens, with my bariatric practice fairly evenly divided between the two places, was that the numbers of cases for either were not quite high enough. However, if I limited my practice to either place, the threshold easily would have been met.

I made a proposal to expand the program at Stevens Hospital, which was all but agreed upon, until one of the surgeons blocked me. This colleague took a weekend course and announced that he, too, was a bariatric surgeon. As a weight-loss surgery (WLS) newcomer, he was no threat. However, he was in the process of recruiting a capable, fully-trained bariatric surgeon, hopefully to keep him out of trouble. Perhaps I should have approached him to work together as a team, but I couldn't bring myself to do that.

Although I still had the run of the place in Ballard, remember that Ballard had been taken over by the much larger Swedish Hospital. We gave away the ranch, as it turned out. After the merger, the Swedish administration began systematically closing services at Ballard. The Vascular and Neurosurgery service were first to go.

By this time, I was performing two to three weight-loss procedures per week at Ballard. We had upgraded our wheelchairs, toilets, X-ray facilities, and OR tables to accommodate the ever-increasing size of our patients, and by this I mean all the patients, not only mine. Obesity was rising to epidemic proportions. Our new OR table could accommodate up to 1,000 pounds. The older ones were rated only to 500.

Yet, I was getting no respect from the main Swedish campus on First Hill. They invited me to join a committee to explore the feasibility of a bariatric Center of Excellence program on First Hill, as if one wasn't already going full bore in everything but the name, at Ballard. They paid me such grudging lip service at the exploratory meeting I attended that I opted out of further participation.

Soon enough, First Hill brought in their own bariatric surgeon, a Canadian with moderate previous experience, at best. Next they closed the Ballard Intensive Care Unit. They knew that I needed Intensive Care Unit back up, even though it was a rare bariatric case that I ever put into the unit. They knew that I wouldn't dare schedule a bariatric operation in the absence of an ICU. They had the nerve to tell me, after disrespecting me for years, that I was welcomed to take my patients to First Hill. Obviously, they wanted my numbers and the revenue and prestige that would come with them.

I had no interest in doing that. I took all my bariatric patients up to Stevens for the last four or five years of my practice. Despite the administration having reneged at the last minute on a deal to set me up as director of a full-service weight-loss program, the OR was good to me. I had my own dedicated staff. The hospital engineers fashioned several instruments to my design, and I more or less peacefully coexisted with the two other surgeons who were offering bariatric surgery.

I was to make one more big play at establishing a formal program, this time at Northwest Hospital. But that, too, flopped, despite considerable effort on my part, again because of back-room dealings by another surgeon. This was particularly hurtful, as I had brought this man in as an associate, only to have him leave my practice after a few months, set up shop at Northwest and, worse, take Lisa, my long-time, personally-trained office assistant with him!

Competitiveness I can deal with, but subterfuge and ingratitude are particularly painful.

***

It should not come as a surprise that in all the years I did this work, I had some memorable cases. What follows are a few of the highlights—and a few bad scenarios, too.

One husband and wife, who both qualified for the surgery, asked me whether I would do them together in one day and have them admitted post-operatively to the same room. I asked who would be taking care of them for the first week or so at home. They said they had a sixty-nine-year-old mother who was willing to undertake the assignment, which included watching their three little children.

I asked how big the grandma was; they said about 125 pounds. The husband-wife tag team weighed in at a total of 650 between them. I turned down their request. One of my colleagues had done this the year before as a sort of publicity stunt, but I wasn't into that sort of thing. I staged the two operations a month apart, and everyone ended up happy and healthy.

Through the years, I performed WLS on every possible family combination: mother and son, mother and daughter, father and son, and father and daughter, plus several sets of siblings, and three husband/wife combos.

One time, in the old Ballard Hospital operating room, as I was deep in the abdomen of a very large person, the lights went out. Ballard had a back-up generator, but nobody had tested it recently. Now it was on the fritz. We had to do something. The circulating nurse found a flashlight, and on we went, operating away, with the anesthesiologist hand-bagging oxygen via a portable tank, until the power went back on. This lasted for ten minutes or so, although it seemed like hours.

I helped a young Mormon wife shed nearly 200 pounds with surgery, whereupon she split the sheets (meaning she left her husband). This was not an uncommon event after successful weight loss surgery.

Sometimes the wife, with a new svelte figure, developed enough self-confidence to leave. Or she began "getting the look" from guys other than her significant other, which made him jealous and unable to cope with the change, and he left.

This woman left the church, began frequenting bars, drinking and smoking, which horrified her strait-laced family. Although she had two younger siblings both weighing over 300 pounds, the family would not dream of letting me get my surgical gloves on them. Probably they came to regard bariatric surgery as the root of, or route to, all evil.

I always wondered whether significant weight loss might diminish vocal power in singers. I know that Pavarotti, Deborah Voigt, and Renée Fleming famously had undergone WLS, and it appeared to me as though they still manifested plenty of volume. The Seattle Opera asked me to consult with one of their stars, who weighed well over 450 pounds and had become an object of derision. I would have been happy to take the case. But sadly for her, she demurred. Word came back to me that she had once lost over fifty pounds and had noted (pun) weakness in her voice.

Although the diva never came to see me, I did operate on a well-known Christian music and jazz singer. She started at 475 pounds and lost an amazing 300 pounds. She claimed that after the surgery, her voice became more powerful. She shared her success story with the opera singer, who remained obdurate and consequently no longer was employed by the Seattle Opera.

Through the years, I had some dealings with psychiatric patients. I am not talking about depression here, which affected as many as half of my morbidly obese patients. And this should come as no surprise. They thought they were thin people trapped inside a huge body, struggling to get out. Many of them could not be weighed on standard scales. On several occasions, needing an accurate weight to submit to the insurance company—and we never fudged on a weight, which others in the field had been known to do, in some cases egregiously—I had to send patients over to use the scale at a meat-packing factory. What an indignity.

Most of my patients were so thrilled about the weight coming off after surgery that they would weigh themselves every day, sometimes twice a day. Although I tried to discourage this obsessive behavior, who could blame them? It was important for them to realize that half of their weight loss would occur in the first three months, with a gradual decrease in subsequent weight loss over the following nine months. This could be explained by the simple fact that the effect of drastically lowering caloric intake would be greatest while a person was at his or her heaviest.

Still, some of my patients would get somewhat wigged out when they stopped losing. I offered reassurance and challenged them to keep following dietary and exercise guidelines to ensure that they not start regaining. Indeed, many did fall by the wayside and experienced variable degrees of re-accumulation of weight.

Most hardly could keep from admiring themselves and their new shapeliness. Yet, one lady, slightly crazy, who had not looked in a mirror for years when she was at her fattest, took a look once she became a hundred pounds lighter, and then decided that she was fat. Thing was, she was now down under 155! I sent her off to therapy.

I operated on a woman with multiple personalities. I wasn't keen on the idea, but the psychiatrists claimed they had stabilized her, more or less. In a desperate attempt to reduce her weight. she had attempted to cut off one leg. Fortunately, she didn't get too far into it. I made her wait an extra three months to make sure that she was mentally stable. During that time, she told me that she had gotten a consensus from her thirteen personalities that it would be acceptable to proceed with the surgery.

She turned out to be more compliant than most, a model patient, really. She lost well over half of her preoperative weight. The last time I saw her, I inquired whether her numerous personalities were pleased with the results.

She told me that nine of them had gone away, and

that the other four were getting along fine now. What a success story. One person, losing all that weight and all those people!

Less successful was my foray into working with a bipolar male. He came to me in referral from the nutritionist at the Naval Hospital in Bremerton who sent me dozens of cases through the years. There was a bariatric surgical service at Madigan Army Hospital near Tacoma, but their complication rate was pretty high. This worked to my benefit, as I felt I was doing my part for our men and women in the military by accepting a deep discount in my fees. Most of my bariatric surgical colleagues were unwilling to do as much.

The Bremerton patients, mostly military wives, tended to be, on average, ten years younger than my other patients. This translated to fewer concomitant medical problems and, therefore, lower risks and better results. They formed a burgeoning support group, which generated a lot of referrals.

At any rate, back to this bipolar guy. He weighed in at 365. His psychopathy seemed well controlled, and his military psychiatrist gave us the green light. The surgery went without a hitch, and he lost nearly 200 pounds as a result. He looked great, but he stopped all of his psychiatric meds, perhaps because everyone kept telling him how well he was doing. I suppose he must have thought, "If I am doing so well, I don't need to be medicated any longer."

I recall him sitting in my waiting room, telling a roomful of patients, a number of whom were coming in for their initial consultation, "You don't want to see this guy. He's a butcher, and he will fuck you up just like he fucked me up!" Each time he returned for follow-up, we got him out the door as quickly as possible, but he would always manage to disparage my work vociferously. And, sure enough, he found a surgeon at the military hospital he was able to browbeat into reversing the surgery. The last I heard, he weighed over 400, but, hopefully, at least he was back on his meds.

Reversing bariatric surgical procedures can be done, but the operations involved tend to be hazardous, even though the patient usually weighs a lot less than at the time of the original surgery. Furthermore, the weight lost is always regained and then some. I never reversed any of my patients, but there was at least one other case of mine where the bypass was taken down. This involved a middle-aged woman with severe diabetes. Her daily insulin requirement was a whopping 360 units. Amazingly, she was totally off all insulin within three weeks of the day I performed a bypass on her!

How can that be, you may well ask? After all, there is only so much weight that can be shed in three weeks. The fact is the drastic drop in caloric intake after the reservoir capacity of the stomach is decreased to one-twentieth of its previous size will allow the patient's own insulin production to keep up with demand.

This woman should have been thrilled. She was off all her diabetes medicine, and she had marvelous weight loss of over nearly half of her (total) preoperative weight. But she was on a mission to be reversed. It was the old, "I have lost my best friend" complaint, i.e., the ability to eat with impunity. I told her repeatedly that she would be right back on boatloads of insulin if she reversed the surgery. She kept asking; I kept refusing. Eventually, she talked somebody into reversing the surgery. She reunited with her "friend" and was back on insulin, as all the lost weight came back.

Indeed, the name of our association was changed to reflect the dramatic control weight-loss surgery affords diabetics—to the American Society for Metabolic and Bariatric Surgery (ASMBS) from the American Society for Bariatric Surgery (ASBS). The idea was to convince endocrinologists that we were no longer a fringe group doing experimental surgery for dubious indications, or whatever it was they thought of us.

WLS lessens, if not eliminates, most of the treatments required for control of not only diabetes, but also high blood pressure, fluid retention, joint pain, obstructive sleep apnea, and urinary incontinence. Some are able to come off their antidepressants. One woman was taking fourteen different pills a day for treatment of her panoply of obesity-associated medical conditions—at a cost of over $1,000 a month. After her surgery, she came off all medications and off the CPAP device she needed for sleep apnea. The fact is, she now requires multiple vitamins, B12, extra iron, and calcium, but the cost is minimal.

Plus, you never saw a happier person! She went to all the support groups she could find and sang my praises. But, as I maintained with all my WLS patients, I took credit only for giving her the tool with which she could regain her health. Truly, to hear her tell of getting back on her bicycle and hiking, you would think she had found the Fountain of Youth that evaded Ponce de Leon in Florida.

A year after her surgery, she sent me a photograph of herself, easily fitting both legs into one side of the pants she once had filled out. I received numerous before and after photographs from others as well, many of which we displayed in our office break room. They validated my specialty and made me grateful for any assistance I might have been able to provide these deserving and often desperate individuals in their struggles to achieve a healthier life.

Many of my patients would tell me that they felt ten years younger, once they got beyond the immediate recovery period. I was so thrilled to hear such stories that I put a number of them in my book, *Overcoming Obesity Through Weight Loss Surgery.*

Out of the many WLS cases I had, only once did I need to revise my work because the patient lost too much weight. This woman underwent a simple stomach stapling in Astoria. She started off at nearly 300 pounds, lost to 120, and she stayed there for nearly ten years. Then she began losing weight again, largely because she was going through a traumatic divorce. She got down to eighty-seven pounds, nearly died from malnutrition and electrolyte imbalance, was placed on high-calorie intravenous therapy, and gradually regained her health.

Although she went into therapy and got her life back in order, she could not keep her weight at a stable, safe level. I revised her outlet from the surgically-created upper pouch into the remainder of her stomach, reinforcing the newly-created opening and sealing off the older one. This did the trick, and she again stabilized at around 120 pounds.

Revising gastric stapling or gastric bypass is a tricky business. As a result, many bariatric surgeons prefer not to do revisions. To me, this is as much as admitting that they are unable, or unwilling, to deal with their own complications. The fact is, no matter how experienced a bariatric surgeon is, there will be complications.

Some of the more common reasons for revision are staple-line leaks, bowel obstructions, enlargement of the outlet below the stomach pouch (which may have been too large when created), and stretching of the stomach pouch to excessive reservoir capacity (which, again, may have been made too large in the first place).

I was willing to revise the work of other bariatric surgeons, as well as my own, when indicated. If a patient had simply outeaten the previous operation, I was understandably reluctant to offer a revision, because the odds were high that second operation would fail as well. Revisions were fraught with a considerably higher risk of complications. Death is the ultimate complication. Fortunately, none of my revisions resulted in fatality, although some did have complications.

The fact is many morbidly obese patients do not follow directions regarding proper eating and drinking after surgery. Sadly, they may not have been properly instructed or were not followed closely enough. Most of my colleagues saw their patients only a few times in follow-up after surgery.

My program included seeing patients on a regular basis for six months and then every six to twelve months thereafter. To give them incentive to continue to come back to see me, I did not charge for follow-up visits, even years out. But then, it also was my practice not to charge other physicians, their immediate family members, or even nurses beyond whatever insurance paid. Call me old school, if you will. That was the approach taken by my parents and uncle, and I was proud to follow their lead.

I made myself available as needed for as long as necessary, even to the extent of giving out my email address to patients after I retired. I still hear from patients with questions or issues related to their surgery. All of my patients were given careful dietary, vitamin supplementation, and exercise instruction. They were clued in preoperatively and made to practice eating smaller amounts, chewing forty times before swallowing solids, avoiding liquids during meals, reading food labels, and setting up an exercise program. They were given the appropriate chapters from my unpublished manuscript, *Overcoming Obesity Through Weight Loss Surgery,* pre- and post-operatively.

Of course, not everybody followed my guidelines. It is possible to "out-eat" these operations, although doing so requires a great deal of effort. If a person were to consume high-calorie liquids relatively constantly over the course of the day, or if he or she were to drink during meals, thereby helping food "slosh through" the small opening beneath the reservoir pouch, or not exercise, the resultant degree of weight loss would be unsatisfactory. Pregnancy within the first year particularly was to be avoided, because the extra degree of hunger nearly always would lead to staple-line disruption or enlargement of the pouch or the opening below it.

One woman came to me having failed two previous attempts at WLS. She became pregnant two months after the first operation and three months after the second. And this second pregnancy was twins. I refused to re-operate on her on grounds of total lack of compliance.

For one reason or another, I turned away quite a few

patients. Take, for instance, the eighteen-year old who was brought over from Wenatchee by her mother. It was clear to me that she was only willing to undergo the surgery because her mother wanted her to do so—not because she was particularly motivated. I recall a man in Astoria who wanted to drop his wife off for WLS, while he went hunting with his pals. He said he would pick her up on his way back. I said no thanks, even if he were to pay me with a life supply of elk steaks.

There is immense joy in helping people accomplish what they could not do on their own. The simple fact is that only five percent of those who are morbidly obese can take off, *and keep off,* the necessary amount of weight without WLS. Even the most compliant and better educated can only achieve transient success at significant weight loss. Unlike the rest of us, morbidly obese individuals seem not to have a properly functioning satiety center. When it comes to eating, they simply do not know when enough is enough. There always seems to be room for more.

Each prospective patient was queried about the most they had ever lost before coming to see me. One man, who weighed over 400 pounds, told me he had lost a hundred pounds. I took that to be a sign of great potential for successful WLS. So I asked him what his second best attempt had been. He said, "A hundred pounds."

I asked the obvious question, "How many times have you lost a hundred pounds?" He told me six times! *Wow,* I thought, *Is this ideal, or what?* So I told him to go out and try again, and to call me when he was just about there, so that we could put him on the schedule and do the WLS before he ballooned up again.

I have noted that men have an easier time taking off massive amounts of weight than women. Perhaps this is due to more muscle mass and a greater capacity for exercise. Some have suggested that it is a matter of stronger will power and discipline. I could be bordering on a sexist remark here, so I'll let it go.

At any rate, this particular man called me seventy-five pounds later to say that his non-operative weight loss was about done. I put him right on the schedule, and today he weighs about 225. Considering that he is six foot five, he is right at his ideal weight.

The only person I ever operated on who was less than morbidly obese was 5' 2" and weighed 200 pounds. I sent her to Vic Hayes for a psych evaluation. He felt I should operate, because the extra weight was driving her mad. Otherwise, she was psychologically, intellectually, and compliantly acceptable as a candidate.

After her surgery, she brought her weight down to 115 (which, by the way, she has maintained for twenty-four years), became a dance instructor, learned to play the accordion, and wrote five books. One of them, *From Housewife to Dominatrix,* sounds more titillating than the biography of Harvey Cushing. But I could be wrong...

Quite a few post-operative patients wanted body-contouring work. This was to be expected. When a person sheds over forty percent of his or her total preoperative weight, there is almost always a lot of redundant skin.

I estimate that over ninety percent of successful bariatric patients could stand to have a nip here or a tuck there. Interestingly, in my patient population, it seemed like only fifteen percent actually underwent plastic surgery. Of course, my population was nearly one half military, and the military rarely would agree to pay for non-essential plastic surgery.

I had two or three very fine plastic surgeons with whom I worked, but none were willing to take the deep discounts that I accepted. In fact, their fees were often far in excess of mine, for work that involved much less risk as a result of successful WLS.

I heard so much belly-aching (another pun) about the inability to find affordable plastic surgeons that I finally began doing tummy tucks and arm recontouring myself. I had to relearn the techniques, as it had been over twenty years since I rotated on a plastics service.

My friend Truman Ellis, an able physician's assistant, who assisted me on so many of my bariatric cases, encouraged me to go this route. Because he had scrubbed in on so many cases, he knew the correct location for the big incisions that were required. I think I ended up doing at least twenty-five tummy tucks and ten or more arm reductions. The patients loved my work, and they especially loved my prices, which undercut the plastic surgeons by more than fifty percent. I did this work primarily as a service to my patients, and they were most grateful for it.

Well into my career in bariatric surgery, Joie Whitney, a professor from the UW School of Nursing, asked if I would be willing to participate in a wound-healing study. The idea was to put warm patches over the midline incision after wound closure every six hours for two days, to see whether we could demonstrate enhanced healing, i.e., fewer wound infections than the expected norm. We also tried placing tiny catheters on either side of the wound for supplemental local oxygen infusion.

Because a large number of patients were needed for statistical significance, five or six other surgeons also were invited to participate in the study. Since I was so busy, my patients comprised nearly half of the total study population. Most of them were happy to sign up for the study, as it meant extra home visits by university R.N.s, free of charge. Results, although disappointing, were published in a prestigious journal.

MISBEGOTTEN MANUSCRIPT

I wrote my first book, *Overcoming Obesity Through Weight Loss Surgery*, because I was appalled to see unscrupulous physicians heaping abuses upon this desperate population. One would hold the little finger of a 500-pound woman, look her in the eyes with seeming compassion and sincerity, and say "I see you as a size six." Irresistible to a woman paying three times as much for a size thirty-four outfit at a plus-size store as someone buying the same outfit in size fourteen at a department store. Another doctor actually bribed patients with gifts if they agreed to let him do their surgery.

I asked a medical student who was moonlighting as a house painter about her interests in medicine. When I told her what I did, she responded, "Oh, I had that surgery."

I looked at her, and could see that she weighed about 140, so I said, "My, you had a really nice result."

"Haven't I? I am forty pounds lighter," she told me, proudly.

Her statement horrified me. "You mean you only weighed 180, when you had a bypass?" She said that was just about right. "Of course, I am not exactly sure. They never weighed me."

I'm thinking, *"How can they get insurance approval for weight loss surgery without submitting this critical piece of data?"* and *"How could they, in good faith, subject a person weighing a mere 180 pounds to the risks of this surgery?"* I could see from her height that she had been perhaps forty percent overweight, but guidelines existed at that time only for people who were at least eighty percent overweight. So I asked, "Why did they advise you to have this operation?"

"Because they said I might get cancer if I didn't get all that excess weight off."

Shocked at what I had just heard, I suggested, "You must have paid out of your own pocket for the surgery."

She said no, it was fully covered. This meant that they fudged her weight where required on the insurance authorization request.

She told me that she decided to have her surgery at another, more prestigious institution, because the first place she went to was ordering too many tests. I couldn't help myself. This second hospital where her surgery was done has a solid national reputation. "They must have advised you not to undergo surgery."

I knew that some of my unscrupulous colleagues would have handled this situation by telling the patient to go out and eat up a storm and come back at 250 pounds. But this poor woman was taken right to the OR. And the surgeon at the second hospital didn't have her weighed, either! To top off this saga of medical malfeasance, she had a bowel obstruction post-operatively and had to have a second operation. In spite of all this, she was thrilled with her new size-ten figure.

That did it for me. I decided to write a book to help guide prospective weight-loss surgical candidates to and through safe surgery. I divided the book into three parts.

The first part was "What You Need to Know About Weight Loss Surgery." Chapter 1 explained how WLS works: either by restricting intake, impairing digestion, or a combination of both. In the second chapter, I discussed the evolution of WLS and the different surgical options available. The third chapter was about the training of the bariatric surgeon and setting up a hospital program. Finally, Chapter 4 was about the costs involved.

Part Two was "Making Decisions." The first chapter helped readers determine if they were appropriate candidates. The next concerned itself with the best surgical procedure for them. For some, one procedure might be best and for others a different one would be better. The last chapter in this part offered suggestions on how to choose among surgeons and hospitals.

The third part was "Getting Ready and Going Through It." Chapters were organized around the patient's role in preparation. This included gathering and providing the appropriate medical history, learning better ways to eat, and initiating an exercise program before the surgery. Also included was what to expect while in the hospital, going home, and what types of early complications to watch out for.

The last part, "Life After WLS," emphasized proper post-op eating, vitamin supplementation, and exercise. Also included was information on later complications and how to prevent or at least minimize them, follow-up care, and maintenance of the proper weight.

I invited Ed Mason, my mentor and the originator of both simple stomach stapling and bypass, to write the Foreword. I excerpt the following:

> *Dr. James K. Weber has written a book explaining the questions that should be asked by any person contemplating an operation for weight reduction and control. Potential candidates will benefit from his expert advice in making choices that will affect their health, comfort, and length of life...*
>
> *The choices that you are about to make are vital, and Dr. Weber guides you through the possibilities logically and with clarity. Do not be hasty or rash. We want you to live a long and healthy life, but there are many risks based upon your decisions.*

Wiley & Sons and M. Evans and Company both were interested in publishing the book. We went with the higher bidder, which was M. Evans. Although smaller and less prestigious than Wiley, they had published Dr. Atkins's original diet book. They had very deep pockets as a result, and their independence in the complex world of publishing takeovers appealed to me.

What happened next is a tale of woe. The owner/publisher of M. Evans passed away, and his widow sold the company to a mega firm, Rowman Littlefield. They set the galleys but never moved to publish. When their rights expired, I got my book back. By then, it was four years behind the times and would have required revisions and a search for another publisher. As I was rapidly losing my enthusiasm for surgery in general and weight-loss surgery in particular, I let the matter rest.

One day, not long ago, I found two copies advertised on Amazon for $2,400 apiece. I did not know that advance copies had been printed. I wrote the bookseller a nice note and told them the story behind the book. I said I would be willing to purchase one or both for a reasonable price. I never heard back. The next time I looked up the book, it was listed for $2,750. I passed.

The hundreds of hours of my work on that book were not for naught, however. Individual chapters proved exceedingly useful as teaching aids for my bariatric patients. I got as far as an author can get without his book seeing the light of day. Chalk it up to experience.

Sort of like Moses getting a glimpse of the Promised Land, but not quite reaching it.

METAMORPHOSIS

Why, then, after such lengthy, prestigious training and so many surgical successes, would I want to chuck it all just before my sixtieth birthday? There were a host of reasons to keep on doing what I had done for so many years. I saw some every day in my office, in particular, the gratitude in the eyes of so many of my patients. Websites like obesityhelp.com were filled with any number of glowing tributes and testimonials to my work. I knew in my heart that God had blessed me with the requisite skills, judgment, personality, education, patience, and determination to help many people alter their lives for the better through WLS.

But there were even more reasons to close this chapter of my life. Reasons related to health, finances, emotions, and timing. Intellectual reasons. Other opportunities. I had to do make a radical change, and I should have done it sooner.

For several years prior to closing my practice, on June 30, 2008, I had been contemplating a life beyond medicine. I could not countenance the thought of ever being forced into retirement due to erosion of cognitive or motor skills. I wanted to exit on my own terms.

I never for a moment considered traditional retirement. It was always a matter of finding another field. Teaching, always near and dear to my heart, immediately came to mind. I called the secondary school my daughters had attended and discussed the possibility of my teaching there with the Headmaster. I pointed out that I had been teaching throughout my career in medicine, and that I could teach English, Biology, or Music History. She said that she would put me on the substitute list and thanked me for my call.

I never heard back. Schools, other than medical or nursing, simply do not employ physicians as teachers. Lawyers, yes; doctors, no.

Getting back to Mary. She had re-entered my life in a big way by this time. Soon after she moved to Seattle, she mentioned that I was getting round-shouldered. And no wonder. By the time we reconnected in 2004, after a 27-year separation, I had performed well over 12,000 operations. I was spending most of my waking hours bent over a table in the OR.

Yet, Mary supported my continuing to work as a surgeon. She would pack a lunch for me, snacks for ZsaZsa, our French bulldog, and send the two of us off to work. She pitched in as office receptionist when needed; she even watched me perform a gastric bypass, which was quite an initiation to the OR for a person with no medical background.

Mary first introduced me to yoga to improve my posture. This suggestion turned out to be key to my exit from medicine. She also suggested I take the Myers-Briggs Type Indicator test to gain better insight into myself. It opened my eyes to the reasons why I never really felt

I was like the other surgeons. I am an ENFP, a lot more extroverted and intuitive than your average surgeon. In addition, I am more prone to feeling rather than thinking, more about spontaneity than planning ahead. In short, I have the personality of an entertainer. The Bard Hall Players and singing groups. Remember?

But it was an elf hat that really convinced me how different I was from the other physicians. Yes. An elf hat! One of my patients made it for me, and I wore it on Christmas Day, as I rounded through two hospitals. The patients loved it. The nurses loved it. I must have seen at least fifteen other M.D.s that day on the wards, stairwells, or hospital common areas. Not one so much as acknowledged my hat. They would sneak a peek and move on, without so much as a "Ho, ho, ho!" Hard to believe, yet true. I thought to myself, *What am I doing here? I am not a bit like these other doctors.*

I could see the link between stress and coronary artery disease; indeed, I was a textbook case. And I had a family history for heart disease. But I had none of the other risk factors. My diet was always healthy; I was careful about not eating too much salt or high-cholesterol foods. I exercised regularly: biking, running, weights, calisthenics, and almost always took the stairs.

But I could not have chosen a more stressful career. Imagine the stress of nicking the pulmonary artery and witnessing blood loss of two pints in half a minute, or trying to control blood welling up through a keyhole while looking through a long tube into the chest, or attempting to resuscitate a nine-year old dying on the operating table from complications of appendicitis. Or try being sued twice on the same day. I could go on, but I'm sure you get my point.

On top of that, I could not control my hours enough to ensure restful, adequate sleep. I had not taken call to the ER, except on rare occasions, for years, because of my coronary artery disease. Even so, I had to take call for my own patients. Other surgeons did not know enough about WLS to troubleshoot properly, let alone intervene for emergent complications, and many simply preferred not to get involved. WLS was the reviled stepchild of general surgery. All the usual societal biases were in play: "These fat people are just looking for an easy way out;" "It isn't right for surgeons to be offering such risky 'elective' surgery;" "I don't want to get sued;" and, most insensitive of all, "Fat people are disgusting."

Consider that the creation of a new stomach pouch, at one-twentieth the size of the original stomach, requires drastic adjustments in eating. Old habits can be hard to break, and many patients were inclined to test their altered anatomy. Net result: somebody was always calling to say they had been throwing up. And most waited until the middle of the night to call, despite throwing up during the day. No matter that they had been told, over and over, how to eat and drink after the WLS. No matter that I had given each of them pertinent chapters from my unpublished manuscript. Most of the time, telephone advice sufficed. Yet, the possibility of a serious obstruction requiring re-admission, hydration, even reoperation, had to be considered. And there were other emergent complications. A conspiracy against good sleep hygiene.

Long days in the OR, having to round on patients in two different hospitals, coping with dermatitis on my hands and wrists from repetitive scrubbing, lecturing to support groups, doing consultations, office hours three days a week, dealing with lawsuits from patients who, instead of suing, should have put me on their Christmas card list for saving their lives, lingering legal and emotional issues secondary to the divorce from Edie—I could go on. All these things created mega stress. Off-the-charts stress.

I feel stressed just thinking about it now. My lifestyle was more than endangering—I was literally killing my-self. It is no wonder that none of my four daughters considered a career in surgery, not even for a minute. Frankly, it is no wonder that a recent study showed that a majority of physicians advise their children not to go into medicine. The closest any of mine came was el-dest daughter Emily, who became an occupational therapist.

Financially, I was treading water those last few years. What with payroll, office expenses, insurance write-offs, reduced hours to comply with my disability coverage, and having to give ex-wife Edie half of my net income, I am sure that I must have been the lowest-paid general surgeon in the country. My take-home had dwindled down to $40,000 a year. It was barely sustainable.

There was an emotional downside as well. My practice had had started to feel like a prison. The Swedish and Stevens administrations did not afford me appropriate respect. I felt alienated from the other surgeons, which more than likely was the psychological residue from my traumatic residency.

Another reason I was becoming disenchanted with surgery was that I had been phased out of my role as Surgical Liaison with the Family Medicine Department. That was because I was putting in fewer hours and doing less and less general surgery, which meant there were fewer opportunities for residents to learn surgical principles. Not teaching residents contributed to a growing feeling of intellectual stagnation for me.

Worst of all were the lawsuits. One came from my non-bariatric surgery work: a complicated bile duct and liver abscess case, where there was a one-day delay in diagnosis, mostly caused by the ER doctor. No money was paid out, but the depositions and meetings with the attorneys drained me emotionally.

And then there were the litigations involving WLS cases. In one case, I was sued because the patient had severe post-operative pancreatitis with a markedly prolonged hospital stay and convalescence. Never mind that I rounded on her every day while she was in the hands of the intensivists (ICU docs) at the Swedish First

Hill Campus. And never mind that I had to convince the entire Radiology Department that she wasn't too heavy to undergo a CT scan, thus averting what would have been an unnecessary abdominal exploration. The family was convinced that I must have done something wrong. The case was settled out of court with no monetary award. The woman ended up 200 pounds lighter and never thanked me for saving her life.

Imagine being served with two different subpoenas in one day! These came from a bottom-feeder law office. Neither suit had merit, but the firm managed to engage the former head of our bariatric surgical association as a witness for the prosecution. This man had performed the first laparoscopic gastric bypass and was well respected, that is, until he started to help patients sue their surgeons. It turned out that he had lied in court on a case of his own. My lawyer, John Graffe, a great fellow, whom I got to know quite well through the years, discredited him. Both cases were dropped.

From time to time, attorneys asked me to review the evidence in malpractice suits. As a matter of principle, I never agreed to serve as an expert witness for the prosecution. In a few cases, I did tell the physician's defense attorney that I thought that the medical care had been badly handled. Please note that there can be a great deal of difference between an adverse outcome and medical malpractice. Sadly, jurors are not physicians, and their decisions are all too often based more on the way the lawyer presents his case than the way the events actually unfolded.

The most annoying lawsuit of all—although, in retrospect, the most laughable—came from a civilian firearms instructor who tried twice, unsuccessfully, to get me into court. I had performed a gastric bypass on him. He lost 150 pounds and achieved his ideal weight. When he developed a superficial wound infection, I treated it at bedside with simple drainage and antibiotics. He healed and came in a few times for follow-up, looking great.

Unfortunately, when his wound infection again flared up—which they sometimes do—he chose to go to the Naval Hospital in Bremerton, where an inexperienced general surgeon examined him. X-rays revealed a circular foreign body in the upper abdomen. Instead of calling me to discuss the findings, the radiologist and the surgeon both erroneously inferred that I had left part of a drain in the patient, and this was the cause of his wound infection. The surgeon operated to remove the ring.

The patient found an ambulance chaser to represent him, and they sued for negligence. Graffe wrote a letter to the other side's attorney, explaining that this was not part of a drain left behind by accident. Rather, it was a marker intentionally sewn into the bypassed part of the stomach as a target for the interventional radiologists. (It otherwise would be hard to identify and fill with contrast material, should the need arise.) He explained that I sewed such a device onto all my by-passed stomachs, all patients were made aware of this, and all signed a special consent form acknowledging as much. The lawyer, seeing no money in it for him, advised his client to drop the case.

Amazingly, almost two years later, I was again served with papers regarding this case. Again, Graffe wrote an explanatory letter. Yet this time things went a bit further—the claimant stated that he was never told about the marker ring. We produced the Power Point from my prospective patient presentation (how about that for alliteration?) and the consent form from my office, plus the one from the hospital, both signed by the patient and both specifying the insertion of the ring. His lawyer tried to claim the signatures were forged. We had multiple signatures on multiple documents, all of which matched. And that was that.

In another lawsuit, I took full responsibility for not draining a small abscess, even though I had several consultants who should have shared the blame. Indeed, none of us thought further surgery was indicated in this case. Had the patient not had a series of complications eventuating in her death, there would have been no case. But my malpractice company advised that we offer a financial settlement, which the plaintiffs accepted. My insurance rates doubled for three years as a result. At one point, I was paying $72,000 a year for malpractice insurance.

I had always felt I was better suited for a career in pediatric surgery. Pediatric surgeons, in general, tend to be kinder, friendlier, and more compassionate than other surgical specialists. In fact, more like primary-care physicians. That was my goal from the start of residency, but lack of support from my department chairman prevented me from moving into that field. It's something I regret. Likely, I would have been happier.

I never considered a career in family medicine until I started mentoring the residents, but by then it was way too late. According to the Myers-Briggs, primary care would have been the best fit for me in medicine.

At the same time, as my surgical career was winding down, something new was unfolding. I had started practicing yoga and was being drawn toward a more peaceful lifestyle. I took an Intro to Yoga class. At first, I didn't get what yoga was all about.

Supportive as ever, Mary took the course with me. Once, I turned to her and hissed, "I have no idea what I am doing."

She replied, "Your Downward Facing Dog is growling. Hush."

I retook the Intro course. I found myself competing with other students and, worse, with myself. After all, being competitive was how I got to Hotchkiss, Yale, Columbia P&S, and the University of Washington. It took a while for me to learn to accept things as they are, to accept that "good enough" was the proper mantra for a balanced life. As in my poem:

A Real Reach

Yoga is something else altogether—
We never did any of it when I was a kid.
Now exercise I can understand
Especially when competition is involved.
Learning to bat, or dribble, or row.
The idea is to hit it further,
Fake the other guy out of his shoes,
In some way or another find the way
To finish first, else bust a gut trying.
Yoga to me seems kind of weird—
You don't win or lose doing it.
Never even break much of a sweat.
Some people say stretch first,
Others say no—always afterwards,
After you have tired yourself out,
Before you make a beeline straight
For that cold one you promised yourself.
Just try it, they say, you'll like it.
These kinds of stretches seem so foreign—
Associated with yogis and other
Very thin people, who probably
Mostly just eat to live, when they are not
Meditating or chanting.
Me, I like to play hard (at times)
And sit up in the stands for hours,
Yelling at umpires who cannot hear me
And chowing down stuff I do not need.

I feel I am not suited for yoga—
I'm afraid that I am stiff as a poker.
In fact I know it. I proved it one day
To every single person in yoga class
Who watched my miserable attempts
To arch my back, holding on for dear life
With left hand and right foot, while
Lifting right hand and left foot.
I looked (and felt) ridiculous.
I was talked into trying yoga—
Had no business being there,
Wanted to apologize to everyone.
Of course I snuck in kind of late,
Hoping that I could put my mat in the back,
But the only spot was right up in front.
Right in front of the teacher, who
Smiled serenely (They all look that way)
And said I was perfectly welcome.
There I was contorting like never before—
Trying impossible positions while
Surreptitiously looking at the clock,
Unable, though patiently instructed,
To clear my mind of much of anything . . .
Yet, who would have guessed it, after a bit
I was feeling less inept and less out of place.
We partnered, and I heard people on all sides
Saying they didn't know what they were doing either.
When the class mercifully was over, I thought—
To myself—Maybe there is something to it,

Maybe it really helps, maybe I should try
Again some time. Not right away, mind you,
But after a while, after a workout or a hard day.
Before I knew it, I was actually looking forward
To another crack at yoga, and it really made
Absolutely no difference how bad I was at it,
Because there was no competition going on at all.

I think this poem describes pretty accurately how awkward I felt in my first yoga class. Steep learning curves had never before daunted me, but, in this situation, I was way out of my comfort zone.

I was impossibly stiff for months. A friend who teaches yoga in Ojai, CA, evaluated my early, miserable attempt at the cross-legged sitting pose. It took propping me up on six folded blankets to get my back upright. And to think, today, I can sit in full lotus position. Well, maybe not for very long and, at that, only after a full warm-up and practice with attention to hip openers, but still...

I started doing yoga poses in the OR after long operations. It felt really good to open up my back and shoulders. The first time I got down on the floor to do a few twists, the OR personnel thought I was having a stroke or another heart attack. They vividly remembered the one that I had in the OR some years before. Back then, I was my own worst enemy. Now I was being kind to myself. I suspect they could see the difference.

What really made the difference was the teacher-training course I took, again at Mary's suggestion. I wasn't sure that I could do this at age fifty-nine, but I decided to give it a go in late 2007. I thought, *If I can get through the training, being a yoga teacher might just be the right move.*

Let me tell you, the training was no walk in the park. The twenty of us (nineteen young women and yours truly) met Friday through Sunday evening once a month, with a second weekend added in two of the six months. We had a two-hour-plus vigorous practice in the morning, followed by focused pose work, didactic work, and then practice teaching in the afternoons.

I absolutely revered our teacher, Catherine Munro. I probably represented an anomalous pet project for her, being so much older than everyone else. Although I was in great shape for the Seattle-to-Portland bicycle race, or when I ramped up my running to 200 miles a month, none of that compared with the shape I was in at the end of the yoga teacher training program, because Catherine trained me in mind and spirit, as well as in body.

The philosophical and historical parts came easily. Training the body to perform the poses well enough to demonstrate to the class was the challenge. Meanwhile, I was winding down my medical practice and planning for a smooth exit.

I could see that this new career would offer me a stress-free opportunity to reach more people. My aim was to teach more and also to have more time for other interests, like writing, traveling, doing things with the family, working on my coin collection, and reading. I knew that yoga was my real professional purpose in life. I began to realize that I was saying things to my students during the opening meditation that emanated directly from my heart. I could put together coherent, challenging or calming sequences, without any forethought, just by assessing the needs of my students at the beginning of class and modifying as we went along. My students enjoyed my ability to make helpful adjustments in their body positions. They were more inclined to let me do this, since they knew that I was a physician.

The timing was right. I was matching my new life with Mary to a new career. And I relished the challenge of making it in an entirely new discipline.

So, goodbye to surgery. Hello to yoga. No regrets. We had a surprise party to celebrate my liberation. Office staff, family (including our dog, ZsaZsa, of course), friends, OR nurses, and even patients showed up.

I had two lab coats, each inscribed with my professional name. Mary made use of both. One became a patch for my custom yoga bag; the other was given to our friend, Danner Graves. For a number of years, Danner put it on, assumed an air of sincerity and compassion, and modeled as James K. Weber, M.D., F.A.C.S.

for ads requiring a doctor. And I say, all to the good. I was done with the coats and what they represented anyway.

Not to be outdone, I, too, have done a bit of modeling on the side. For my first foray, in a Filipino fashion show, of all things, I made sure that a couple of dozen folks from the hospital were in the audience to cheer me on. Later, various parts of me were used in physical therapy demonstration films, because they wanted an older guy in reasonably decent shape. To be sure, I stuck to my day job. Even when I gave up one for another.

RE-GROUNDING

Loving Monet's *Bridge over a Pond of Water Lilies*

Imagine you wake up
With a second chance: The blue jay
Hawks his pretty wares
And the oak still stands, spreading
Glorious shade. If you don't look back,
The future never happens.

Rita Dove, "Dawn Revisited"

MERKA

MISSTEPS

Love allows second, sometimes, third chances.

Ojals

One day, in late September 2003, I came back to my Ballard office to find a blue Post-it note prominently displayed on my computer screen. It read:

I chose not to return the call. We had not communicated since Mary left me twenty-seven years ago. For the second time.

***

Mary and I met in March of 1969. I was in my junior year at Yale, and the Alley Cats had just given an evening concert at the College of New Rochelle, a women's college just outside New York City. It was a good gig. First of all, it paid. It wasn't too far away, and we could use a live-audience run-through of our material before the upcoming Singing Club Jamboree.

The venue was fine, and the all-women audience was especially appreciative. The school gave us a snacks-and-sherry reception afterwards. And there was this girl who appeared out of nowhere and unexpectedly insinuated herself into my life. Blue cardigan over white blouse, brown, knee-length pleated skirt, navy blue knee-high socks, brown loafers. She was gorgeous, with medium brown hair down to her shoulders, perfect posture and figure. And she was charmingly shy, yet smart, cheerful, and funny. Wow.

We talked. And we talked. And we talked some more. Two hours of talking. We talked about her extensive ballet background. We talked about my aspirations to be selected for the Whiffenpoofs, following the jamboree. She was an English major, so we had that in common.

I told her about organic chemistry. I mentioned that my brother was living in South Africa, and that he had been a champion swimmer. I boasted about my uncle and his White House connections. She laughed when I told her that Uncle had Enrico Caruso's cribbage board on display in his office. I laughed when she remembered Admiral Nelson's first name.

She casually mentioned that she was a model. I wasn't surprised. She certainly had the looks for it. I told her that I was hoping to return to my hometown for medical school.

We talked about everything. About anything. About nothing. We didn't talk to anyone else. We didn't look at anyone else.

The bus came, and it was time to leave. As Business Manager, it was my job to round up the troops. But I was busy. Let somebody else do it. I was otherwise occupied.

I didn't want to leave. I kissed the girl on the cheek, said goodbye and hopped on the bus. I remember feeling a little sad.

Did we exchange phone numbers? No. Did we make promises to write? No. Were there any expectations from this all-too-brief encounter? No. Our worlds collided for a brief two hours, and that was that. Or so it seemed at the time.

Little did we know at that moment that we were fated to get serious about each other, split up, try again, split up again, and finally make things right.

About 35 years after we first met, I asked Mary why she left me—the first time, that is. Seemed like a fair question.

Without hesitation, she said, "I didn't feel I was smart enough, witty enough—or enough of anything compared with you." Let me try to explain.

Mary, or Merka as she was called by her Hungarian grandmother, was educated in Catholic schools from grade school through college. Between her studies and after-school ballet practice, she had little leisure time. Whenever possible, she preferred to be alone, reading, dancing, or simply processing.

When it came time for college, she wanted to go to Sarah Lawrence and pursue a major in dance. Her father had other ideas. If he was going to pay for it, it was to be more Catholic education. So, it was off to the College of New Rochelle. Where she met me in 1969. Not that anything came of it. Not then.

***

Fast forward to a crisp, cool, arrestingly beautiful day in October of 1970, more than a year later. The sky is a deep azure blue, not a cloud to be seen, the trees are exploding with a palette of vivid red, orange, and purple. There's a little nip in the air—this was no day to sit indoors and study biochemistry. No, this was a day to get into the car and drive far away from the concrete, garbage, and congestion that is New York City.

There is freedom to be enjoyed in the bounty of Nature. Freedom for the soul to soar, the mind to take respite, and the body to feel the exuberance of youth once again.

Picture me, now in med school, driving alone, on a beautiful Fall afternoon:

I have no particular destination in mind; I'm blissfully unaware that Destiny is calling. I head north on the Major Deegan Expressway. Windows are rolled down, the cool air smells fresh and is smelling fresher by the mile. Fewer and fewer apartment complexes and, pretty soon, none at all. More and more foliage.

This is what's happening in my head:

> *Where am I? There's a sign: New Rochelle. Wait a minute, isn't that where that girl was going to college? What was her name? Oh yes, Mary... Mitchell. That's it. Oh, she was so sweet. I really liked her. What year was she? A sophomore... or was she a junior?*

No, I am sure she said sophomore. That means she must be in her senior year now.

I'll pull off the highway, find a phone booth, and see if she is listed in the phone book. I'll call. See if she's home. See if she remembers me.

My side of the ensuing dialogue must have gone something like this:

"Hello. Mary Mitchell? Yes? Well, this is Jim Weber. Remember me? The Yale Alley Cat concert... a few years ago... You do? Well, I just happen to be in the neighborhood... And I thought I'd give you a call to, you know, see if you wanted to join me for a cup of coffee. Do you have a few minutes to spare... You do? Cool. So, how do I get to your dorm? Oh, you are living off campus... Okay, I'll find it. See you in a bit."

And there she was, as charming as I remembered her. And demonstrably glad to see me. What was it that we found so interesting to talk about that afternoon? I remember asking her about boyfriends, telling her about Amee. She told me that she was finished with ballet and modeling. I said that I was not yet finished with singing, and I might try my hand at putting together a Christmas choir.

I don't know—there must have been a lot more things to say, because I ended up staying well into the night. Never got off her living room sofa until the wee hours. Time flew by.

This time, in saying goodbye, there was a bit more than a peck on the cheek. And definite promises to come back again. Soon. And often. I would say that we had fallen in love.

***

Now, flash forward 33 years to September of 2003. After looking at that Post-it note for two days, I still wasn't sure what to do.

My thoughts:

> *If I do not return the call, won't she just call back? Or will she leave well enough alone, and let sleeping dogs lie? Why would she think that I would want to talk to her, to see what she wants from me, after all these years?*

I should have been seeing patients, but I was day-dreaming about something that happened back in 1977. It was so pathetic:

> *I'm in Mary's living room at her apartment in Seattle, not knowing what to say. I don't have a word to adequately express the fu-nereally hopeless sense of loss. It was Mary, not I, who requested this final meeting. What's the point? To inform me that she is leaving town? To make me feel bad, even*

though it was her choice to leave in the first place, (and in the second place, too!)? Am I supposed to ask her to stay? Beg her to stay? So that she can leave, yet once more?

She tells me what she has been doing during the past six months since she packed up and left the home we shared in Bellevue. I am not going to remember much of what she said. She looks beautiful, as always, but sad. She says something about working in public relations for a firm in downtown Seattle.

I make an excuse about having to leave. I am sure she is relieved. Perhaps she thought there was to be a rapprochement, or that I would beg her to stay. Perhaps I have gone there with that in mind. But here we sit—two proud, stubborn lovers in a stalemate of epic proportions. Neither will let their guard down. Not now.

She has a job lined up back East. She can see that I am fine with letting her go. In my mind, she is already gone.

I have little choice in the matter. I am treading water at the University, barely able to keep my head up, fighting for my professional life. I have nothing left in me to fight for anything else. I am physically and emotionally bankrupt.

My nurse buzzed me, and I was jolted back to the present; I really had to see some patients. No more time for dredging up old memories. I was not about to return that call. Certainly not then. Maybe not ever.

***

Yet, later that day, I found myself recalling the happy times that followed my spontaneous drive to New Rochelle. Back in 1970 and 1971, when we were dating. We saw each other on weekends, mostly in New Rochelle, as I was the one with the wheels. On two occasions, I took Mary down to the family house in Gramercy Park for dinner. We ate and ran. I am not sure we were there long enough for my parents to get much of an impression of Mary. I am sure they would have loved her, had they had a bit more exposure to her charm.

I frequently drove the eighty miles from the medical center to her parents' house in Yardley, Pennsylvania. I would drive around to the back of the house, and Mary would be right there, waiting. Her mother, Lillian, would be puttering in the kitchen, pretending not to listen. We would hide behind a door to sneak a kiss. Lillian knew that we were in love, *even if we never told each other.* It was failing to speak these three little words that would create major difficulties for years to come.

The day we saw *Love Story* together, I was pulled over for speeding through a small Pennsylvania town. I remember telling the magistrate, whose courthouse was right over a feed and grain store, "But, your honor, there are extenuating circumstances." There really were. I wasn't paying any attention to my speedometer. We were in love. Just not saying so. We paid a certain price, both at the courthouse and in life. But we would reap the benefits, eventually.

Those three words. I never heard them spoken at home. Not once did I hear my parents express their love for each other, or for me, for that matter, although I felt the love must have been there, at some level. Mary's situation at home was strikingly similar.

I must have told Amee I loved her during the four-and-a-half years we were dating. We were an item all through my college years. Mary was something I didn't plan on. But Mary was not to be denied. Except over school vacation periods, when Amee was back from her senior year at Skidmore. Poor Mary would be placed on the backburner for the duration. But there was an electricity between us that kept flowing. It would be telephone calls only for a couple of weeks until Amee was back at Skidmore. But it was always Mary I was longing for.

We continued to date. I shot the photograph that she used for her senior yearbook. Her eyes eloquently expressed joy at our being together, for that moment in time. Yet, I was unable to attend her graduation. Maybe

I was at Skidmore that weekend for Amee's graduation. I don't remember. I did know that this situation couldn't last. Not the way it was. Something had to give.

***

Mary's father expected his daughters to go on to graduate school after college, as he had. He wanted Mary to go to law school. When she refused, he insisted that she go to a professional school, Katherine Gibbs. His plan was that she'd become a legal secretary, get exposure to law, see the error of her ways, and end up in law school. Mary dutifully learned to type and to take shorthand. These skills came in handy throughout her career.

Her first job after Katherine Gibbs was with a prestigious law firm in Trenton, New Jersey. It was a disaster. Mary would not be going on to law school. Her next job, which was in the hospitality industry, was more to her liking. And it offered attractive employee benefits.

With this job, she was able to get us a complimentary suite at the Holiday Inn in San Juan, Puerto Rico. And off we went for a three-day weekend. There were *piña coladas* on the beach, a drive through the *El Yunque* tropical rainforest, and a walk through the huge casino. We didn't gamble; we just watched. And we wondered if anyone else was having as much fun as we were.

But the fun stopped, and the gambling started abruptly the day Mary told me she was engaged to a graduate student at Princeton. It came like a bolt out of the blue. She had always known about Amee and was tired of being on my "B list." I was at a loss for words.

I should have said, "Wait a minute! You can't do that. You're in love with me. And I cannot imagine life without you." But I didn't. Instead I mumbled, "Oh no! Not a Princeton man."

Disappointed to the core, I'm sure, Mary said, "How very Noel Coward of you." And I gave a half-smile and walked away, shattered. Cowardly, I am ashamed to say.

The worst day of my life was paradoxically the first day of the rest of our life together. I cannot tell you how I came to know the date, time, and place of Mary's wedding. The particulars of that piece of sleuthing are lost to me. Nor can I remember the drive to the Princeton campus that day. I had only been there once before for a football game. I got hopelessly lost and missed half of the game.

Somehow, on this day of days, I found my way, which was ironic, since the way I should have been going was lost to me. I was early. And, of course, I hadn't been invited. I waited in a side chapel, one door removed from the sanctuary. Why was I there anyway? I guess I just had to witness the event for myself, to know that it was really happening. I found it so hard to accept.

The church started to fill. I stayed where I was, out of sight, listening. First, I heard the wedding music from

Lohengrin, "Here Comes the Bride." Tears started falling; there was no point in trying to hold them back. How could I have known that as Mary and her father walked down the aisle, he actually was encouraging her to back out? Prescience? Probably so.

I could not make out the exchange of vows, which was just as well. I might have lost my self-restraint and tried to break up the ceremony, as Dustin Hoffman did in *The Graduate*. It was on my mind. But no, not me. I was far too reserved. I waited for the opening strains of Mendelssohn's "Wedding March" and slipped into the sanctuary. There was an empty pew near the back. I moved close to the center aisle. When she was about halfway down the aisle, Mary saw me.

Our eyes met, and time stopped long enough for us to seal a bond that never could be broken, come what may. Nor has it been. Nor will it ever be. I slipped back out, without a word to anyone. I made it home, despite the tears clouding my vision.

Certainly, a day to remember. A day that never could be erased from memory, no matter how many layers Life piled on top of it.

A few months later, I married Amee. What reason did I have not to? She was a lovely young woman—smart, talented, motivated. We had been dating for over four years. We were compatible. Just maybe not so much in love. More like a comfortable habit.

On the day of my wedding, Mary had an eerie

feeling. She was walking by the Plaza Hotel in New York, and her thoughts turned to me. That evening Mary told her mother about the experience; she had felt my presence around her all day long. It was almost as though she had expected to see me. Clarification came from *The New York Times* the next day in the form of my wedding announcement. The reception had been at the Plaza.

Coincidence? Some people, I increasingly among them, believe that there is no such thing as a coincidence.

While I remember Mary's wedding vividly, I cannot recall a thing about my own reception.

***

Another day went by. Perhaps a hernia repair or a gastric bypass. Perhaps both. The blue Post-it note was still there. I debated with myself:

> *Go on. Do It. Call the woman. You know you will. Why keep putting off the inevitable?*
>
> *Why? Inevitable? Don't I have any say in the matter? Don't my feelings count? Why dredge up old hurts? Don't I have enough problems, trying to atone for my infidelity to Edie?*
>
> *On the other hand, what harm would there be in returning a phone call? After all, she only wants to talk about weight-loss*

surgery. Wait a minute. How does she know that I am doing bariatric surgery? And why call me? There are plenty of other people out there doing the same thing, doubtless closer to where she lives, wherever that may be.

The curiosity was getting to me. Yet I hesitated, still reluctant. Was it anger or resentment? Could it have been fear?

I needed to think some more. My office was the best place. I could think between patients. Better yet, I stayed in the office after closing and thought, while not to my heart's content, nonetheless, a lot. Things were so tense at home; it was better not to go back there any sooner than was absolutely necessary.

It hadn't always been that way. For years it was fun being home with Edie and the girls. Always hectic, but always appealing. Not any longer. I messed up big time, and I hadn't been able to make things better.

***

I am transported back to a dark day in 1977...

I am thinking about Mary and again bemoaning the loss of what might have been. Several years previously, I had heard that she moved to Cairo, Egypt.

We haven't spoken in over six years.

I don't know what's motivating me. I still have her family's telephone number in my address book. I could give her mother a call. I guess I just need to hear that one of us is doing all right. I certainly am not.

I make the call. Her mother, Lillian, answers. I tell her I am inquiring about Mary. I only want to know how she is doing. Lillian says, and I can almost see the twinkle in her eye today, "Just a minute, she's right here. She can tell you herself."

My opening gambit is something banal:, "How are you?"

I could have done better. Oh well... it's a start.

"Not terribly well, but better for hearing your voice. How are you? And where are you?"

"No longer in the City. Now I'm in Seattle."

"Really? I think I heard something about your moving." So, I realize that she has been keeping tabs on me.

"Thought you were in Cairo."

"I came home last week."

"Yes, okay, so tell me why you said that you are not terribly well."

From there, I got more of the story. Mary had been hospitalized in Athens with typhoid fever, and her husband was, shall I put it, less than supportive of her need for TLC. She told him that she wanted to fly back to the states to recuperate, whereupon he said something to the effect of, "If you do not leave with me tomorrow for Cairo, the marriage is over." Mary asked to have her things shipped back to Yardley. That was that. My day was getting brighter by the minute.

I told her that I would fly east to see her the following day.

I cannot remember what excuse I gave the Department Chairman—something about serious illness in the family. John Schilling was rather avuncular and considerably kinder to me than his successor, Jim Carrico, ever was. He let me go.

In all, it took me less than 24 hours from the time we spoke on the phone to be with Mary again in person…

> I knock on the door. Lillian answers, hands me the keys to her beach cottage, says, "I think you two have much to discuss," and leaves.
>
> Discuss we do, but not until we hold each other for half an hour or more without speaking. Tears, yes; words, no. This time around, we waste no time. We pledge our love, bemoaning the fact that we had not

done so seven years earlier, and go from there.

We are a couple now. The only thing to resolve is how long it will take for Mary to move to Seattle, since I am enslaved there for upwards of two more years—assuming that I make it through the training.

I fly back to Seattle with a new lease on life. It doesn't take long for Mary to join me. Our lives are now in order, and we are finally where we are meant to be. No matter what happens with my draconian surgery program, we are a team. Finally. We celebrate. We thank God. We are on our way.

***

Mary moved in with me to my home in Bellevue. Sad to say, she didn't stay but three months. I was putting in up to 130 hours of work a week, and I was exhausted. All my energy was used up during the long days and nights at the hospital. When I got home, I was short of temper, unresponsive to kindness and love. I hated myself, but I couldn't help it. I never confided in her the full horrors of the abuse I was subjected to. I was too ashamed.

Mary blamed herself, thinking that it must have been something lacking in her that caused my unhappiness.

One night, I came home to find her gone. She had rented an apartment in Seattle. She left a note, but not a phone number.

This was almost the last straw for me. I never have been suicidal, but I came close. My resolve hardened into a determination to make it in surgery, and to hell with everything else. Including Mary. Her leaving me twice was enough. More than enough. I must have been crazy to think that things would be different this time. They could have been. They should have been. But I had been transformed into an automaton, completely unlovable.

Mary moved back to the East Coast and made quite a name for herself. She spent 14 years in public relations, representing such musical greats as Jean-Pierre Rampal, James Galway, Dietrich Fisher-Dieskau, and Alfred Brendel.

In 1992, she began writing a column for *The Philadelphia Inquirer*, "Ms. Demeanor" (Don't you just love that *nom de plume*?). Two columns per week, with national syndication by King Features. Ten years in all, which amounted to over 1,000 columns—without once missing a single deadline.

Her first book, *Dear Ms. Demeanor* (1994), was a compendium of the columns from her first year with *The Inquirer*, a *succès d'estime*. Letitia Baldrige, former Social Secretary at the Kennedy White House, admired her work, and the two began a close friendship and collaboration.

Mary's next book was *The Complete Idiot's Guide to Etiquette* (1996). It was followed by *The First Five Minutes* in (1998). In 2000, she brought out *The Complete Idiot's Guide to Business Etiquette*, as well as the second edition of *The Complete Idiot's Guide to Etiquette*. *Class Acts* followed in 2002, and the third edition of *The Complete Idiot's Guide to Etiquette* came out in 2004, shortly after we got back together.

***

Back to October of 2003, and the Post-it note. Another day passed, and by now the curiosity was killing me. Frankly, I couldn't figure out why Mary Mitchell would have wanted to talk to me about obesity surgery. She always had been so slender and lithe.

I finally returned the call. In the final analysis it would have been rude not to. Say what you will about me, I am never rude. Well, hardly ever.

"Hello, Mary? This is Jim."

"What took you so long? I called you three days ago."

"Well, you know. Busy." I already was on the defensive, fumbling for words. I didn't know what to say, so I blurted out, "Are you still in good shape?"

We talked for well over an hour, because we had nearly half a lifetime of catching up to do. I mentioned that I had four girls. She told me that she remarried in 1990. I asked her if she had any children. She said no. (Years later, she confessed to me that the only babies she ever had wanted to have would have been mine.) The conversation paused. We were way off what I thought was supposed to be the subject at hand. This I felt was likely my fault. Mary always was much more focused.

She gently reminded me that the reason for her call was business. She needed help writing a chapter for her latest book. I wondered, "What book? She's an author?"

She told me that this was to be her seventh book; she wrote books on etiquette, translated into eleven languages. She was probably thinking, *Take that, Ms. Skidmore! I have creds now, too!*

Not to be one-upped, I told her that I had been contemplating writing a book of my own. A book about weight-loss surgery.

She was persistent about needing help. She envisioned a chapter on obesity in the third edition of her *Complete Idiots Guide to Etiquette*, but could not get the information she needed from the morbidly obese people she had met. She thought she might get better assistance from bariatric surgeons, and my name turned up in a computer search.

Enough background. Cutting to the chase, she asked whether I could deliver what she needed. All business.

I thought I might be able to help her. A few articulate

patients came to mind. I could persuade them to talk with Mary. Besides, I knew a thing or two about societal issues as they conspire against the extra-large—things like airplane seats, turnstiles, and armchairs.

There were more calls. For the most part, we stuck to the subject at hand. Mary was enthused; help was on its way. We returned to my idea for a book. She told me that she might be able to help. *Quid pro quo.*

What exactly did I need from Mary? So many thoughts and emotions were flooding in at once. It was very hard to stay focused.

Once Mary realized that I was serious about writing a book, she sent me the Outline for a Nonfiction Book Proposal. It was a kind of trial by fire. She thought I would never have the patience to jump through the many hoops in this exceedingly author-unfriendly proposal.

By dint of the persistence and hard work, which has always been my trademark, I put the proposal together. In the meantime, our conversations were roaming further and further afield of business and encroaching upon each other's crumbling personal lives. Neither of us was happy in our marriage. I had brought on the downfall of mine by breaking my vows. In Mary's case, it was more about lack of support while she was dealing with a severe neck injury and puzzling, unfair isolation from her niece and nephews enforced by their mother, her sister.

We agreed to meet in New York City in November. Mary would introduce me to her agent and an editor at the M. Evans publishing house. Unspoken was that something bigger may have been in the offing.

***

A Short Scene: Noon, on a cool, sunny, late November day. St. Patrick's Cathedral in New York. Minds—and hearts—at work.

MARY: *He said he would meet me here; I distinctly remember. I am sure he said noon, on the steps of St. Patrick's Cathedral. Of course, I arrived early; I am always punctual. It's one of my finest attributes. How could it be otherwise? What credibility would I have, as an etiquette authority were I ever to show up late?*

"Project Pang," we called it, my hairdresser friend, Gail, and I. I am decked out in my finest fur, splendidly accessorized. Ah, there he is, on the steps, where he said he would be. He looks different: a beard. He's looking right at me, not moving. Is it possible that he doesn't recognize me?

I am simply going to stand here. Let him come to me. He keeps looking, but not moving. Do I see a tear in the corner of his eye? Wait, he is walking right toward me. Yes.

JIM: *Phew! I made it to the steps of St. Pat's, right on time. Where's Mary? She was always punctual, almost to a fault.*

Good God, there are thousands of people walking by. She knows where to look for me, but will I be able to find her amidst this massive throng of humanity?

It has been twenty-seven years since that saddest of days, when we last saw each other. Does she look different now? How about me?

If she does show up, should I offer my hand? Or give her a hug? Maybe a kiss on the cheek? What will we say to each other? Was this a big mistake, coming here like this today?

Wait, there she is. I am certain it is she. Nobody else could look that elegant, that beautiful. Suddenly, the streets are not crowded. There isn't another soul in sight.

She sees me. She keeps looking at me. She is not moving. I must go to her.

Why won't my feet move? This is not a dream. I am in control of my muscles. It's my emotions that I cannot control. Nonetheless, I must walk down the steps. I must go to Mary.

Yes.

***

In theory, this was to be a business trip, and it was, partly.

We took my book proposal to her agent, Nancy Love, who saw possibilities in it. Meaning profit for her, and for her buddy, the co-editor I never needed. Nor was my book published, as I said earlier. But that's okay; I got back my Mary out of the deal. And an opportunity to put my life in order.

MIRABILE DICTU

And just like that, Mary moved to Seattle. But not without an understandable modicum of apprehension. This decision had required some serious reinforcement from friends, all of whom had told her, without hesitation, to go for it.

This was not to be "déjà vu, all over again." This time, it was for good.

We were married in the fall of 2005, by the Ballard Hospital chaplain in my divorce attorney's conference room. Mary's surrogate mother and mentor, Letitia Baldrige, gave the bride away by teleconference, and my brother was best man by virtue of the same technology.

We initiated this third chapter in our lives together in a two-bedroom apartment in Fremont—a funky, busy, always-interesting part of Seattle. It's known, with tongue firmly in cheek, as "The Center of the Universe." You get the idea. The multi-story building houses an organic-food supermarket, open from 6 a.m. until midnight, which is like having the world's largest pantry five floors down.

Our apartment provided plenty of space for the twenty-odd bookcases we accumulated, besides a multitude of eclectic art and knickknacks. One treasured object is an old postcard Dad sent me when I was about ten. In it, he referred to me by his pet nickname,

"Chips." Mary seized on that name for me. And why not? I call her Merka. Seems fair.

We got plenty of use out of the nearby Burke-Gilman trail, which runs for twelve miles paralleling Seattle waterways. Our French bulldog, ZsaZsa, loved to take long walks along it. minette (Lower case "m" is the way we wrote her name; that was her decision.), a rescue dog, strongly preferred to run in the hallway or, better yet, recline on the bed. But she, too, often led us down to the trail, mostly to do her business.

In November 2005, after some protracted negotiations, we bought a home from one of my former WLS patients. It floats on Lake Union in the middle of Seattle. We were charmed by the Dutch front door and front porch, the second-floor porch (perfect for breakfasts, from May into October), and the fabulous, panoramic view of Lake Union and the Seattle skyline from the rooftop deck. Seattle is rather famous for its floating homes, especially since the movie *Sleepless in Seattle*, which was filmed right across the lake from us.

Admittedly, a second residence might have seemed superfluous. Yet this situation was handy when we had out-of-town visitors, or when work needed to be done in one place or the other. The Fremont apartment transitioned into our offices and library. I established a lovely little yoga studio in the living room for our own practice and for private clients.

Having the apartment allowed us to extensively renovate and enlarge the 110-year-old floating home, starting from the cedar log raft and working all the way up to the rooftop deck. The project took nearly three years but considerably improved the place. The net result was that we de-accessioned, closed the apartment, and moved full-time to the floating home. Household furnishings and clothing that had filled a large storage unit ultimately were donated to an immigrant Ukrainian family. My grandparents certainly would have approved.

Unloading the bulk of our library, in the interest of not sinking the floating home, presented a bit of a challenge. Although our Theodore Roosevelt collection was gratefully accepted by Dickinson State University, the Seattle Library system tried to cut us off as we inundated them by donating many of our other books. Undaunted, we resorted to a bit of chicanery: friends were given box loads to drop off at different branch libraries.

Sleeping on the lake is much quieter than in bustling Fremont. I can feel my blood pressure and heart rate fall every time we drive down the hill toward the water. The (mostly) gentle rolling motion is particularly soothing. Sunsets frequently are spectacular. And the neighborhood is ideal for dog walking.

Mary and I had a fifteen-year streak of unbroken attendance at the Oregon Shakespeare Festival, brought to an untimely end by the COVID-19 pandemic. We may have different interests, but we certainly share a deep and abiding love for Ashland, Oregon, and Shakespeare. Call it a hobby. We prepare for every Shakespeare play we see: we reread the plays, listen to audio lectures on tape, and read from among five or six compendia of critiques. Starting in college, where we both were English majors, and with our play-going history since then, we have seen the entire canon of thirty-seven plays, many of them numerous times.

We both enjoy classical music. Mary approaches it from the perspective of a dancer, whereas I bring to it a lifetime study of music history. Whatever. We enjoy dressing up and going to symphonic concerts together. Date night. We sit there holding hands, Mary blissfully choreographing what she hears, while I let the music wash over me amidst eddying currents of biographical bubbles. Sadly, that, too, has been curtailed by the pandemic. Thank God for Spotify.

We also enjoy traveling, and hope to resume doing so when it again becomes safe. Katie's wedding in Italy marked the first time I had been abroad in forty years. Since then, we have visited the U.K. several times, and we celebrated the start of my eighth decade—you know by now, how touch and go it was to get that far— in Eastern Europe.

More and more, however, we ascribe to the "See America First" approach. So much to see, and so little time, it seems.

***

Mary wrote a chapter in *The Experts' Guide to 100 Things Everyone Should Know How to Do*. The editor, Samantha Ettus, found 100 contributors, "painstakingly selected from among their distinguished peers as *the* expert on their subject."

Mary was among this select group, which reads like a "Who's Who." I will not list the whole group, but I suspect you may have heard of Larry King, Steven Covey, Dean Ornish, Nicole Miller, and Donald Trump. Of course, Letitia Baldrige also was a contributor. Her subject was handshakes. Mary's topic was "Give and Receive a Compliment." Trump's contribution, "On Negotiating

Deals" (What else?), is sandwiched between Mary and Letitia's. You would think he might have learned a bit of couth by osmosis, but it appears not.

In her piece about paying a compliment, Mary wrote: "Be sincere... be specific... don't compare." For the recipient, she recommended, "Never dispute, disparage, or diminish a compliment. To do so is to insult the giver by questioning his or her judgment, standards, taste, or, worse, sincerity. Much better to smile, say thank you, and savor the moment. And watch for the next chance to offer that great feeling to others!" Good advice by which to pattern one's life.

And with that, Mary chose to stop writing. No more books, no more columns. Instead, she designed a special social and communication skills program for the University of Pennsylvania Biomedical Post-doctoral Department. From that, for the past fifteen years, she has devoted considerable time to working with multicultural post-doctoral fellows, at programs all across the country, even in Saudi Arabia.

She has touched the lives of hundreds of bench scientists, via lectures and one-on-one sessions, designed to give them the tools necessary to advance their careers. This work has brought her message to others in a more personal way than any of her celebrated, more formal writings on etiquette.

I flatter myself into thinking that our new directions in work reflect the joy and fulfillment we feel finally being together. Both of us reach out to others in a more direct way than ever before. The objects of my attention no longer are anesthetized. My yoga classes and writings are intended to help others reflect on their own experiences.

Mary has told me several times that I have made God seem more real to her. This never fails to stun me. (How could there be any better compliment?) I never fail to thank her for saying that, once I regain my composure.

To be sure, we practice gratitude every day. That we love each other is only half of it. That each of us makes the other feel complete is the other half.

Sandy Peck, a dear friend, has studied astrology for over forty years. Sandy did my natal chart, and recently Mary's—never having met her. She also did a combined chart. Just the other day, she told us that she had never seen a more astrologically compatible couple!

Her explanation was too complicated for me to try to explain. Suffice it to say that, while we appreciate the affirmation, we celebrate the reality of it daily. As we gratefully move forward together, we maintain our commitment to serve others—even while we have changed our methodology—by being the best possible stewards of whatever communication gifts we have.

HIGH GROUND

Taking a page from Rizzi's *Let the Good Times Roll*

O Me! O life!... of the questions of these recurring;
Of the endless trains of the faithless—of cities fill'd
with the foolish;
Of myself forever reproaching myself, for who more
foolish than I, and who more faithless?
Of eyes that vainly crave the light—of the objects
mean—of the struggle ever renew'd;
Of the poor results of all—of the plodding and sor-
did crowds I see around me;
Of the empty and useless years of the rest—with
the rest me intertwined;
The question, O me! So sad, recurring—What good
amid these, O me, O life?
Answer:
That you are here—that life exists, and identity;
That the powerful play goes on, and you will con-
tribute a verse.

Walt Whitman, "O Me! O Life!"

MOVING ON

MEMENTO MORI
{literally: "Remember that you must die."}

In hindsight, I'd say my spiritual awakening, that is, what became a true heart opening, was occasioned by the loss of our beloved ZsaZsa. She was my best friend, the friend I never had as a child, through my schooling, nor after I started in medicine. Through her, I learned the meaning of devotion and unconditional love.

She died of an inoperable brain tumor when she was not quite seven years old. It was truly devastating. Yet her short life touched me on a deeper level than I knew was within myself.

Later on, I tell the rest of the story, how she came into our lives, the fun we had and the book she inspired. She left us on her own terms, but she continues to make her presence known to us. ZsaZsa, in case you have forgotten, was our beloved French bulldog.

And after her, through an extraordinary chain of events, came another. And yet another. The way had been prepared…

MISADVENTURES

Almost immediately after closing my surgery practice, I was invited to join the Kerala Ayurvedic Clinic. The deal looked pretty sweet at first. They gave me an office, which afforded me a bookcase to hold the best of my medical and surgical books, as well as walls on which to hang my diplomas, fellowship and board certifications, and a few photos.

In return, I gave the Kerala Clinic the pick of my office furniture and supplies. The rest was donated to charity. My office adjoined a small yoga studio where I held classes and did yoga therapy. It looked like I had landed on my feet and quickly, at that. It turned out to be a transition, for which I remain thankful.

The Kerala people were overjoyed to have a Western-trained M.D. on the premises as an adjunct to the acupuncturists, naturopaths, and massage therapists, all of whom were supervised by natural medicine practitioners at other Kerala Ayurvedic clinics in California. I was promised a salary for my consultations, plus reimbursement for the classes and yoga therapy. As an added incentive, I was invited to join their 500-hour Ayurvedic Counselor certification program.

Although the three California clinics and the one in Seattle were bankrolled by a highly successful company in India, they proved to be losing propositions. As a result, promises were made, and promises were broken. My role as medical advisor was eliminated, although they asked me to stay on as a yoga therapist and teacher. I had been promised a trip to India; it was canceled.

In frustration, I left. Within a few years, the U.S. operations closed. My mentor, Dr. Suhas Kshirsagar, moved to Florida to collaborate with the celebrated Dr. Deepak Chopra. Both men, by the way, were among the original appointees of the Maharishi Mahesh Yogi, when he introduced Ayurveda to the West, following his great success with Transcendental Meditation.

I stayed long enough to become a certified Ayurvedic Counselor, which has informed my yoga therapy practice. What I learned has been helpful to Mary and me as well, in terms of dealing with our *doshas*.

Simply put, in Ayurveda, *doshas* represent the three varieties of personality and physiology that are found in differing proportionality. They are easily disturbed and, consequently, they can be a root cause of illness.

My particular makeup indicates strength in the arts, ideas, and leadership. At the same time, I am not cut out to be a follower or much of a team player. How true. Yet this does not preclude a deep sense of loyalty to principles and people in whom I believe.

These strengths, if out of proper balance, can lead a person with my profile toward anxiety, depression, joint pains, heartburn, and coronary artery disease, among other problems. At various times, I have manifested each of these. It appears that there may have been more in play than adverse effects from my surgical career and the untrammeled pursuit of entertainment events. Enough said.

Another false start was with the UW School of Nursing. As I mentioned previously, I had started doing research in 2005 with their Biobehavioral Department. We were studying the effects of delivering extra warmth to the midline incisions and boosting oxygen levels in the soft tissues around the incision in bariatric patients. My weight loss surgery program—three times busier than that of the University of Washington—was used to gather demographic and pre-operative weight loss information on over 800 consecutive patients. This data was correlated with post-operative outcomes.

Accordingly, my teaching appointment was transferred to the School of Nursing from the Department of Surgery in 2008. I was asked to develop and teach a course in the evolution of yoga from its Eastern roots into a bona fide complementary alternative medical modality, i.e., yoga therapy. I was very enthusiastic about this project; it came with an office and a monthly salary. I put many hours into the design of a course for the post-graduate nursing students.

Unfortunately, it turned out that there was a great deal of professional jealousy between the nurses and this one doctor—me. Also the Department was running out of funding and preferred to use the grant money for other purposes. So my course was scuttled at the eleventh hour.

I think a big part of the decision to abort had to do with the fact that my salary was due to be quadrupled as soon as the actual teaching began. Hence, I was out yet another office and, for a time, my hard-earned faculty appointment. The latter I recovered as a condition for teaching, now on a pro bono basis, an annual suturing class for nurse practitioner students. This keeps my hands in the field, however remotely.

It became increasingly clear that I needed to simplify the trajectory of my new direction. Yet I do believe each stop along the way had a purpose.

MANTRA

Early on, my yoga workweek included teaching five classes at a gym and four at two studios, all near our apartment. I resigned from one studio after only a year, as the owner was far too controlling. I had enough of that kind of thing during my residency. The other yoga studio was run as a cooperative venture and simply was a losing cause for all concerned.

I taught at this first gym for four years and had a great following there. The only problem was that this owner, too, was extremely difficult to deal with. Not just for me. All of us, staff and members alike, tried to keep out of her way as much as was humanly possible. Four years of this was all I could take.

Meanwhile, I found a perfect place for studio teaching—spacious, full of natural light, and surrounded on two sides with beautiful trees—where I taught Level One and Two classes for several years. This, too, was not to last. The owner sold her business to a company that served women only. This caused quite an uproar—which one might not expect from yoga practitioners—as one quarter of the clientele was male. And here I was, the sole male teacher!

I seriously considered becoming a part owner of a downtown facility, to have included chiropractors, massage therapists, and a Reiki Master. Again promises were broken. I bailed out, which was a fortuitous decision, as the enterprise failed within two years.

My yoga career picked up from there. I saw that LA Fitness was opening a new facility in Ballard, so I contacted the regional fitness director. I told her that, with my credentials, I wouldn't work for less than twice the normal starting pay for LA Fitness instructors. She got the okay, and I became a fixture at the Ballard LA Fitness from the day it opened. My classes were extremely popular. Twice, we packed a room with over seventy students!

A student who has become a good friend, Liz Talley, studied cello with another friend and former yoga student, Miriam Shames. Liz often played her cello at my yoga classes. Another of my students, Glenn Frank, a gifted guitarist, often performed duets with Liz during class. This was so special. Between the yoga practice and the synchronized musical accompaniment, the students were blissed out. So was I.

What better way to integrate my lifelong love for live music performance with my newfound devotion to helping others achieve a balance of mind, body, and spirit through yoga. Shakespeare was right: music soothes the soul. Management was happy, too. My yoga classes, featuring live music, became a marketing tool.

Sadly, my ten-year affiliation with LA Fitness was a casualty of the coronavirus. They offered no online teaching options for me, and I was no longer comfortable teaching there in person. It was a great run while it lasted, but all things must end, sooner or later. Even the pandemic.

The Washington Athletic Club hired me to fill a vacant yoga therapy position and teach two yoga classes a week. Soon, this became four classes, and then a fifth was added. I taught several series of Introduction to Yoga classes. It is always great fun for me to get students started on the right track, just as I was.

A loyal following has resulted. Often students will come up and tell me if they are going out of town. They clue me in about personal issues, often asking for medical advice and perspectives. Many have become friends. When the WAC considered canceling two of my morning classes, the students put up such a ruckus in protest that management had to relent.

Teaching at the WAC is a pleasure, even remotely, as is the case these days. Everybody treats me with respect; members and co-workers call me either Dr. Jim or Dr. Weber. They recognize that I bring unique qualifications to my work as a certified yoga therapist: years of experience as a surgeon, my training and years as a yoga teacher, and my grounding in Ayurveda. I often play classical music in my classes and occasionally spice them up with musical historical vignettes. Can't help it.

I specialize in one-on-one interventions for clients (constantly reminding myself to call them that and not patients) with specific medical or psychological conditions, for which yoga therapy has been shown to be beneficial. These include: cancer patients and people with acute and chronic back pain; obesity; pulmonary insufficiency; depression; and recent ortho-pedic surgery. Typically, I evaluate the client and set up a home yoga program, utilizing individually-designed sequences, with periodic follow-up visits as indicated.

Some of my clients have been particularly challeng-ing. One lady was so debilitated that she no longer could get down to or up from the ground, nor could she make it into or out of her car. I made house calls to her place for eighteen months and gradually got her to the point where she had achieved enough self-sufficiency to do her own shopping. And get down on the floor and back up without assistance. She was pleased, and her husband was ecstatic.

I worked with a client with advanced prostate can-cer for over a year, modifying sequences as his disease progressed to the point where he was no longer able to sit—secondary to radiation therapy damage to his anal region. Yet he continued with standing poses and inversions, every day, right up until ten days before the cancer took his life.

The International Journal of Yoga Therapy published my article, "Square Pegs and Round Holes: Should

Evidence-based Medicine Apply to Ayurveda?" in their November 2009 issue. The first part of that title could apply equally well to this book and much of my life, for that matter.

The problem of achieving good, randomized, controlled clinical trials pertains equally to Ayurveda, yoga, and yoga therapy research. Everyone with any experience knows that these modalities work. Yet providing solid evidence basis that holds up to the same level of scrutiny applied to drug trials is well-nigh impossible.

For example, yoga cannot readily be standardized, either in the teaching or in the performance of poses. How deep should the student go? How long is the pose to be held? Besides, the quantification of the spiritual benefits bedevils researchers. There are other difficulties as well, but I won't go into all of them here. Just take my word for it. Or read my article.

All the same, yoga continues to get good press. Witness, for example, an article from *The New York Times* on December 22, 2015, discussing the value of yoga in osteoporosis prevention and amelioration. The student who pointed this article out to me told me that her bone density had increased by eight percent in the few years since she began practicing yoga. Another article shows a link between yoga and preservation of mental acuity (*NYT* 6/1/16). Still another points to yoga three times a week as a good way to stave off depression (*NYT* 11/20/19).

Teaching yoga to the track and field and cross-country athletes at Seattle Pacific University was a special treat. The students loved doing yoga; the administration was less excited. For one thing, it was an extra expense for their already bare-bones athletic budget. For another thing, the idea of yoga with its Hindu roots did not exactly jibe with the relatively fundamentalist Christian ethos of the school.

I am proud to say that after a couple of years, the faculty and staff started participating in their own yoga program. I think that they saw that the athletes were comfortable, even enthusiastic, while remaining just as fervid in their Christian religious beliefs as ever.

I am especially proud of the fact that there were no serious hamstring injuries among any of the athletes over the six years that I taught at SPU. Alas, the yoga program is now in-house and sporadically taught at best. This helps their budgetary bottom line, but I fear it may not help the athletes' hamstrings.

Indeed, yoga is compatible with any religion or even agnosticism. The Observances and Avoidances that form Steps One and Two of the eight-step approach to Raja Yoga are very much akin to the Ten Commandments and certainly are predicated, as all religions are, on the Golden Rule.

It has ever been my practice in teaching yoga to start with a short period of grounding, followed by a centering meditation. The emphasis is on compassion, contentment, truthfulness, and gratitude. Yet I try to keep things from getting too serious; we work hard, but we also have fun.

I especially enjoyed doing adjustments, which are readily accepted by virtually all of my students, since they know I am a physician and can see, in many cases, that I am at least as old as their parents. Of course, the COVID-19 pandemic has changed all of that.

Currently, all my yoga classes are online, with much uncertainty about when, if ever, I will go back to teaching in person. I must admit that there are advantages in not having to factor in any travel time. Yet, I do miss the personal contact. Handshakes and hugs seem slowly to be making a comeback; perhaps adjustments in yoga class will, too.

I have been fortunate to work with so many talented and intelligent students. Really fascinating people. There is no doubt in my mind that I am helping more people—and more interesting people at that—and having a lot more fun in this second career than I ever did in my first.

Richard Seven, a columnist who wrote about my transition to yoga from surgery for *The Seattle Times*, understood as much. He summarized his article by quoting me:

> *"I feel I belong in yoga. As I look back, I had sort of made myself belong in surgery.*

Yoga has given me a totally new perspective. I am learning that there is unity and value in everything. I hope I was always compassionate, but I feel I am more at peace now. And I'd like to share that."

In 2013, Mary got me a gig teaching yoga for four years for the Association of American Medical Colleges. This meant two classes a day for three days at their annual Early Women in Medicine Symposium. These physicians finally had a chance to quiet their minds, limber up, and get the kinks out from sitting through lecture after lecture.

Mary had been teaching social skills at this conference for three years prior to bringing me aboard. She talked the organizers into providing a wellness component, hitherto unheard of at medical conferences.

From my experience with my mother and many other women in medicine, I suspected that quite a number of the attendees were emotionally repressed. I encouraged them to open up to their inner feelings, honor their breath, and live in the moment. Mary, a certified Zumba instructor, then got them to shake their booties and finish by literally skipping around the room. It was like "Open Season for the New You" at the conference.

This was great fun for me. Here I was, the token male amidst 140 young women physicians. Mary had fun, too. Chaperoning me.

Mary taught Zumba at the Ballard LA Fitness for a year or two. She switched to Aquafit (water aerobics) and Silver Sneakers, a fitness program for seniors, much easier on her back than Zumba.

You might have trouble believing this, but the fact is I also taught a weekly Aquafit class for several years. I had the best time, playing my old rhythm and blues, rock 'n' roll, and doo-wop tunes, shades of the Bluenotes and Sha Na Na, while getting a pool full of people, admittedly mostly seniors, to work out and dance with me to the music.

I'd like to make more time for my own practice, yet I find that Life keeps getting in the way of yoga. Daughters and grandchildren. Poems, books, and plays to be read and reread.

Opera on demand. Movies to watch. TV series to get hooked on. Memoirs to write. Football and baseball games. A dog to walk. Cooking techniques to learn. Plants to water. So much to do. We seem to be busier than ever, as we adjust to the restrictions necessitated by the pandemic.

All things considered, for the first time in my life, I am content with my work-life balance and, moreover, with myself. I feel that what I have is enough. I want nothing more but time to continue as I am and time to continue my spiritual development. Helping others goes without saying.

This poem emanated straight from a place deep inside:

Om

Yoga to me:
The thing is a discipline,
A blend of breath control, meditation,
And physical positioning—both dynamic and static.
The aim is to balance mind, body,
And spirit, all three together.
When a person strengthens and enriches
These areas from within, he is
Then ready to take the benefits of the
Practice from mat to the world beyond.
God knows the world would benefit from
Such serenity. Would the world had eyes
To see the glaring need, or ears to hear the
Calming breath across the throats of
Those who practice. Yoga
Endures in the vastness
Of serenity—as a refuge
At the edge of the abyss of cacophony.

MERCI

In 2012, the organizers of the Second Annual Copper Mountain Medicine and Yoga Symposium invited me to present a lecture. My talk, "Heal Thyself: A Prescription for Self-Betterment," was well received. What a thrill it was to see M.D.s and yogis communicating with each other! Of course, this group of M.D.s was, by definition, more enlightened than most of their colleagues. Sadly, the conference was not well attended. It was discontinued after another year for lack of interest.

Recently, I had occasion to return to the Operating Room as an observer. This was a validating experience. Nearly seven years had passed since I donned scrubs, and I did not expect to do so ever again. Here's how this came about:

Mary's manicurist was found to have a pancreatic tumor on a CT scan, performed as follow up for a history of hepatitis. It appeared to be a non-hormone producing solitary lesion. The oncologist referred the woman to a general surgeon.

She shared her history with me and asked for my help. I reviewed the data and agreed that surgery was indicated, but felt that there was a better man for the job, one of my former junior residents who had extensive experience with pancreatic surgery. With the patient's permission, I called the oncologist, who turned out to be new to the community, suggesting a change in surgical referral.

The woman was quite apprehensive about her operation, although she was comfortable with the man I suggested. She asked me if I would observe the operation in the OR—as her guardian angel. This was a new role for me, and I could hardly refuse the request. I then called the surgeon, explained how I had become involved, and obtained his permission.

I showed up on the appointed day, put on my scrubs, and went into the room as they were setting up. The surgeon walked in with his assistant and began to do his thing. What was odd about it was that he made not the slightest effort to acknowledge my presence, let alone introduce me around. A man I had known for over thirty years—especially after I had been responsible for getting him the case. This was awkward, to say the least. Frankly, I was shocked.

Finally, the robotics company rep introduced herself and showed me where to sit to observe the proceedings via a monitor screen. During the three or four hours I was there, I made a comment or two, perhaps a suggestion or two, and offered a few "Atta-boys." I might as well have been talking to myself.

Once the critical work was done, I mumbled my thanks, said I needed to get going, and left the theater. Nobody appeared to notice. I stepped out into a nice sunny day, thanking my lucky stars that I had been brought up with better manners than this surgeon.

You might have guessed that he, too, was a Dallas-to-Seattle transplant, part of the Texas "Mafia." They had managed to get to me, one last time.

On a happier note:

Through the years, before and after my "retirement" (a term I prefer not to use), grateful patients have sent me a host of acknowledgments. To have been able to help them regain control of their lives through bariatric surgery is what made all that training, all the mental and physical abuse, all the nightmares—which persist to this day, fourteen years after closing my practice—worthwhile.

Although I thought all the cards and letters had gone to the recycling bin, I came across one the other day, as I was cleaning out some drawers. It was a letter celebrating the third anniversary of the day the woman had her surgery, which she said had made her life worth living. She gave credit to herself and to me for working hard to achieve her goals, saying that she now was able to keep up with her grandchildren as a result of her weight loss. It embarrasses me to relate that she called me the greatest man to walk the earth, fortunately qualifying the acme of praise by saying that was in her opinion, (thereby implying that not everyone necessarily would agree).

Hyperbole notwithstanding, you can see why I felt blessed to be doing what I did for all those years. Despite the obstacles I had to overcome to get there. Also why I had kept this one note!

MANNERS

Ah, but there is another side to what I do these days. I co-authored an etiquette book! Here is how that came about.

Alpha Books, an imprint of Random House, contacted Mary to write a shorter etiquette book as one of the six titles they hoped to bring out in their new *Complete Idiots Guide Fast-Track* series. They stipulated a length of 130 pages, all original writing, and few, if any, bullet points.

Mary had real concerns about paring down the essence of etiquette into a book this short. Her other books were two to three times as long. But I thought it might be fun and certainly an interesting challenge. So off we went on this venture.

Mary asked me to write the chapter on table manners. She flattered me by reminding me of my privileged upbringing, my attendance and participation in many of her table-manners lectures, and my writing skills. I took the bait.

I passed it back to her, requesting that she fill in the appropriate language for dealing with certain situations. She asked me to interject a bit of humor into a chapter she had written. Thus, a pattern developed.

Emboldened, I offered to write another chapter, and then another. She agreed. Furthermore, she said, "You're the doctor; you write about 'Courtesy for the

Disabled'," handing me a few useful references, among the best of which were her previous writings on the subject.

And so it went until the book was done.

As the ultimate Father's Day gift, Mary had the publishers list me as co-author. And in so doing, I was given a very important bragging point: I can lay claim to be the best-mannered surgeon and yoga teacher you ever will meet!

The book, as it is now constituted, is perfect for Millennials. It gives concise information on what they need to deal with the majority of etiquette issues. It is affordable and a quick read. Entertaining, even.

Now that I have bona fide etiquette creds, I give occasional talks on table manners and interviewing skills. The ninth graders at Buckley annually assemble to hear my pearls of wisdom. It's a good way to show my gratitude for the excellent educational start the school provided.

I was a last-minute substitute for Mary at a meeting of microbiologists in San Diego and later jetted to Sioux Falls, SD, to lecture to a roomful of medical students, residents, and attendings. In both cases, the organizers had requested Mary, but she felt that I would be a better fit, considering the nature of the audience. One thing I have learned is that doctors have a hard time accepting anything from laymen. However, they will listen another doctor. They may not agree with what they hear, but they will listen.

The yoga and meditation groups at MD Anderson invited me to lecture and teach a class. I traveled there with Mary, who was engaged to help the post-docs improve their social skills.

Who knows? Perhaps in the future, I will lecture more and teach a bit less.

Perhaps. Certainly, I am writing more—this book and at least two collections of vignettes and essays, the first already in print. Meanwhile, I intend to continue teaching yoga. As long as I can. I love this work.

Several years back, I made a Level I yoga DVD, now available as an mp4, sold at cost simply as an aid to my students. They can take me with them when they travel. So far, I have been taken along to Australia, Kenya,

Mexico, England, Italy, Spain, Japan, China, Thailand, India, Bali, and the Philippines. Without leaving home.

I have recorded several of my Zoom yoga classes, which I email, gratis, to anyone who requests them.

Somewhat reluctantly, I shut down the free Wednesday afternoon Zoom restorative yoga class—the one I originally intended as part of my college 50th reunion—substituting an open Friday class for peace in Ukraine, which will continue until Russia is compelled to end this unjust war.

MIRACLES, MINETTE, AND THE MONARCH

We move on to my most important message: Miracles can happen. I believe in miracles, and I have witnessed a few in my time.

The first was the miracle of surviving not one but four heart attacks. But more than just surviving, the real miracle was being able to return to a productive life. And to pay it forward by helping others. Through surgery, in particular WLS. Through yoga. Through love of family and friends. Through this book and my other collections of shorter pieces.

When I finished my most recent treadmill stress test, going halfway through Level Four, the nurse compared my results to age-controlled norms. She said I achieved what was expected for a fit 45-year-old or a sedentary 35-year-old. I told her I thought I probably could have done better. Maybe next time.

The second miracle was having a third chance with Mary. We have met a few couples who got things right the second time around, after more than half a lifetime of separation. For us, it took three tries. It is possible we weren't mature enough for each other the first two go-rounds.

No doubt, we have differences in personality. Mary is very much an introvert; I am an extrovert. She is a planner par excellence; I tend to fly by the seat of my pants. She says that I thrive in chaos. Yet we are alike in certain important ways, both of us being intuitive and sensitive. We like many of the same things, baseball and opera being notable exceptions. No doubt, we are living proof that *amor vincit omnia!*

The timing simply wasn't right for us, not in 1971, not in 1977. We were meant to wait, to experience more of life. We were given the opportunity to seize the third and final gold ring, and we did. During those intervening years, Mary wrote her books to the benefit of thousands of readers, and I had my children—each, in their own way, admirably productive members of society. We had our separate lives and careers. Finally, we get to do life together. It is miraculous!

Now we come back to ZsaZsa. To be more accurate, she came to us. In retrospect, we both feel someone else was pulling the strings the whole time. We three were meant to be together.

ZsaZsa was a miracle.

Neither of us ever had been exposed to French bulldogs until the afternoon we found ourselves at Jon Watling's pumpkin carving party. The Watlings' two English bulldogs were running all over, trying to catch up with a laser pointer. In walked a couple with two Frenchies that similarly began to tear around the place. Finally, in came two more people with a chihuahua.

I assessed this calamitous dog situation *in toto* (a pun, if you remember the Oz that preceded Mehmet) and concluded that the French bulldog must have evolved by crossing an English bulldog with a chihuahua. Think about it; you will have to admit that I have a point, size-wise and ear-wise.

Some months later, at the office, I heard that the Frenchies had produced a litter of puppies. Since Yalies can't resist bulldogs, naturally I gave the matter some thought. Almost eight minutes, in fact. Not about whether or not I wanted a pup. That was certain. The question was whether Mary would go for the idea.

I fibbed a bit. Told Mary I was taking her out for brunch. The residential neighborhood we drove into made her suspicious that something was up. The house we entered was a real mess: tiny poops and pups all over the Persian rug just inside the door. One toddled right over to Mary and sat on her shoe.

This was our introduction to ZsaZsa. She picked us. Pure and simple. At two and a half weeks old.

It took Mary three days before she said any words about the pending puppy situation. And they were, "So what do you want to name our pooch?"

It didn't take long for us to realize that ZsaZsa had quite the sense of humor. She would egg us on to play with her, developing a remarkable talent for playing with balls. I don't know what it was about balls, but they had special appeal for ZZ.

When it came to walks, ZZ displayed superior skills. We realized early on that she was just fine off leash. In fact, she was more malleable off leash than on.

The thing about bulldogs is that you cannot force them to move forward when they are of a mind not to do so. They have this way of slamming down all four paws and letting a person know it. Stubbornness is a big part of their character. Actually, mine too. ZsaZsa may have grown to a mere 21 pounds, but she could stop us in our tracks.

ZsaZsa was always happy to let humans cross our threshold. In fact, she was pretty much of a party animal. But she always was on high alert for canine interlopers. Early on, she learned to scramble up and down the circular stairs to the roof of our floating home. She would position herself at the corner of the roof, which afforded her the best view of both docks, the parking lot and the street. From there, she would announce to any and every dog that she was at home and not to be trifled with. She would sit up there for hours on end, so long as it wasn't raining.

The entire dock was her turf. She would take either one of us, or both, down to the end of the dock every night before turning in. I think she was just doing her evening patrol to make sure that everything was in order. She would go all the way to the end, look out over the water and turn right back.

Of all the office assistants I ever had, the best, in terms of patient popularity, was our French bulldog. The patients so enjoyed having ZsaZsa as greeter and entertainer that, when making follow-up appointments, they would inquire whether ZsaZsa would be there. If the answer was no, many would opt to reschedule. No kidding.

Norm's was ZsaZsa's favorite restaurant, mostly because Norm's was the only restaurant in Seattle that welcomed dogs indoors. From her favorite corner booth, she could keep an eye on the comings and goings of the other pooches. She would allow them to slink by, with nary a growl, so long as they showed proper obeisance.

Norm's displays an original drawing from *Woofs to the Wise*, showing ZsaZsa, front and center, in the place of honor opposite the bar.

Woofs was really the brainchild of Mary's best friend from Philly, Nessa Forman. Nessa and ZsaZsa, who by now had her own email address (and why not?), had started to correspond, after Nessa was diagnosed with cancer. The emails flew back and forth for a few months. ZsaZsa could say things to Nessa that neither Mary nor I would ever dream of saying, such as "Get a grip." And this she did. More than a few times.

For her part, Nessa never seemed to mind catching it from ZsaZsa about not being in the moment or not fully explaining her terminology or motivation. ZsaZsa needed to unload her frustration over the absolute cluelessness of her long-time boyfriend, Peloton, a puggle. ZsaZsa was also contemplating a new job, since I had closed my office and therefore no longer needed her to be the greeter. She also perceived that Nessa might share her vast experience in mentoring divas.

Nessa saw that a book of pithy epithets, savvy in-struction, and sage advice was taking form. It didn't take much convincing to get Mary and me to buy in. ZsaZsa needed more convincing. Once she understood that this would be her book, no matter that humans would be listed as the official authors, she went whole hog (dog) for the idea, two paws up, as it were.

The book had a plot line: enjoying every day, while communicating clearly, being gracious and kind. Subplots included handling bad manners and "faux paws"—the foil for which was ZsaZsa's boyfriend, Peloton—the path to becoming an enlightened, modern-day diva, and how to deal with adversity of all kinds.

Through the course of the book, ZsaZsa absorbed more and more wisdom and life lessons from Nessa, until the tables turned. Toward the end, Nessa came to depend more and more upon ZsaZsa for help in dealing with the last months of her life, as she faced insurmountable odds against long-term survival with pancreatic cancer.

Oatley Kidder, Mary's dear friend, who painted a number of remarkable murals in our floating home (and who has illustrated this book, as well as my book of short reflections, *Joie de Vivre, As I See It*), contributed twenty-five original drawings. We hired a vanity-book concierge company. They guided us through the process of self-publishing, which was something new for Mary and, ultimately, the way I was to go with my books.

My role was behind the scenes, adding content here and there wherever ZsaZsa saw fit or needed help typing, providing continuity between sections. When Nessa died before the book was completed, Mary channeled her inner Nessa and took her part in the dialogue. It was left to ZsaZsa and me to continue with the responses. Well, in truth, it was mostly ZsaZsa.

We coaxed a fine Foreword out of Letitia Baldrige and secured some great endorsements and cover blurbs. The publishing company put us in touch with their editor, who took two passes through the book.

The final result was a lovely, entertaining, instructive, memorable little book, of which we all were proud, especially ZsaZsa. Proceeds from sales were earmarked for arts education in the public school system of Philadelphia.

The book was launched first at the Philadelphia Free Library before a crowd of nearly one hundred.

Dog-friendly Norm's Restaurant in Seattle was the site of the second launch.

We had bookmarks, calling cards and posters made up. Mary held a number of book-signing events with ZsaZsa, who made it clear that she wasn't inclined to have her paw dipped in ink for every customer who wanted an autograph. So we inked her once and had a stamp made of her front paw.

Unquestionably, we learned much more from ZsaZsa than we ever taught her. In fact, Mary devotes half of one of her most engaging talks, "My Two Greatest Teachers," to lessons she learned from ZsaZsa. Her other greatest teacher was Letitia; I am only slightly miffed at being passed over.

Mary put her finger on it early on when she turned to me and said that ZsaZsa was "an old soul." I was more prosaic in my calling her "a little person in a fur suit." Both descriptions apply.

ZsaZsa passed away eight months after her book was published. The book serves as a beautiful memorial to three larger-than-life characters, Nessa, ZsaZsa, and Peloton, who died two years later. All are sorely missed.

ZsaZsa spared us the painful decision to euthanize. In my opinion, she literally managed her own death in such a way as to preserve for herself a certain dignity in dying. A dignity that I confess few of my patients were able to experience, owing to the propensity in Western medicine to push therapy to the extreme.

Out of the blue, the last evening of her life, while Mary was holding her, she became very lucid and looked deeply and for a long moment into Mary's eyes. Mary knew immediately what was going on. Ten minutes later, while I was holding her, she rallied and gave me the same deep, lingering look. She was looking right into my soul, and telling me that it was her time to go.

ZsaZsa's body was respectfully cremated, her ashes given back to us in a lovely wooden box. We had a beautiful paperweight made out of some of her cremains.

But this wasn't the end. It was the beginning of a new phase of awareness of subtler realms. You see, ZsaZsa had not left us. She was, and still is, very much in the picture. She sends us messages in times of need, generally in the form of tennis balls at the side of the road, or floating in the water near our home. You say coincidences, maybe synchronicities? Try affirmations.

Since ZsaZsa's death we have noted many of what some would call "strange happenings." I won't describe them all, yet I hope my readers will concede that there is much we are not given to understand about the non-physical or spirit world.

To give one example, on several occasions, Mary found herself inviting ZsaZsa to inspire her Zumba or Aquafit classes, only to clearly visualize her sitting quietly in the corner. These events were preceded by her seeing ZZ in a dream, front and center, dancing.

Through yoga, ZsaZsa, and perhaps through a shamanic process known as soul retrieval, I am coming to a better understanding and acceptance of a higher level of existence.

Perhaps I am getting a bit too "woo-woo" for some of you. It is your option not to read any further, to skip ahead, or perhaps you may read and not accept. Yet, I hope that some of what I am trying to describe here will strike a chord and get you thinking, feeling, and opening yourself up to possibilities and potentialities.

Mary and I both have had shamanic soul retrievals and along with them, a past-life reading. This is predicated on the belief that our souls live on and come back in different bodies. Shamans believe the reincarnation is always human. Hindus and yogis believe such things not to be species-specific.

Nothing in what I learned at the Brick Church or in reading the Bible prepared me for my session with the shaman. Frankly, I was quite skeptical about the whole thing. Yet, I was open-minded enough to give it a try, and what I learned was surprising—even revelatory. Certainly, it has given me much food for thought ever since.

Soul retrieval is a fascinating process. A shaman, with the aid of his or her spirit guides, searches for parts of the soul that were lost due to trauma. It can be done in person or, remarkably, remotely.

Here is what I found fascinating during mine: as the shaman was doing her thing, I had a clear sense of a pulling sensation. First, I was generally aware of it, as if I were being drawn or sucked toward something outside of myself—but not uncomfortably. Next, I felt the pull through my mouth; it moved to my nose and, from there, to my hands. Then, strangest of all, my mouth opened and not because of any nasal congestion. I attempted to close my lips, *yet I could not do so*. Finally, I felt a sensation in my feet.

The shaman, who was supplied with no background information, came back on and told me what she had been allowed to see. She saw me as a dark-skinned, huge man working on something in a very dark place. Not a mine, but perhaps a blacksmith shop.

I was alone and others feared me, despite my being kindly, with compassionate intentions toward all—a keenly observant witness to life, not welcomed in the community. She saw this man dying at an old age, again all alone.

She saw my mother at the time of my birth, fearful that she couldn't be a good mother to me. There was an image of me at one or two, terrified of being left alone. She could see me, at age four, sensing the fear of others, crying on the inside, losing connection with everything, yet retaining a good soul and sense of kindness. There was a glimpse of me learning to explore at six or seven. Possibly forgetting about the dark cave.

I was exhibiting superior intelligence by nine, trying to connect with others by being helpful; yet, others remained afraid of me. By the time I was eleven, the shaman was told that I realized that others would not accept help from me, even though I knew what they needed. By thirteen, I was turning to books and living for the future, as day-to-day experience was not making sense. She said she saw me attempting to teach the teachers, who were threatened by this and also were somewhat afraid of me.

The shaman said that typically she loses the picture of her clients at an age between twenty and thirty, but that she could follow this past life of mine up to forty. She saw clearly that I now could help people, even though they remained afraid of me. Sadly, I had not developed the spiritual resources to enjoy that life.

She summarized by telling me that I always wanted to be accepted and listened to. That I had missed a love connection for almost two lifetimes. And that I had searched through spirituality to find this.

She told me that I was healed and now I could

search with joy and peace. That my life is no longer about the future. And on some level, I always knew this.

Finally, she assured me that the present will take on a whole new color. And it has. I greet each new day with enthusiasm and heartfelt gratitude. Sunsets are more spectacular, roses and lilacs smell sweeter, even food tastes better. My meditation guidance comes more directly from the heart. This book conveys a far more powerful message than the simple autobiography I originally envisioned

I asked the shaman about power animals. I had been told that shamans and freed souls have such things. Power animals serve as guides to help a person fast track into the spirit world. My shaman has three but was using only her panther.

This next part is what really floored me. She said that for the first time, as she was observing this panther, it opened its mouth, not to roar, but to let something either in or out. She said she was amazed when I described the way my mouth opened and could not shut while all this was going on.

I told her that I felt I already had my power animal in ZsaZsa, and that I wanted no other. She agreed, emphatically.

***

While nothing could ever replace ZsaZsa, another lovely dog (or should I say spirit animal—or, better yet, spirit) came into our life.

We never thought we wanted another dog after ZsaZsa. After all, what animal could possibly follow that act? Yet, suddenly the image of a poodle came into my head. I mentioned it to a few people, and almost everyone to whom I spoke had had gratifying, personal involvement with poodles.

I googled a bit, and minette's little face popped up on a dog rescue site. We drove out to the pet rescue kennel in West Seattle. There were dozens of little dogs jumping up and down. Sitting quietly in the back was minette, locking eyes with Mary. What clinched the deal for me, however, was the name she had been given in the shelter. Reminded me of my pet frog, Vmin.

Her survival on the the mean streets of LA was a miracle in itself. She had been found by the dogcatcher and shipped up to Seattle. She was in bad shape on arrival—emaciated, with eye, skin, and urinary tract infections.

She remained at the rescue center for nearly three months, the limiting allowable length of stay. The attendants could see that she was exceptional and were amazed that nobody wanted to adopt her. Had we not come along, she would have been euthanized.

We asked a dog channeler whether ZsaZsa would be okay with our possibly bringing minette into the family; we got the green light. The shelter required three references. They brought the mins to us on Christmas Eve, Mary's birthday, but would not give her over without first completing a site visit.

They told us that she really did not like to be picked

up or held. Wrong. That she was mostly poodle. Wrong again. Try minestrone. Whatever blend she was, minette settled right into her "forever home," jumped right up on the bed and all the chairs and snuggled right in. She felt the love from Day One, and so did we.

On that first day she arrived at the apartment, we noticed a rainbow on the floor of Mary's office; it only lasted a few minutes. The same thing happened within minutes of minette's first introduction to the floating home. It was as if ZsaZsa had sent rainbows to let us and minette know that she was welcomed!

People write and speak of the Rainbow Bridge in describing a place across which departed pets accompany their guardians as they are reunited for eternity. Makes you think.

minette (who approved the lower case "m") fit in amazingly well. For a rescue dog, she was very well adjusted. She exhibited a great talent for adaptability. We think she was mostly Havanese, as she showed the same circus dog, companion dog, and watchdog traits that typify the breed. And she was very intelligent.

She was quite unlike ZsaZsa. For one thing, she seemed more like a dog. She was more agreeable when it came to changing directions on a walk. She had absolutely no interest in balls; she had three identical bunnies that she would attack briefly before settling down with her head propped up on one. She got along with all dogs and humans, although she barked and carried on when almost anybody came to the door.

She liked dear old Peloton well enough, but there was no special link between them. The special link is between Mary and me and Peloton's guardians, Scott and Sheela Tallman. At their request, and in honor of ZsaZsa, we have unofficially adopted them!

We six, dogs included, spent a lovely Thanksgiving together. Peloton was thrilled finally to be welcomed back into our apartment. He had stopped by the door every time he walked by for the preceding year and a half since ZsaZsa had died. Sadly and totally unexpectedly, he died in his sleep a few nights later. He and ZsaZsa are reunited and waiting by the Rainbow Bridge.

minette grudgingly accepted the Tallman's new dog, Noci. He is younger and smaller, more easily bossed around. They had frequent sleepovers in a state of more-or-less-peaceful coexistence. Four in a bed, her place or his.

She communicated very clearly when she wanted a treat, needed to go out, wanted to be put back on the bed and was too lazy to jump up herself, and especially around mealtime. She secured our attention and then looked in the proper direction to communicate her need at that particular moment.

She, too, was capable of thinking ahead. You could almost "see the wheels turning," as Dad used to say. She, more or less patiently, taught us new tricks. Thank God, we still were trainable.

Gradually, she became the boss around our house. We would organize our days around her needs. And we were delighted to be in service, because she was such a wonderful, loving companion.

Really all she ever wanted was to be with us. That and having her food right on time. And plenty of treats. We almost never used one-word commands with her; we spoke to her in full sentences. And she understood.

Her age, when we adopted her, was estimated at three or four. Six years later, she was started on medication for a leaky heart valve, the same valve issue that nearly had taken Mom's life. Apparently, small dogs—she weighed ten pounds—are prone to degeneration of the valve between the right side of the heart and the lungs.

For three months, the medicine did the trick. This took us into the time of COVID-19 sequestration. minette was really happy, as she had us to herself all day long.

On her last day of life, she took us on two lengthy walks. By this time, she was taking us wherever she wanted to go. And up hills we went, albeit at a slower pace than before.

Suddenly, as we finished the second walk, she fainted. She revived for a few hours and then began a rapid downhill course. She refused to eat, drink, or take her meds. Her heart and respiratory rates went way up. She was in fulminant cardiac failure, something we were forewarned would happen, sooner or later. We were hoping for later.

We held her in our arms all night, anticipating that she would not survive until morning. When she did, even appearing to rally, we made the mistake of asking our-selves whether anything could be done to save her. This decision has haunted us ever since.

Because of the sequestration, we were not allowed to stay with her at the veterinary hospital. Where she died, alone and, we imagine, frightened. Instead of in our arms, where she would have been comforted and soothed as she passed. Her still warm, lifeless body was brought out to us. We had a lot to say to her, which we hope she heard. A lot of kisses to give her, which we hope she felt...

The hospital reception area featured a photo of two dogs standing together on a hill. One was a Frenchie; the other a poodle mix. The two were looking out at some unidentified object. It was ZsaZsa and minette, from afar, looking at us!

I had had a dream two nights before ZsaZsa died. She was in a pool of water, smiling calmly just below the surface. I also had a dream two nights before minette died. We were playing happily in a field, until she ran away from me. I was confident that I would find her, until it got dark. She was gone.

For two nights after she died, minette again ap-peared in my dreams:

In the first, she was there to be walked in the midst of a hectic situation, after which there seemed clear direction regarding what needed to be done.

In the second, she led me onto an elevator to get me away from an irritating, know-it-all former resident.

The door was nearly closed behind her, but I reached the button just in time. minette and I were alone in the elevator, going up.

That same day, Mary had a vision, much like the ones she had when ZsaZsa had passed on. Coming up the stairs, she clearly saw minette, sitting in one of her favorite spots, looking directly at her.

The dreams and the visions assured us that our beloved friends were still very much in the picture. They helped assuage the intense grief.

Yet, what really brought us peace were the return of the rainbows:

The first came on our bedroom ceiling upon waking up in the form of two linear rainbows at right angles, which merged into a larger rainbow.

The second was a tiny, transient rainbow on the floor leading to the middle of the front door. As if to say: we are together now in looking after you. You can leave your house; we will be going with you.

We are not at all sure why we have been so blessed to have shared so many precious moments with ZsaZsa and minette, but we believe that we have two guardian angels protecting us. Neither is ever far from our thoughts. Indeed, it feels like minette is in the other room, barely out of sight, Mary's vision notwithstanding. We are grateful for every sign they send us, most often during times of need. Both inspire us to continue to be the best possible stewards of our abundant gifts.

The shaman underscored the point about craving acceptance and not ever actually feeling that I was getting it, either in past lives or in this. Mary has told me for years that I am the one she has always needed. I have absolutely no doubt that the same is true of her for me. Yet, ZsaZsa and minette showed me what acceptance actually looks like. Now I can better appreciate what I have, who I am, and why I was put here.

***

In the meantime, another little creature has insinuated himself into our lives. Months after coming to grips with our grief over the loss of minette, we were at it again—opening our hearts to another rescue dog. Louis le Premier du Lac, as we call him, a chihuahua/Italian greyhound mix, was at a kill center in Modesto. Fortunately, he was removed from there, at the eleventh hour, and made his way to us, all nine pounds of near-toothless fearlessness.

Within a few weeks he had taken charge of our exercise schedule, commandeered the middle of our bed, and brought us his special brand of joy. As different from ZsaZsa and minette as can be, yet an equally resolute companion, Louis shows us that, no matter how full our hearts may seem to be with love for each other, for family and friends, human and otherwise, alive or departed, there is always room for one more.

Louis, now over twelve, heroically survived a near-fatal attack by a vicious Great Dane. Residually minimally impaired, he now inspires us to stay fit during daily long walks, by insisting that he be carried at least half of the way.

MORE TO COME

I am not a particularly reflective person. Character-istically, I have been more about action, or, when not active, assimilating. I am a teacher. And I am a collec-tor. At one time I collected stamps. I still collect coins, books, facts, and, especially, memories. That shouldn't come as a surprise to anyone who has waded through all of these pages.

Mary, on the other hand, is supremely effective at self-evaluation. She is much more capable than I of pondering the deeper meanings inherent in the dispa-rate events of one's life. She patiently has taught me the meaning and value of gratitude, as well as forgiveness as a healing mechanism. I believe she has changed me profoundly.

After proofreading an earlier version of this man-uscript, Mary put her finger on what was missing... a proper summation. In the end, what meaning did these struggles, achievements, and missteps have? Looking back over my life to write this book, I unlocked many memories. Those memories expanded into stories, and, in stringing the stories together to become a book, I had occasion to describe the major events of my life. Certain themes became apparent. Insight, however, was lacking. I never delved into why things happened the way they did and what they meant.

I began to ponder over some serious questions that I should have asked myself before, had I been more reflective:

o *Did I have a happy childhood?*

Certainly, I achieved a measure of success in academics and music. Success did not come without hard effort. Perhaps I should have put more effort into cultivating stronger and more lasting friendships. My parents had as much success in their studies as I, yet they both were more prone to socializing than I. Unquestionably, they had more friends. I am not sure that any of us had any idea what true happiness was about. It took me more than half a lifetime to get to that point.

o *Was I scarred by Mother's alcoholism?*

Without a doubt, alcoholism is not limited to the alcoholic; it afflicts the entire family. I have many treasured memories of my mother and harbor no resentment for the indelible scars I wear from that destructive turn she took in her life. I forgive her for what she could not control. Yet, I cannot forget. There is always a residue of sadness at the bottom of every glass of wine I enjoy with a meal.

- o *Did I reveal personality traits in childhood that should have warranted psychological intervention?*

Both of my parents were physicians. If I needed help, they might have been expected to perceive this. But then, when it came to health care for their children, they were what I would call therapeutic nihilists. I remember going more than ten years without getting a physical exam, from age eight, until I was in college. Dad simply filled out the medical forms every year. Besides, I am sure that, by my parents' standards, I was perfectly well adjusted. My teachers never reported any major concerns, nor did I express any. Which I take to mean, "No."

- o *Shouldn't we have talked more about feelings?*

Thinking back, I would have to say that, growing up, I was not troubled by feelings of loneliness or unhappiness; I was simply unaware that there was any imbalance in my life. I certainly did not lack for intellectual or financial support. Nor were my parents unavailable; all I had to do was ask. Of course, I rarely did so, just as they never looked to each other for help.

What was lacking were demonstrations of affection, other than the fact that we always kissed on greeting or leave taking. The word *love* never came up, in any context, so far as I can remember, except for the weeks in 1970 that Mom lay unconscious and near death in the ICU after her open-heart surgery. One time, Dad temporarily softened up a bit and told me that I always was "the apple of his eye," but I think I must have been at least twenty before he made this admission.

From my perspective, everything in my life seemed about right, other than Mom's alcoholism. But then, perhaps I was too busy trying to excel to notice otherwise.

- *Was I somehow reliving what the shaman described as a solitary past life as a smithy in a dark cave, wanting to help and to be liked and loved, yet feared by others?*

My achievements were satisfying, just not fulfilling. Staying so involved in school activities was, to a large part, an effort to be well-liked. At the same time, I became proficient at building up protective walls, whenever necessary. My parents were past masters at this, and my brother arguably is the most secretive and closeted of all of us.

- *Was my confinement to all-boys' schools deleterious to normal emotional and social development?*

It well may have been contributory to my lack of success in previous marriages. Gratefully, fathering four daughters has, among myriad other blessings, provided plenty of compensatory experiences.

o *Have I done a better job as a father than my dad?*

I wish I could say so, but then, he stayed with Mother, while I left Edie and let my family down. One of my daughters has never forgiven me for that. I let my first two wives down, too. I made numerous poor decisions in my social life, which I deeply regret. Many are documented herein. I should have known better. I make no attempt to gloss over the shame I feel.

Had I opened up about my feelings to Mary that first year of medical school, I would have broken up with Amee. But then, I never would have met Edie, who was an exemplary mother to our four daughters.

I would have married Mary in 1971. Clearly, that wasn't part of the plan in the greater scheme of things. I would have to say that my girls are my proudest accomplishment. They are intelligent, highly motivated, and successful, beautiful young women. They grew up well aware of my struggles and accordingly have chosen careers that allow them more time for family. They all are married. Three have two lovely children each.

Without question, my surgical residency training was brutal and traumatic. I suspect that those of you who have read through my frank account of the harassment, the uncertainty, and the misery of those years will have been shocked. The emotional scars from those years are permanent; bad memories replay in my dreams to this day. As I relive those years through writing this book,

I realize that I have suffered ever since from a subtle form of post-traumatic stress disorder.

Did I make it sufficiently clear that from the day I finished my chief residency, I never went back to the University of Washington Surgery Department? Not for a meeting, not for Grand Rounds. Not once. How could I?

I deeply resented certain of my mentors for the callous, almost sadistic way they treated me. As I said, I never felt like other surgeons, and I didn't want to be like them. Why, then, would I associate with them? Oh, I kept up with the surgical journals and attended plenty of out-of-town conferences and review courses. That was to fulfil continuing education requirements, while still preserving a protective degree of anonymity.

When I opened my practice in Seattle, I felt a strong commitment to teaching residents. I wanted to keep my hand in academics. Of course, considering my negative feelings toward surgeons, I had no desire to work with surgical residents.

Instead, I mentored family-practice residents, with whom I felt a great affinity. It was bothersome enough that I was forced to hold my academic appointment through the Surgery Department. I never was required to report back; I simply received periodic notification that I was progressing up the academic ladder.

Although typically I had a resident working with me for six months of the year, I didn't care that I wasn't being salaried; I just loved to teach. The opportunity of inspiring and gently molding young individuals into compassionate physicians was recompense enough. I was able to show my family-practice residents the kindness that had never been proffered me.

For that matter, I never worried about the massive write-offs from my surgical work. I was happy to help others as a general surgeon, especially in bariatrics. I felt blessed to be able to deliver quality care and make a difference in peoples' lives.

I sustained my own practice, with no supervisors or colleagues looking over my shoulder telling me what to do. I could not have countenanced a career in surgery any other way—neither in a group practice nor in academics.

The transition to being a yoga teacher, where I now work as an employee, has been challenging after so many years being my own boss. And, while I've never been accused of arrogance, this has been a humbling experience.

Learning a new skill set at age fifty-nine was a tonic. Were it not for Mary, I never would have embarked on the path of yoga. Were it not for my heart attacks, I would likely still be slogging through a relatively grueling work schedule as a surgeon.

Frankly, I like to work. I like to keep busy. I like to contribute, to pay forward. I like to help others. Teaching is breathing for me, natural and essential. This is a particular gift that has been given me, and it is the attribute for which I am most grateful.

Edie, rather cynically, told me once that I did volunteer work to stroke my ego; she was referring particularly to my extensive involvement in swimming organizations and the Seattle Symphony. I suspect there is some truth in what she said, yet I think she missed the main point. I was born to serve, to help others help themselves.

I mentioned earlier that following my first and second coronary events, I spent some time in therapy. Edie, with the best of intentions, sought out a therapist who had gone through a heart attack himself. The idea was to get me to slow down. Yet, these interventions were doomed to failure.

I had been inculcated from my residency years with a drive to accept all referrals and to push myself to the limit. Fierce competition with others, beginning in grade school, had nurtured an inner "need to succeed." Whenever others were not in the arena, I would compete with myself.

I really could not countenance taking time to "smell the flowers." I was so overcommitted with swimming activities and musical, theatrical, and professional athletic events that I hardly ever took time to catch my breath and reflect. Besides, reluctance to ask for or accept help has been a persistent character trait (or defect) of mine since childhood.

Without a doubt, I would not be alive today had Mary not taken me off that hyperkinetic merry-go-round. It was a Dance of Death, but I didn't realize it. Even before the advent of the coronavirus scourge, we gradually had given up season subscriptions to theatre groups and baseball games. We had become more selective regarding theatrical offerings. We limited ourselves to a handful of symphony concerts a year, where previously I would have attended closer to twenty.

Our floating home is a haven of quietude. No street noise to awaken me at night. This is much appreciated, as I am a very light sleeper, and it doesn't take much to jolt me awake. My idea of a perfect evening is to lie in bed alongside Mary, watch a PBS Masterpiece Theatre program, an episode or two from a new series, or a streaming movie—or simply read a book. Mornings are for reading our three newspapers over a cup of coffee.

Then, of course, there is yoga. Nothing relaxes me more, whether I am doing my own practice or teaching. I find peace every time I lay down my mat. My opening messages to each class are more heartfelt and, in turn, help my damaged physical heart grow stronger. I now have the insight to teach others not to compete in yoga, not with other students, not with themselves.

Sheltering at home afforded us time to reset our priorities. More time to write and edit, to read, and to collaborate on projects with Mary. I have become much better about staying in touch with old friends and more facile at making new ones. I am enjoying long walks with Mary and Louis every day. Between that and all the yoga, I am in better shape now than I had been for some years.

There's more time for reflection. Time to nap in the afternoon, when I feel the need. I pick books off our shelves—and there are a lot of books and shelves, even after de-accessioning—that I never had a chance to finish in college or that I want to reread. And then there is that biography of Harvey Cushing, which sits prominently on a shelf, directly in view as I practice yoga. A bright red reminder of how far I have traveled since I was a boy, fantasizing about growing up to be a neurosurgeon.

Occasionally a dream remains vividly etched in my memory. I have described a few already. Here is yet one more:

> I am with my father. He has just returned from a trip somewhere. He places his suitcase on the bed, and I open it up to help him unpack. There are red pajamas on top. He also is carrying a paperback book, something dealing with the subject of why medicine really matters.
>
> I say to him that I would really like to read the book, but that doing so would

be too painful. I tell him that I had been really good, before giving it up. I ask him whether he could see it coming, the fact that I would relinquish my surgical practice and take up a different endeavor.

He tells me he could. There is no sadness or criticism in his voice. Only a clear assertion that it did not surprise him.

This dream came seven years and four months after I closed my practice—nearly seventeen years after my father's death. I felt that the dream underscored some residual ambivalence about ending my surgical career, until a deeper interpretation was offered. If I were to look at my father in the dream as a representation of myself at a more mature level, his acquiescing to my leaving medicine suggests an end to any ambivalence. That makes a lot of sense.

What have I learned from ZsaZsa? To be of the moment, to communicate clearly, to give unconditional love. minette, although arguably less a teacher, was all about love. Louis is our special fitness advisor, with his love of walking, especially up and down hills. Mary is the very essence of gratitude, honesty, and selfless service. My brother is a shining example of patriotism.

As for my daughters, Emily is demonstrating the right way to balance a career with parenting her children, Moses and Miriam. Katie reminds me of the value of diligence and protectiveness, as she cares for her daughters, Olivia and Raffaele. Sadly, because they live in Italy, and because of the pandemic, I don't get to be with them as much as I would like. Thankfully, Emily's children live nearby.

Betsy has taught me how to live patiently in hopes of reconciliation, so that I may participate in the lives of her sons, Henry and Theodore. Joey influenced my thinking regarding forgiveness—how to do it, why we should do it, and when best to offer it.

I am blessed to be surrounded by teachers. And I am twice blessed in that I now am more open and, as such, more capable of absorbing their messages and life's lessons. I am a better teacher now than I ever was before.

The shaman indicated that I lived a past life of solitude, in a dark cave. I wanted to reach out to others, but my efforts were spurned, because I was feared. The residue of that life in this one helps explain many of the problems that have beset me. If she is correct seeing me emerging from the dark cave, I have much to look forward to.

Maybe the shaman is correct that ZsaZsa is my power animal. Maybe she is something even more significant. The truth is that ZsaZsa provided the key that allowed me to unlock the door holding me in that dark place. And remember, ZsaZsa brought minette to us, welcoming her with rainbows on her very first day with us. And the two of them in turn led us to Louis. Our lives have been enriched immeasurably by our close association with these old souls in canine costume.

I see a world outside now, full of color and light. Incidentally, my sense of smell has returned for the first time in over 30 years; this in itself is no coincidence. I am becoming aware of possibilities, of choices, of potential as never before.

At the same time, I am cognizant and greatly appreciative of the light within. Mary walks with me on this journey, hand in hand, step by step. I cannot overstate my joy of having her as a companion. She is patiently teaching me the value of simplification. Letting go does not come easily, yet I realize that I must strive to do it. Only by relinquishing the unnecessary can we come to a fuller appreciation of what really matters.

I referred to *The Book of Questions* at the outset of this book. I reviewed the 217 questions proposed by Dr. Stock. Eleven particularly caught my attention. Of these, I found that I had already dealt with one in the first chapter and most of the rest in this chapter. Perhaps I am becoming more reflective, after all.

Here are the remaining three:

Question: *What do you like best about your life? Least?*

Answer: Best—Waking up every morning next to Mary.
Least—Difficulty making and retaining close friends.

Question: *Your house, containing every-thing you own, catches fire; after saving your loved ones and pets, you have time to safely make a final dash to save any one item. What would it be?*

Answer: The two little wooden boxes con-taining ZsaZsa's and minette's ashes. I never would be able to choose one over the other.

Question: *What do you strive for most in your life: accomplishment, security, love, power, excitement, knowledge, or some-thing else?*

Answer: Without hesitation, love.

***

I close with a little poem I wrote about getting back with Mary. It was written following a long period of si-lence and emotional closeting. We gave it as a me-mento to attendees at our D.C. wedding reception, along with a few photos and, of course, a Shakespeare quote (from *King Lear*), to wit: "The wheel is come full circle." For the final, key line, I thank the great Pacific Northwest poet, Raymond Carver.

Coming Home

You, emerging from the crowd, while I
Stick, statue-fast, to the steps of St. Pat's—
Time-traveling, years blurring by. My life.
Twenty-seven years. No, further: thirty-five—
Back to the beginning. Before that, even.
Rebirth. Salvation. Dream quest made real.
"Old college friend," you said. My response:
"What in God's name took you so long?"

BACKGROUND

Inspired by Rembrandt's *Canal with an Angler and Two Swans*

Seek always to bring out the best in others,
Thereby bringing out the best in oneself.

Felix Adler,
Founder of Ethical Culture

MÉLANGE

MENTIONING

Mary has proofread the entire opus in each of its various iterations, which has taken up an enormous amount of her time. An author is only as good as his editor, and Mary is a terrific editor. She has superior writing skills and is without question a better speller than I ever hope to be. She knows when and how to make necessary changes, and just when to let slight errata slide. A split infinitive, however, is where she draws the line. This invariably draws out the red pen. Mary was scrupulous about not altering the content; that she left to me. I am greatly in her debt for her patience with me, as I spent countless hours writing and revising my book.

Mary Gwen Dungan had exactly the right combination of editorial skills and spiritual acumen to take this book to a higher level. I am forever grateful to her for her excellent suggestions, appropriate deletions, and forbearance. Putting me indirectly in communication with Sri Sai Baba added timeless perspective and experience to my message.

My dear friend, Penny LeGate, a talented television personality and humanitarian, has made valuable contributions. Bill Kenower, an author and memoir coach, helped me put the book into better focus. Danna Faulds, whose yoga-inspired poetry is unparalleled, graciously has allowed me to use one of her works in the introductory section.

I must give thanks to minette, who served as a marvelous muse for me. She was almost always right at hand, either on the bed while I typed at my desk, or under the table, the times I worked from the laptop at the floating home. She gave me encouragement in the form of kisses, playtime, or walks—whenever a break was needed. Now she is watching over me, as my special angelic advocate, in concert with ZsaZsa, as Louis has taken on the earthly responsibilities. Perhaps the three of them are manifestations of the same celestial being. Perhaps there is another story there...

A memoir is an iffy proposition at best. One can and must pick and choose from among the myriad experiences of life, emphasizing and de-emphasizing as one goes along, according to one's personal whims. Readers, especially those who know me, will find certain possibly glaring omissions, and, quite likely, some inaccuracies. I beg their forgiveness, and remind them that, *au fond*, I am only human, and hope to continue to be for a goodly number of years hence.

I hope that my book has stimulated some thought, brought forth a few chuckles, perhaps occasioned a few tears, and, most of all, has proved to have been entertaining.

My message?

Happiness
Isn't a birthright.
It is a precious gift,
Devoutly to be sought,
Gratefully to be appreciated,
And generously to be shared...

MONITI, MELIORA SEQUAMUR

{Motto of the Hotchkiss School, from Virgil, *Aeneid*, Book III; meaning: "Having been instructed, let us reach a higher level."}

"Because in the end, you won't remember the time you spent working in the office or mowing your lawn. Climb that goddamn mountain."

So penned Jack Kerouac, in *The Dharma Bums* in 1958, when Jim was a youth growing up in the tony neighborhood bordering Gramercy Park in New York City.

And that is exactly what Jim has finally done, as he meticulously chronicles in his memoir *Cutting Out*, beginning with his pampered youth of private schooling, through privileged education at one of the finest New England prep schools and then two Ivy League Universities, through his sometimes tortuous training and career as a surgeon (in the process burning out on many things, including three wives), and culminating as he currently perches atop his "goddamn mountain" as a Yoga Master Instructor, a calling he turned to at the urging of his "true love, his soulmate," his fourth wife Mary, who was, ironically, his first love, way back in his undergraduate days at Yale.

Cutting Out, pun clearly intended, is so full of engaging anecdotes that it could be made into a movie. But the movie would never be as good as the book, because there is too much pith, too much detail, too many fascinating personalities who circle in and out of *Cutting Out* for today's fidgety audiences to countenance in a 120-minute big screen feature—truly a film editor's nightmare, with miles of film left piled on the cutting room floor. Maybe a ten-episode Netflix mini-series would begin to give enough screen time to develop some of the intriguing ancillary characters he encounters in his fifty-year post-college practice for life...

It has been a long journey of roads taken and roads not taken. Comedic, enlightening, tragic, amazing at times (he has read *Moby Dick* something like three times), Fowlesian (John, that is) in its recitation of detail, are all apt depictions of this narrative of a man who, as a Romantic lover of music and literature extraordinaire, is now following a different and, for him, more heartfelt calling of service to others.

Bob Small, tax consultant and
photographer par excellence,
keen observer, superb writer, and steadfast friend

MINUTIAE

Jim Weber, born and raised in Manhattan into a medical family and fortunate to have been educated in elite schools, has lived in the Pacific Northwest for nearly half a century. He gave up a busy surgical practice to follow his bliss, becoming a yoga teacher. Given a third chance to do life with his college sweetheart, he finally made it happen.

Married to one of the world's leading authorities on etiquette, he cowrote with her a book on manners. Virtually automatically, this qualifies him as the politest surgeon-turned-yoga-teacher on the planet.

This is his fourth book. The third, a collection of vignettes and essays, called *Joie de Vivre, As I See It: Reflections on Youth and Maturity*, an antidote to the dark days of the pandemic, was released last year. Stay tuned for *Scribbling In My Spare Time*, a sequel of sorts.

Website: prescriptionyoga.com.
Email: yogadoc@hotmail.com.

***

Oatley Kidder, a long-time friend of the author, is a celebrated sculptor, muralist, and book illustrator—nota bene her imaginative contributions to *Joie de Vivre, As*

I See It—who transformed the Webers' small bathroom into an expansive jungle scene and painted memorial murals of their dogs on the stairwell. Her work adorns a multitude of walls in southern California.

CPSIA information can be obtained
at www.ICGtesting.com
Printed in the USA
LVHW101402240123
737840LV00016B/351/J

9 781665 728553